Patrick O'Brian's
NAVY

Patrick O'Brian's
NAVY

The Illustrated Companion to
JACK AUBREY'S WORLD

RUNNING PRESS
PHILADELPHIA · LONDON

EDITOR AND INDEXER: Philip de Ste. Croix
DESIGNER: Philip Clucas MSIAD
ILLUSTRATIONS: Hardlines, Oxford
© Salamander Books Ltd
ART DIRECTOR: John Heritage
PROJECT MANAGER: Antony Shaw
COLOR REPRODUCTION: Anorax Imaging Ltd
PRINTED AND BOUND IN: China

THE CONSULTANT EDITOR
RICHARD O'NEILL is a writer and editor who has specialized in military history for the past 40 years. He is the author of *Suicide Squads*, a history of the weapons and missions of the Special Attack units of World War II. He has contributed to many books on weaponry and military history, including *The Complete Encyclopedia of Battleships and Battlecruisers*, *The Illustrated Encyclopedia of 20th Century Warships*, *The Vietnam War* and, most recently, *An Illustrated History of the Royal Navy*.

CONTRIBUTORS
CHRIS CHANT is a highly experienced writer on military matters who has more than 90 published books to his name; he has also contributed to numerous partworks dealing with military history and aviation. He has written extensively on the navies and warships of the world, and was co-author (with Richard O'Neill) of *The Complete Encyclopedia of Battleships and Battlecruisers*.

DAVID MILLER is an expert on naval matters who has written many books on modern warships and naval subjects. He is also interested in the Georgian age and has been writing on Napoleonic era nautical and military subjects since the publication of his books *The Wreck of the Isabella*, which describes the true-life adventures of a group of shipwrecked people in the Falkland Islands in 1812, and *Lady De Lancey at Waterloo* about a young woman at that most famous of all land battles.

DR. CLIVE WILKINSON (PhD, University of East Anglia) is a historian of 18th century maritime and imperial history. He has a special interest in naval administration and ship's logs. Presently he is based at the National Maritime Museum, Greenwich, England, where he is involved in an international project to reconstruct the climate of the world's oceans from 1750 to 1850 from ship's logbooks.

Patrick O'Brian's Navy
Created by Salamander Books Ltd,
64 Brewery Rd, London N7 9NT,
England

Copyright © Salamander Books Ltd
2003
A member of **Chrysalis** Books plc

First published in the United States in 2003 by Running Press Book Publishers All rights reserved under the Pan-American and International Copyright Conventions

9 8 7 6 5 4 3 2 1

Digit on the right indicates the number of this printing

Library of Congress Control Number 2003091057

ISBN 0-7624-1540-1

This book may be ordered by mail from the publisher. Please include $2.50 for postage and handling.
Published by Courage Books,
an imprint of
Running Press Book Publishers,
125 South Twenty-second Street,
Philadephia, Pennsylvania 19103-4399

Visit us on the web!
www.runningpress.com

Note: Currency conversion
Monetary values in this book, as in the Aubrey canon, are expressed in pounds sterling (£). To convert pounds to US dollars ($), multiply the sum by 1.5.

Contents

Introduction

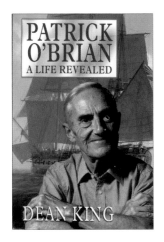

Above: Patrick O'Brian was an enigmatic figure who guarded details of his private life closely. Dean King's biography is the only account of his life currently available (2003).

Above: Whatever may happen ashore, the Aubrey-Maturin novels are very much the story of Britannia triumphant by sea.

Patrick O'Brian, born Richard Patrick Russ in Chalfont St Peter, Buckinghamshire, in 1914, died in Dublin in January 2000 at the age of 85. His somewhat complex private life—documented in Dean King's biography *Patrick O'Brian: A Life Revealed*—is outside the scope of this book. Our aim is to provide a factual background that may help the reader to a fuller appreciation of one of the greatest achievements in modern fiction: the 20 novels that make up the "Aubreyiad" (the term is appropriate, for reviewers and obituarists alike did not shrink from mentioning O'Brian and Homer in the same context), the adventures by sea and land of Captain "Lucky Jack" Aubrey, RN, and his friend Stephen Maturin, physician, natural historian, and British espionage agent.

Something must be said, however, of O'Brian's earlier literary career, where themes that were to be of importance in his major work may be discerned. He was a precocious writer: his first novel, *Caesar*, a fantasy of natural history, was published in 1930 when he was 15 (under his true name, Richard Russ; after 1945 he published as Patrick O'Brian), and his second book, *Beasts Royal*, animal stories, when he was 19. The love of natural history which is so great a feature of the Aubrey canon was with him from the very beginning. In the 1950s-60s, O'Brian attracted some favorable critical attention but small sales with such novels as *Testimonies* (1952) and *The Catalans* (1953); the greater part of his income came from his translations from French of such writers as Simone de Beauvoir and André Maurois.

In 1956 there appeared *The Golden Ocean*, O'Brian's first novel of the sea, based on Commodore George Anson's dramatic and tragic voyage of circumnavigation in 1740-44. A second novel, *The Unknown Shore*, took up the story of one of Anson's ships, HMS *Wager*, shipwrecked on the coast of Chile. The prototypes of the major characters of the Aubrey canon are dimly to be seen in these two books. In *The Golden Ocean*, Midshipman Ransome of HMS *Centurion* is given to making, and laughing immoderately at, the most dreadful "clenches" (puns)—one of Jack Aubrey's endearing failings. The central characters of *The Unknown Shore* are the stalwart and resourceful Midshipman Jack Byron—based on the later Admiral John "Foulweather Jack" Byron (1723-86), grandfather of the poet Lord Byron—and the surgeon's mate Tobias Barrow.

O'Brian had brought together a man of action and a more reflective man of science and learning, but it took him some years to perfect the characters and give them the appropriate setting. In the latter, choosing to set his novels during the Napoleonic Wars, he may have been a little influenced by the success of the "Horatio Hornblower" novels of C.S. Forester. But in the perfection of character and narrative style he had one predominant influence, that of the greatest writer of his chosen period, Jane Austen. (Many readers must have noted the initial coincidence of JAne AUsten and JAck AUbrey.) It is her lucidity, limpidity, wit, and complete lack of pretension that inform O'Brian's books. Some of his characters (for example, Jack's mother-in-law, Mrs Williams, snobbish, greedy, and avid to procure prestigious partners for her daughters) would have particularly delighted Miss Austen. It is worth remembering that although, as has been often noted, Jane Austen's novels pay little attention to the Napoleonic Wars, in her private life she must have been concerned with naval matters, since her brothers Francis and Charles were naval officers, ending their careers as Admiral of the Fleet and Rear Admiral respectively. Naval officers are almost invariably shown in a favor-

Right: Locked together with her starboard anchors fouled in the French vessel's shrouds, HMS *Brunswick* and the *Vengeur* hammer away at each other during the Battle of the Glorious First of June in 1794. Jack Aubrey would have approved—he was fond of quoting Nelson's maxim "Never mind manoeuvres: always go straight at 'em." After about four hours, the *Vengeur* struck her colors. The painting is by Nicholas Pocock.

Above: *Glasses of grog to hand, a seaman regales his messmates with a story of past glories in George Cruikshank's cartoon entitled "The Sailor's Description of a Chase and Capture." Part of O'Brian's brilliance lies in the way that he brings such scenes to life in his novels, so that we feel that we understand how everyone serving on a warship of the period—from captain to humble powder boy—lived and behaved.*

> ❝ **Captain Wentworth had no fortune. He had been lucky in his profession, but spending freely, what had come freely, had realized nothing. But, he was confident that he should soon be rich;—full of life and ardour, he knew that he should soon have a ship, and soon be on a station that would lead to everything that he wanted. He had always been lucky; he knew he should be so still.** ❞
>
> *Persuasion,* Chapter 4, Jane Austen

Commander, first novel of the Aubrey canon. Here it will be useful to list the 20 novels of the canon. They run in chronological order: O'Brian once said that he sometimes regretted having chosen to begin his story as late as 1800, but resisted what must have been a temptation to produce a "pre-quel" to *Master and Commander.*

Master and Commander (1969)
Post Captain (1972)
H.M.S. Surprise (1973)
The Mauritius Command (1977)
Desolation Island (1978)
The Fortune of War (1979)
The Surgeon's Mate (1980)
The Ionian Mission (1981)
Treason's Harbour (1983)
The Far Side of the World (1984)
The Reverse of the Medal (1986)
The Letter of Marque (1988)
The Thirteen-Gun Salute (1989)
The Nutmeg of Consolation (1991)
The Truelove (UK: *Clarissa Oakes*) (1992)
The Wine-Dark Sea (1993)
The Commodore (1995)
The Yellow Admiral (1997)
The Hundred Days (1998)
Blue at the Mizzen (1999)

O'Brian had intimated that *Blue at the Mizzen* was to be the last of the series, but it is known that he had completed some chapters of a further title before his death.

Although the Aubrey novels attracted early critical praise, acclaimed by such disparate authorities as the master mariner Sir Francis Chichester and the great historical novelist Mary Renault, and appeared with some success on both sides of the Atlantic, they remained the province of a discerning minority of readers until 1991, when the cover of the book section of the *New York Times* hailed the series as "the best historical novels ever written…subtle artistry…[reminding us] that times change and people don't, that the griefs and follies of the men and women who were here before us are in fact the maps of our own lives." Like Lord Byron, although at a much more advanced age,

able light in her novels: one thinks particularly of William Price in *Mansfield Park* and Admiral Croft and Captain Wentworth in *Persuasion.*

That O'Brian had succeeded most brilliantly in recreating the "Wooden World" of the Royal Navy under sail was at once apparent in 1969 with the appearance of *Master and*

Left: *Jack Aubrey has no qualms about taking on enemy ships much bigger than his, much in the way that this British sloop,* Bonne Citoyenne, *tackled— and defeated—the French frigate* La Furieuse *on July 6th, 1809.*

Below: *A cartoon showing a gluttonous John Bull being fed by his admirals—Nelson, in the foreground, is holding out a plate labeled "Ragout from Aboukir."*

O'Brian found himself famous almost overnight – no longer "the best author you never heard of." From that time, all his novels were best-sellers in both the USA and Britain (and as this book was being written work was underway on the first movie based on the Aubrey canon: *Master and Commander—The Far Side of the World*, with Russell Crowe as Jack Aubrey and Paul Bettany as Stephen Maturin, due for release in 2003).

In August 1992, writing in the *Washington Post*, critic Ken Ringle, who was to be numbered among O'Brian's friends and most perceptive interpreters, had praised the canon equally highly. It was Ringle (after whom O'Brian

named the captured American clipper *Ringle* of *The Hundred Days*) who, at a seminar sponsored by the Smithsonian Institution in November 2000, pointed out that there are six great literary themes: Man against God or Fate; Man against Nature; Man against Man; Man against Woman; Man against Society; and Man against Himself. O'Brian, said Ringle, "...skillfully and profoundly explores not just one of those themes, but *every* one. *Every* one in *every* book."

CHAPTER ONE

The World That Jack Knew

Hardly a breeze was stirring off the French naval base of Brest on January 2nd, 1793 as Captain Robert Barlow (captain by courtesy—he was a "Master and Commander," like Jack Aubrey in the Sophie*) allowed the flood tide to carry his brig-sloop HMS* Childers, *armed with 14 or 16 guns according to different sources, toward the harbor.*

Barlow's mission was to gather intelligence on the state of units of the French Atlantic squadron at France's major Atlantic and Channel base, lying at the western tip of Brittany, and thereby offering access to either body of water except in the face of any dead westerly wind that would prevent the ships from leaving harbor. On the continent, the forces of Revolutionary France were already in combat with those of Austria and Prussia in the War of the First Coalition. The French army, unexpectedly victorious at Valmy and Jemappes in September and October 1792, occupied much of what is now Belgium, and although Britain and France remained at peace, Britain feared French domination of ports in the Low Countries vital to her trade and security. Hence the importance of Barlow's mission, for information gathered worldwide by the commanders of warships was the mainstay of the British intelligence system.

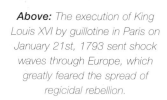

Above: *The execution of King Louis XVI by guillotine in Paris on January 21st, 1793 sent shock waves through Europe, which greatly feared the spread of regicidal rebellion.*

Right: *The British immediately began offensive operations, and the first French prize was the Sansculotte, which was taken by HMS* Scourge *on March 13th, 1793.*

10

spirit as Jack Aubrey accepts the undesirable HMS *Polychrest* in *Post Captain*, having been promised she would be a step to something better. Off Midby, Norway, on March 14th, 1808, Dillon beat off the Danish brig *Lügum* (20 guns)—it was said that the timbers of the British vessel were so rotten that the Danish 18-pound shot simply burst straight through without shattering them—and thus preserved a galliot he had taken as a prize. Later that month Dillon was made post (elevated to the rank of captain), and the *Childers* was broken up in 1811. Nineteen days after the *Childers'* brush at Brest, King Louis XVI of France lost his

Left: *This watercolor by Nicholas Pocock depicts the shore batteries protecting Brest harbor in Brittany as they fire on the British brig* Childers *on January 2nd, 1793.*

❝ ...information gathered worldwide by the commanders of warships was the mainstay of the British intelligence system. ❞

Two artillery forts guarded the approaches to Brest, and as the *Childers* stood in, no more than a mile from the harbor, a cannon ball furrowed the water too close for comfort to the small warship. Barlow hoisted the British ensign to show his peaceful status, but was answered by cannon fire from both forts. Near-becalmed as she was, the *Childers* was a diminutive but sitting target. Barlow ordered his crew to man the sweeps but to his relief a light westerly breeze whispered into life and wafted his ship out of range. One 48-pound shot had struck the *Childers*, destroying a 4-pounder gun but causing no casualties. Thus began the hostilities between Britain and France that were to endure almost without pause for 22 years as the host of complex and interlocking wars that are now generally known as the Revolutionary and Napoleonic Wars.

The subsequent career of HMS *Childers* is worth tracing, as an illustration of how these small warships were literally worked to death in the long wars in which the *Childers* did hard and valuable service, largely as a convoy escort. Having been launched in 1778, by 1807 she was in a condition so poor that her long 6-pounder guns had had to be replaced by lighter 12-pounder carronades. Late in that year, Captain William Henry Dillon accepted her command in the same

life on the guillotine. About a week later, on February 1st, 1793, France declared war on Britain and Holland. Constituting the historical backdrop for the exploits of Jack Aubrey, the Revolutionary and Napoleonic Wars fall into a number of phases, which some historians distinguish by the various "Coalitions" between nations opposing first the Revolutionary forces and then those of Napoleon.

Above: *Lying on the north-western tip of France, Brest was a port vital to French naval interests. It provided access to the Bay of Biscay as well as the North Atlantic, and also offered an avenue of attack against British shipping lanes.*

Above: *A map of Europe as it appeared in 1792. The autocratic rulers of the nations of Europe felt themselves seriously threatened by the possibility of any export of French revolutionary tendencies in 1791, and this led to the War of the First Coalition.*

*The First Coalition was formed by Austria and Prussia in June 1792 and was joined by Britain, Spain, Holland, Naples (Kingdom of the Two Sicilies), and Tuscany. As in later coalitions, not all these allies remained combatant until the end of the War of the First Coalition, which saw Napoleon's conquest of Northern Italy and ended in October 1797 with the Treaty of Campo Formio.

*The Second Coalition was formed in May 1798-June 1799, and comprised Britain, Russia, Austria, Portugal, Turkey (Ottoman Empire), and Naples. The War of the Second Coalition, which saw further French successes in North Italy and on the Rhine, as well as Napoleon's attempted conquest of Egypt and the Middle East, was ended by the Peace of Amiens in March 1802. By that time, only Britain remained combatant, while in 1800 Russia had formed with Sweden, Denmark, and Prussia the so-called Armed Neutrality of the North, intended to curb British naval power in the Baltic. Now, the Revolutionary Wars gave way to the Napoleonic Wars, so-called after Napoleon Bonaparte had become in effect sole ruler of France.

*On May 14th, 1801, encouraged by the fact that the United States had paid tribute in money and ships to secure the release of seamen captured by Barbary pirates, the Pasha of Tripoli declared war on the USA. The Tripolitanian War revealed the United States' growing naval power and was ended in its favor by a treaty on June 4th, 1805.

*Britain was again at war with France from May 16th, 1803 (and would remain so until 1815, regardless of the fates of her changing allies). But she sought allies. Thus the period of April to August 1805 saw the formation of the Third Coalition between Britain, Russia, Austria, Sweden, Naples, and several small German states. Napoleon won great victories in Italy and Germany. The War of the Third Coalition was ended by the Peace of Pressburg in 1805.

*A long-standing dispute with Turkey over territories on the Upper Danube led to a Russian invasion of Moldavia and Wallachia in October 1806 and a declaration of war by Turkey on December 27th. The (Third) Russo-Turkish War was ended by the Treaty of Bucharest in May 1812.

*The Fourth Coalition was formed by Britain, Russia, and Prussia in October 1806. French victories meant that by the time the War of the Fourth Coalition was ended by the Treaties of Tilsit in July 1807, Prussia was overrun and Russia was forced into alliance with Napoleon.

*Following the Treaty of Tilsit, Russia, encouraged by Napoleon, invaded Finland, then a Swedish possession, in February 1808. The Russo-Swedish War, in which Denmark joined Russia while Britain gave some naval support to Sweden, was ended in Russia's favor by the Treaty of Frederickshamm in September 1809.

*The Peninsular War started with the French conquest of Portugal in 1807 and the subsequent invasion of Spain early in 1808. The Spanish resisted fiercely. Landing in July-August 1808, British armies liberated Portugal and, under General Sir Arthur Wellesley (later the Duke of Wellington), finally drove the French from Spain and in turn invaded southern France early in 1814. The Peninsular War ended with French capitulation on April 17th, 1814, after the arrival of the news of Napoleon's abdication.

*The Fifth Coalition was formed by Britain and Austria in April 1809, toward the beginning of the Peninsular War. By July of that year Napoleon's armies had crushed Austria, which in October was forced to end the War of the Fifth Coalition by the Treaty of Vienna.

*British interference with American merchant shipping (often in attempts to retrieve "run" seamen) and American territorial ambitions in Canada triggered the War of 1812 between Britain and the USA. The Americans gained a number of naval victories, but their greatest land success, the Battle of New Orleans, came two weeks after the war was ended by the Treaty of Ghent, December 24th, 1814.

*The War of the Sixth Coalition was triggered by Napoleon's invasion of Russia in June 1812. Britain, Russia, Spain, and Portugal were joined after Napoleon's Russian debacle by Prussia, Austria, Sweden, and some German states. With the greater part of Europe at last united against him by the Treaty of Chaumont (March 1814), Napoleon was driven back into France and, when the allies invaded, forced to abdicate on April 6th, 1814. The Bourbon monarchy was restored in France, and the great powers called the Congress of Vienna (November 1814-June 1815) as a summit meeting to discuss the future shape of Europe.

*The Seventh Coalition was formed by Britain, Russia, Austria, and Prussia, with other allies at the Congress of

Above: *Great Britain and France, represented by Pitt "the Younger" and Napoleon, carve up the world in James Gillray's celebrated cartoon of 1805 "The Plumb-pudding in danger."*

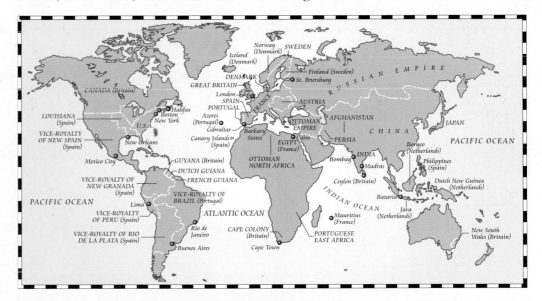

Vienna acquiescing, when in March 1815 Napoleon escaped from his exile on the island of Elba and returned once more to bid for power. The "Hundred Days" campaign ended with Napoleon's final defeat at Waterloo (June 18th, 1815) and the occupation of Paris in the following month. What is sometimes called the War of the Seventh Coalition was ended by the Treaty of Paris on November 20th, 1815.

Above: *The world during the period of the War of the Second Coalition, which ended with the Peace of Amiens in March 1802. All knew, however, that this peace would be shortlived.*

Above: These line-of-battle ships, laid up "in ordinary" at Devonport, highlight the fact that Great Britain was poorly prepared for war in 1793. Her main naval forces were the Channel Fleet under Admiral Lord Howe, and the Mediterranean Fleet under Admiral Sir Samuel Hood.

Comparative Strengths

Leaving aside for the moment the fleets of France's erstwhile allies, figures (although not all historians are in agreement on these) suggest that Britain began the series of wars with marked naval superiority, and this superiority would increase as the wars progressed. A table drawn up in 1810 by Robert Fulton gives comparative strengths in 1790 as 661 British warships, including 195 ships-of-the-line (that is, those with 50 or more guns; see Chapter Three) and 210 frigates, against 291 French warships, including 81 ships-of-the-line and 69 frigates. But these figures do not take into account the serviceability of the ships listed: far more realistic figures are those given by the modern naval historian Brian Lavery, who states that in 1792 the French navy had available 241 warships, including 83 line-of-battle ships and 77 frigates. Again, however, not all of these would have been serviceable. Realistic figures for the Royal Navy show that in 1793 it had 113 line-of-battle ships, but of these only

26 were in commission, the rest being "laid up in ordinary" ("mothballed" in modern terms) whence they might be activated with relative speed, or alternatively under repair.

The Royal Navy had generally good officers but a comparative shortage of ordinary sailors, whose harsh lot was pushing them slowly but inexorably toward mutiny. It was divided into two main forces, namely the Channel Fleet commanded by Admiral Lord Howe with its main bases at Spithead and the Nore, and the Mediterranean Fleet commanded by Admiral Sir Samuel Hood. At the start of hostilities, the British ships were manned by some 20,000 men, but within 12 months this figure had risen to 73,000. Even so, this strength was not sufficient for the full manning of the ships that had been brought back into commission or completed new by the country's yards. This led to the Quota Act of 1795 and also to the enlistment of foreigners. This latter was often forcible, and official letters of the period abound with demands from consuls for the release of their countries' nationals from impressed service. The urgent need for manpower from any and every source becomes all the more evident when one appreciates that the population of Britain at this time was only some nine million, whereas that of France was in the order of 25 million.

France's fleet was in no greater state of readiness. Indeed, in view of the events described below at Toulon, France's major Mediterranean base, at the outset of the wars, it was almost certainly in a far worse state. It is also worth bearing in mind that to a certain extent the physical condition of the ships upon which the French could call was irrelevant. The trials and tribulations of the first stages of the French Revolution, culminating in the internal Jacobin "Reign of Terror" instigated by Maximilien F. de Robespierre and the Committee of Public Safety, and the external successes of the Austrian forces in the fighting for Brussels and Valenciennes, effectively shattered French confidence. So far as the navy was concerned, its corps of professional officers had been purged for political reasons and, after a series of mutinies, its enlisted strength could be regarded as little more than a mob.

The gaping shortfall in the officer corps was redressed by the recruitment of merchant marine officers: these knew ships and the sea, but had none of the professional maritime warfare experience of the naval officers they succeeded. Thus the French navy was hard pressed to man half of its available line-of-battle ships. The situation was further exacerbated by the total and pernicious neglect into which the ships and dockyards had fallen.

In the Reign of Terror, the French navy's officer corps lost about three-quarters of its strength as men were executed, were exiled, or fled abroad. Those who survived were mainly the officers who sympathized with the Jacobin cause, and for these promotion was rapid and, altogether too often, far beyond their capabilities. The speed with which such men were advanced is exemplified by the case of Louis T. Villaret de Joyeuse, who in a period of just three years rose from the rank of lieutenant to admiral, and commanded the French fleet in its disastrous defeat in the Battle of the Glorious First of June (1794).

Above left: Sir Samuel Hood commanded in the Mediterranean between May 1793 and October 1794, a period in which his most important undertaking was the short-term seizure of Toulon.

Above: As commander of the Channel Fleet, Lord Howe scored a stunning tactical victory in the Battle of the Glorious First of June, but a vital French convoy escaped.

Left: Admiral Bruix was dispatched from Brest in 1799 with 25 line-of-battle ships to relieve the French expeditionary force in Malta and Egypt, but he failed. Throughout this period French naval efforts were crippled by lack of capable officers, large numbers of whom had been executed during the Revolution or had fled from France.

Below: *William Pitt "the Younger" was British prime minister between 1783 and 1801 and then between 1804 and 1806.*

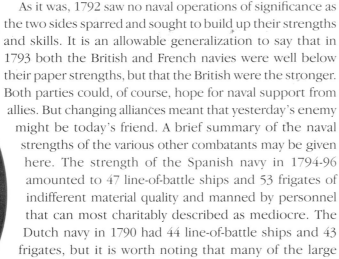

As it was, 1792 saw no naval operations of significance as the two sides sparred and sought to build up their strengths and skills. It is an allowable generalization to say that in 1793 both the British and French navies were well below their paper strengths, but that the British were the stronger. Both parties could, of course, hope for naval support from allies. But changing alliances meant that yesterday's enemy might be today's friend. A brief summary of the naval strengths of the various other combatants may be given here. The strength of the Spanish navy in 1794-96 amounted to 47 line-of-battle ships and 53 frigates of indifferent material quality and manned by personnel that can most charitably described as mediocre. The Dutch navy in 1790 had 44 line-of-battle ships and 43 frigates, but it is worth noting that many of the large

of-battle ships, although of these only 31 were in commission. Turkey had 22 line-of-battle ships and just eight frigates in 1787. Of the small Italian fleets, Venice (controlled by Austria from 1797) had 20 line-of-battle ships and 19 frigates in 1790, and Naples a mere three line-of-battle ships in 1795. In 1790, Portugal had 10 line-of-battle ships and 14 frigates. The US Navy had no line-of-battle ships until 1815; the operations of its frigates, few in number but notably large, well armed, and excellently crewed, are discussed in Chapters Five and Six.

Bases and Blockades

The main naval bases and dockyards in France were those at Cherbourg on the English Channel, Brest, and L'Orient (now Lorient) on France's Atlantic coast, and Toulon on the

Above: *Spain's navy, seen here in the form of a fleet in Leghorn Roads, included some huge ships, but in overall terms it was poorly led and manned.*

Dutch ships were somewhat lighter, in gun power as well as displacement, than those of the other major powers. In 1801, the Danish navy had 23 line-of-battle ships. The strength of the Swedish navy in 1790 was 27 line-of-battle ships and 12 frigates. In 1801, the Russian navy had 82 line-

Mediterranean. By this time France also controlled a number of the ports at the north-eastern end of the English Channel and the southern part of the North Sea. The most important of these French-controlled ports in the Low Countries was Antwerp, which was rightly seen by Britain as the "pistol

> **The primary objective of the Royal Navy was to prevent the ships of the French navy making an escape in any numbers from any of their ports.**

the Great Mutinies of 1797. What saved Britain at this parlous time, when there was apparently a possibility of revolution, when the army was small and inferior to the navy, and when there was a constant fear that rebellion was likely in Ireland, was the presence among the Royal Navy's officer corps of a group of great leaders. This advantage began right at the top with the presence as commander-in-chief of Admiral the Earl of St. Vincent, who had an uncanny gift for the selection of natural commanders. He also knew how to train his fleets by the use of harsh, but effective, methods.

pointed at her heart," and there were also subsidiary French bases in the Pas-de-Calais region at spots such as Calais, where smaller ships and privateers could lurk.

In overall terms, the general superiority of the Royal Navy did not lie in its greater number of ships, for this total was in truth too small for the far-flung responsibilities imposed on the navy by the extent of Britain's world-wide empire and maritime trade. As the French were in the position to select the moment at which to launch an offensive, either at sea or, as became increasingly a threat in the first decade of the 19th century, as a landing on England's south coast, the British were on the strategic defensive, even though this defensive posture was adopted in a manner that was as offensive as possible in the tactical sense. Thus the primary objective of the Royal Navy was to prevent the ships of the French navy making an escape in any numbers from any of their ports.

A strategic blockade of this extent, that had to be maintained right through the year under any and all weather conditions, would have been a difficult undertaking at the best of times. Yet this was not the best of times, for the morale of the British in general and of the Royal Navy in particular was not high. Conditions on board most of the Royal Navy's ships were so bad that they soon produced

The overall direction of the British war effort was vested in the hands of William Pitt "the Younger" as prime minister. Inevitably, perhaps, Pitt planned a war to be fought on the lines established by his father, the great Lord Chatham ("Pitt the Elder"). Lacking manpower and a large army, as had also been the case in the Seven Years' War (1756-63), Britain was to make its major effort at sea. Within the context of the maritime war envisaged by Pitt, the colonies of France and any of their allies were to be taken. As a minister put it in 1801, "it is as much the duty of those entrusted with the conduct of a British war to cut off the colonial resources of the enemy as it would be that of a general of a great army to destroy the magazines of his opponent." The minister was wrong on both counts: France was self-supporting, and her armies lived off the lands they seized.

Above: *In the Battle of the Glorious First of June the French lost seven ships, one sunk and six brought into Portsmouth.*

Thus the reality of the situation was that events in the West Indies, for instance, had little effect on the strength of France in Europe, and in fact caused an unfortunate dispersion of Britain's already very straitened military and naval resources. As the future Lord Barham told a predecessor, the 2nd Earl Spencer, who was the First Lord of the Admiralty between 1794 and 1801: "I think if you see [the secretary of war] it may not be amiss to urge the danger of running after distant objects, while the great object lies still —of hunting the sheep till you have killed the dog....It is this system of unlimited conquest that cripples us everywhere, and diverts the fleet from its natural use." In just the first year of the war Admiral Sir John Jervis took most of the French West Indian islands in a series of notably effective

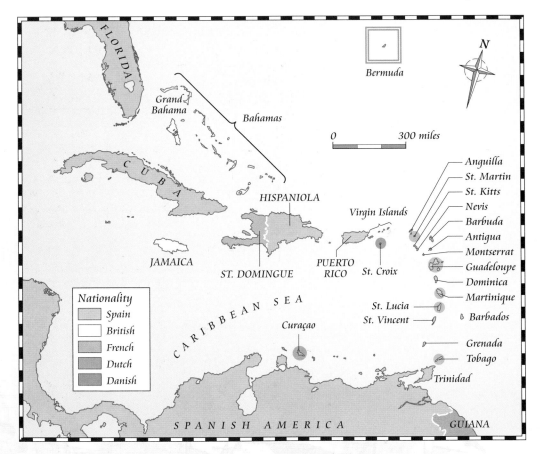

Above: *A map of the eastern Caribbean in 1790 reveals the ownership of islands that were the cause of much fighting.*

combined operations. Relations between the navy and the army were very much of a see-saw nature, but despite this fact the overseas colonies of France, Holland, and Spain continued to fall into British hands.

Action at Toulon

The great politician and thinker Edmund Burke suggested a different approach, however, on the grounds that Britain's enemy was Jacobinism rather than France. Burke therefore urged support from the sea for the French Royalist forces in places such as La Vendée and Toulon. This policy was also adopted, but met with little real success. Admiral Hood's Mediterranean forces, including 21 line-of-battle ships and supported by a Spanish squadron, took Toulon on August 27th, 1793 and his approach spurred a declaration for the monarchy. The British immediately seized the port's great naval arsenal together with some 70 naval vessels including 30 line-of-battle ships that then constituted about half of the French navy's primary strength. The republican French forces responded with speed, and by September 7th had invested Toulon on the landward side. There followed a period of stalemate until the arrival of a capable commander, General Jacques E. Dugommier with Captain Napoleon Bonaparte among his officers. Dugommier accepted Bonaparte's plan of attack, and by December 16th the Republican forces had retaken the forts commanding the anchorage, requiring Hood to pull back his ships and abandon Toulon on December 19th after taking out or destroying 13 of the captured French ships. Spanish incompetence was responsible for another 15 line-of-battle ships surviving to fall once more into republican French hands.

In August 1794 the British seized Corsica, in an operation that cost Horatio Nelson the sight of his right eye, as a fleet base. The various Quiberon expeditions in Brittany all failed, revealing the problems of seeking to support guerrilla forces who were more concerned with gaining local independence than aiding an émigré movement centered on replacing a national government.

The third of the naval strategies adopted by the British, and as events were to prove the decisive concept, was the blockade of France's ports, and in particular the blockade of the country's naval bases and main fleet anchorages. At first each of these blockades had to be of the "open" type: lacking any reserve of ships to relieve those on duty, Howe's Channel Fleet had to adopt a scheme of occasional cruises in force from Spithead into the Bay of Biscay, while at the same time maintaining an observation squadron off Ushant. This was too loose a system to secure any but chance encounters, although it did yield the first

Left: *The Battle of the Glorious First of June, 1794, was a fight between matched fleets each with 26 line-of-battle ships at the start. Admiral Louis Villaret de Joyeuse's French fleet was outfought and broke off the battle.*

Below: *Before they pulled out of Toulon, the British burned or carried away part of the French fleet, but Spanish inaction left 15 line-of-battle ships intact.*

major British naval victory of the war, the Battle of the Glorious First of June, in 1794.

Universally known as "Black Dick," Howe was almost 70 years old at the time of the Battle of the Glorious First of June, and soon after this retired from command afloat, being replaced by the Admiral Lord Bridport, the younger brother of the far superior Admiral Hood. Without any analysis of what was really required, Bridport maintained the "open blockade" of France's northern and western ports and naval bases. The inefficiency of this system was revealed for all to see by the escape from Brest at the end of 1796 of the French fleet carrying French troops toward Ireland. Part of the French force was sighted by Captain Edward Pellew (later Lord Exmouth) in the frigate HMS *Indefatigable*, but he was unable to contact the observation squadron because it was not on station. The Channel Fleet finally succeeded in reaching the scene of the planned invasion a full three days after the last of the French ships had sailed for home after being driven back by the weather. The limitations of the "open blockade" were learned, though, and when two years later another attempt was made to land French forces in Ireland, the observation frigates were able to notify a detachment of the Channel Fleet and all but two ships of the French squadron were intercepted and captured.

Right: *Nelson's inshore squadron blockades the Spanish port of Cadiz. British blockade tactics were based on a lighter inshore squadron that could seek to deter a breakout, but also warn a heavier offshore force of any such attempt.*

Meanwhile in the Mediterranean Fleet's theater of responsibility, Admiral Sir John Jervis had instituted a much more effective blockade system, which involved keeping virtually his whole fleet at sea (off Toulon for 160 days in the first instance). When Jervis took up his command in 1795, he felt that the fleet was in very poor condition but that it had the makings of a superb naval instrument. These makings were to be found mainly in the captains of the ships that constituted the Mediterranean Fleet: Nelson commanded HMS *Agamemnon* and was clearly the man of whom the greatest things could be expected, but there were also other superb commanders in the form of Cuthbert Collingwood, Thomas Foley, T.F. Freemantle, Ben Hallowell, and Thomas Troubridge to name just a few of perhaps 15 excellent leaders. Jervis was a fine teacher as well as a good commander, and soon created a team that was to prove decisive. When given a high command for the first time, three years later, Nelson informed his mentor, now the Earl St. Vincent, "We look up to you, as we have always found you, as our father, under whose fostering care we have been led to fame."

Once captured, the island of Corsica provided good harbors from which Toulon could be watched. This eased Jervis's problems of keeping ships and men at sea for long periods, but even so the supply and replacement situation was so severe that the senior officers of the Mediterranean Fleet had to exercise extreme care in using the ships and the supplies of which they were dependant. In the circumstances Jervis was right when he informed the Admiralty that the Mediterranean Fleet was in a position somewhat different from that of the Channel Fleet and the growing numbers of fleets and squadrons detached to stations in other parts of the world.

Throughout this period Bonaparte was emerging as a leader of genius in his extraordinary first Italian campaign. However, a detached squadron under Nelson rendered insecure the coastal supply route along which the French

> **We have no relaxation in port, where we never go without positive necessity; the officers are all kept to their duty; no sleeping on shore, or rambling about the country; and when at sea we do not make snug for the night, as in the Western Squadron [of the Channel Fleet], but are working incessantly by the lead to keep our position, insomuch as both mind and body are continually upon the stretch.**

Sir John Jervis, quoted in *Memoirs of the Earl of St. Vincent*, J.S. Tucker

Above: *Despite his brilliance in the strategy and tactics of land warfare, Napoleon had a signal misappreciation of maritime affairs. His "continental system" sought to deny the British access to European trade, but his lack of an effective navy left Great Britain to enjoy global trade and power.*

transported their supplies. In the second Italian campaign, some four years later, the ships of Admiral Sir William Keith succeeded to a far greater extent in cutting the French land forces' shipborne supply route, and indeed forced the capitulation of Genoa as it was on the verge of starvation. Bonaparte compelled his men to live off the land, partly because of the speed at which he also compelled his forces to move, and it was this rather than any failing by the British that caused an Austrian collapse at the end of each of the Italian campaigns.

The Austrian collapse combined with an alliance between France and Spain meant that the Mediterranean Fleet was ordered to pull back to Lisbon in Portugal. This was at the end of 1796, a time that must be regarded as one of the lowest, if not actually the lowest, points in the war for the British.

Victories and Mutinies

For two years the Mediterranean Fleet blockaded the southern Spanish port of Cadiz, one of the most satisfactory results being Jervis's great victory in the Battle of Cape St. Vincent on February 14th, 1797. As Jervis said to himself while heading his force of 15 line-of-battle ships toward a fleet of 27 Spanish ships coming round from the Mediterranean in the hope of reaching the French base at Brest, "a victory is very essential to England at this moment" for the combined French and Spanish fleets at Brest would have made French support for a major Irish rising all but inevitable.

Between the Battle of St. Vincent in February and Admiral Adam Duncan's much harder victory over the Dutch at Camperdown on October 11th of the same year, when the Dutch lost 11 of 15 ships to the British in a battle so grim that none of the prizes was worth repairing for British service, there occurred the two Great Mutinies in British waters. If the French had tried to launch an invasion, the mutineers would probably have returned to their duty, as they said they would, and allowed the Royal Navy to tackle the invasion fleet.

Above: *France sought constantly to exploit the capabilities of allies, but without much success. Here Admiral Adam Duncan accepts the sword of Admiral de Winter as the Dutch officer concedes defeat in the Battle of Camperdown in October 1797. The painting is by Samuel Drummond.*

Left: *The British victory at Cape St. Vincent saw 15 British line-of-battle ships defeat 27 Spanish ships, four being taken and the rest being driven back to Cadiz.*

66 In 1796...any thinking sailor would have seen himself as just another of a steadily growing body of pariahs roundly condemned by all ashore... **99**

Although the mutinies broke out on Royal Navy ships in several British ports, it was those in the major elements of the Channel Fleet at Spithead and the Nore that caused the greatest consternation. Caused largely by the brutality of the service combined with poor food and poor pay, the first of the mutinies started at Spithead on April 16th, followed on May 12th by that at the Nore. The Spithead mutiny was not undertaken in a spirit of enormous determination and collapsed as soon as Howe, universally known as "the sailor's friend," took a hand in the matter with promises to investigate and redress the sailors' grievances and also to secure a royal pardon for the mutineers. The fleet's second mutiny between May and October at the Nore under the instigation of Richard Parker was altogether more dangerous for Britain. Instead of sailing from Yarmouth to blockade the Dutch coast, Duncan's fleet moved into the Thames to join the mutineers, at a stroke increasing the strength of the disaf-

Eyewitness

"Well, Lord Howe at last settled the business and came round the fleet attended by his lady and some great gentlemen, and when they landed, the delicates [delegates] hoisted his Lordship upon their shoulders, and carried him up to the house, where they dined with the admiral and a large party. Up went 154 [the flag that had signalled the start of the mutiny]; again the anchors were weighed, and the fleet sailed under Bridport to cruise for the enemy."

"Old Sailor's" account published in *Greenwich Hospital* (1826)

It is easy to see how the generally appalling conditions on British warships could drive the men to consider mutiny, especially as these conditions were long-standing grievances. What is harder to establish is why the mutiny started at the precise moment that Britain's fortunes were at their lowest ebb in the face of a continental enemy that was growing steadily stronger and more antagonistic. One important factor was the long periods of idleness to which the system of "open blockade" condemned ships and men. Awaiting news that "the French were out" and the chance of a decisive battle, the men grew bored with the day-to-day routine of shipboard life. Feelings could fester and, through the efforts of those with the highest levels of disaffection, be brought to the point of open rebellion against authority. Many officers, including Duncan, believed that another important cause of the mutinies was the disaffection of the "quota men." Serving the double purpose of removing "undesirables" of all types from society and at the same time boosting the manpower of the Royal Navy, the Quota Acts of 1795 had led to the drafting into naval service of all manner of "undesirables." One such was Parker, who had been incarcerated for debt after discharge as a midshipman. Parker evidently wanted to get his own back on the navy, and the fact that he had had some education made him a significant figure on the lower decks. Parker was a natural demagogue, but not even his rabble-rousing gifts could sustain the mutiny at the Nore for long. Gradually the disaf-

Above: *"The Devils in Council or Beggars on Horseback" by George Cruikshank—British cartoonists portrayed events with bitter savagery, and particular venom was used on the sailors involved in the mutinies of 1797.*

fection and reducing the Royal Navy's ability to undertake operations in defense of the country. There seems little doubt that the mutiny would also have taken hold in British ships based at Lisbon if St. Vincent had not nipped the matter in the bud by hanging the first offender at the yardarm.

fected ships surrendered to Keith, who had assumed command at the Nore. Eventually Parker and some 29 other ringleaders were hanged.

Efforts were made to remove some of the sailors' grievances, although on a rather spasmodic basis. Improvements to pay and provisions were made, and during the period up to 1810 the more repressive forms of punishment were banned. Even so, not many sailors would have detected major differences in the basic quality of life on board a ship of the Royal Navy in 1796 and in 1806. But the

took naval operations against the French in the Mediterranean in support of the Austrians' left flank. It was clear that the French fleet in Toulon was being readied for action, but British naval opinion was divided as to the probable French objective: some suggested an attack on Naples, but St. Vincent and others thought a descent on Ireland more probable. The Admiralty left St. Vincent with the choice of how best to keep watch on the French in Toulon, but at the same time suggested that the force detached for the purpose should be commanded by Nelson.

Below left: A scene on the middle deck of the Hector. Life for the men seems squalid in this drawing, but the reality was even worse as the height between the decks was lower and the number of men greater. When a ship lay at anchor for long periods, with no prospect of leave or even the excitement of battle, poor conditions and bad food led the idling men to thoughts of protest, and even of mutiny, as possibly the only way available to them to win any improvement in their conditions, food, and pay.

sailors' estimation of their own worth in the eyes of the public did change. In 1806, a sailor would have seen himself as a member of an elite group whose claim to fame was derived from a series of great victories culminating in the Battle of Trafalgar (1805). In 1796, on the other hand, any thinking sailor would have seen himself as just another of a steadily growing body of pariahs roundly condemned by all ashore and currently relegated to long periods of physically, emotionally, and spiritually degrading inactivity as their ships lay at anchor.

The fact that there was no resurgence of mutinous feeling on a major scale is attributable to two basic facts: the replacement of the "open blockade" by the "close blockade," which kept the men fully occupied, and the steady evolution of the arcane art of leadership among the new breed of commanders that the war brought to the fore.

Nelson and the Nile

Early in 1798, Austria informed Britain that it might resume hostilities against the French if the British once more under-

Below: Sailing in line ahead and seeking to get up to windward, a British force—the Arrogant, Intrepid, and Virginie— tries to overhaul a damaged and poorly disposed Franco-Spanish squadron off China on January 27th, 1799. Such excitement became increasingly rare as the war progressed.

Soon to be replaced by Keith, St. Vincent concurred that the possibility of a Second Coalition made it worth the risk of dividing the force at his disposal by detaching 13 line-of-battle ships. Thus Nelson's ships cruised in the Gulf of Lions as the French completed their preparations, but they were driven off station to a point beyond the southern tip of Sardinia on May 19th by a storm that opened the way for the departure of Napoleon's army of 43,000 men on board 13 line-of-battle ships, six frigates, and more than 300 transport vessels. Their destination was not Naples or Ireland, but Egypt via Malta. The Directory which then ruled France had welcomed this suggestion from their young but obviously enormously talented commander. In the previous year, when nominated as commander of the Army of England, he had explained that he could do nothing in this capacity without French

Above: A leader who made much of his reputation in the Mediterranean was Horatio Nelson, whose fleet is here depicted at anchor off Naples.

Above, top: A capable tactical commander, Sir William Sidney Smith held Acre in 1799 and thus checked Napoleon's first attempt to quit Egypt.

command of the sea. Wishing to avoid the danger of leaving so charismatic a figure restless at home and possibly considering plans for his own political advancement, the Directory appreciated the potential of a descent on Malta and then Egypt, thereby crippling British trade in the region and establishing a base from which India might be attacked.

Nelson caught up with the French on August 1st, by which date Napoleon had won the battle of the Pyramids, captured Cairo, and conquered Egypt. The French fleet lay snugly in Aboukir Bay, a few miles to the east of Alexandria, the 13 line-of-battle ships anchored in a line stretching across the bay just 160 yards apart so that they had room to swing at their anchors. The captain of Nelson's leading ship, HMS *Goliath*, led the British line inside the line of moored French ships, and the result of the engagement was a decisive British victory in the Battle of the Nile: only two of the French ships escaped destruction or capture. The establishment of the Second Coalition followed in December of the same year and a rising in Malta, aided by Nelson, led to the besieging of the French garrison in Valletta, where it surrendered from starvation in 1800.

Napoleon's Reverses

The Ottoman Empire was a new ally, Russian and Austrian armies reconquered Italy and moved up to the frontier with France. A Russo-Turkish fleet appeared in the Adriatic, the threat to India was removed, and Minorca fell to the British. In these circumstances Napoleon, stranded in Egypt, opted for an overland return to Europe via Constantinople. Even in this plan he was again foiled by British naval power, and Napoleon later said: "If it had not been for the English I should have been Emperor of the East, but wherever there is water to float a ship, we are sure to find you in our way."

Nelson had left control of operations in the Levant, of an unspecified nature and with only two ships, to Sir Sidney Smith, an extraordinary man who features strongly in the Mediterranean-based books of the Aubrey canon. Learning that Napoleon was marching up the coast of Syria, Smith committed all the forces that he could (largely by stripping one of his ships) to the defense of Acre. At the same time his other ship intercepted Napoleon's siege train on its way from Alexandria. Acre held out against desperate French assaults until plague erupted in the French camp and Napoleon fell back to Egypt, from where the French commander escaped back to France in a frigate, effectively deserting his army.

Smith was a swashbuckling character well able to promote his own capabilities to an impressed public. As events soon proved, Smith could carry off unorthodox and daring strokes when left to his own devices, he was a poor subordinate in more conventional operations.

Before being elevated to First Lord in 1801, St. Vincent had commanded the Channel Fleet for a year. He discovered that the fleet's condition to be worse in all respects than that of the Mediterranean Fleet when he had taken

Above: *Moored in an apparently strong position in Aboukir Bay and expecting a British attack only on their seaward side, the French had not appreciated that part of the British force could pass between their line and the shore, allowing the British ships to fire on the stationary French from both sides.*

command. He soon implemented a raft of measures to improve the situation and, at the same time, replaced the "open blockade" of Brest with a "close blockade." On the first occasion that the Channel Fleet undertook such a blockade, it was at sea for 121 days, but such were the improvements that St. Vincent had implemented that the fleet's 25,000 men suffered only 15 cases of scurvy.

With Napoleon seeking to stir up a naval hornet's nest in the Baltic to draw the attention of the Royal Navy and perhaps inflict major losses on it, in March 1801 53 ships (18 line-of-battle ships) of the Channel Fleet sailed for the Baltic under the command of Admiral Sir Hyde Parker with Nelson as his second in command. The British plan was to deal with the Danish fleet in Copenhagen before the ice in the Baltic broke up: if the allies of the Armed Neutrality of the North were able to combine their fleets, they would have at least 40 line-of-battle ships to the 18 at the heart of the British squadron. The British found 18 such ships at Copenhagen under the protection of armed hulks and floating batteries, but in a fierce five-hour battle on April 2nd Nelson smashed all resistance. Nelson now wanted Parker to proceed to Reval to tackle the Russian fleet, but the cautious Parker demurred and an armistice was signed before the Anglophobe Tsar Paul was assassinated and succeeded by the anglophile Alexander I, effectively ending the threat to Britain's eastern flank.

Below: Admiral Lord Nelson lies dying in the Victory after his triumph in the Battle of Trafalgar on October 21st, 1805. French naval power was shattered.

Little of note then occurred at sea until October 21st, 1805 and Nelson's destruction of the combined French and Spanish fleets in the Battle of Trafalgar. Without losing a single ship, Nelson's force of 27 line-of-battle ships comprehensively defeated the Franco-Spanish force of 33 line-of-

battle ships in a grim five-hour battle. Nelson was mortally wounded, but the Franco-Spanish fleet lost 18 of its ships and with them all possibility of rivalling the British at sea. The war at sea did rumble on until 1814, but there were no more fleet actions.

King George III had described the opening of hostilities in February 1793 as "highly agreeable to me," and it is more than likely that the great majority of British naval officers shared his opinion. For those unemployed, on the beach on half-pay, the war offered appointment to seagoing commands. For those already at sea it offered, in the words of a somewhat heartless military toast of the time, "a bloody war and a sickly season"—in other words, the prospect of immediate employment and speedy promotion.

Enter Jack Aubrey

Among those already at sea when hostilities between Britain and France began in February 1793 was Jack Aubrey. Just where he was early in 1793 we cannot be certain, for all we know of his life before his meeting with Stephen Maturin at Port Mahon, Minorca, in the early April of the year 1800, is what we can glean from his reminiscences in the course of the canon, and these are not always consistent. It seems probable that in early 1793 he was fifth lieutenant in HMS *Queen* (98). We know from remarks in *Master and Commander* and elsewhere that Jack was a sometime midshipman in HMS *Agamemnon* (64). This cannot have been between January 1793 and April 1796, for during that time she was commanded by Nelson, whom we know Jack to have encountered in person only once—at a dinner where Nelson asked him to pass the salt. In any case, in both *The Far Side of the World* and *The Wine-Dark Sea* Jack states that he "passed for Lieutenant" in 1792. (Having been born in about 1770, he is around 30 years old when we, and Maturin, first meet him in *Master and Commander*). We must assume then that his service as a midshipman under Captain (later Rear Admiral) Sir Charles Douglas (a gunnery expert) in HMS *Resolution* (74) was before 1792. It was at some time during this commission that he was disrated and sent to serve for six months before the mast (that is, as an ordinary seaman) as punishment for bringing aboard a black girl—Sally M'Puta, by whom he becomes the father of an illegitimate son, Sam Panda, who makes his appearance in *The Reverse of the Medal* and later parts of the canon—and concealing her in the cable locker. This incident occurred while the *Resolution* was at the Cape of Good Hope, which until August-September 1795 was a Dutch possession.

The conquest of the Cape Colony provides an illustration of a major reason for Britain's remorseless prosecution of

Above: *Ships in Table Bay off Cape Town in South Africa, with Table Mountain evident in the background. The British took the Cape from the Dutch in 1795, and thus gained a vital base on the route between Europe and India, the Far East, and Australia.*

the Revolutionary and Napoleonic Wars. For a naval power, and Britain was then and would for a century or more remain the world's greatest naval power, the possession of a worldwide network of bases is essential for both the successful waging of war and the maintenance of trade. The Cape anchorage at Table Bay (re-established in 1815 at nearby Simon's Bay; later, as Simonstown, an important naval base up to and after World War II) was a major stepping stone on the routes of the British East India Company's ships to India and China. But as a French puppet state from early 1795, the Netherlands (known as the Batavian Republic until 1805 and thereafter as the Kingdom of Holland) was forced to bar the British East Indiamen from the Cape. British naval power had already seized such French West Indian bases as Tobago and Santo Domingo, Pondicherry in India, and St. Pierre and Miquelon in 1793, followed by the conquest of the West Indian islands of Martinique, Guadeloupe, St. Lucia, the Saints, Maria Galante, and Deseada in 1794.

In February 1795 Ceylon was taken from the Dutch, and the conquest of the Cape of Good Hope soon followed. The task was entrusted to a squadron of five line-of-battle ships and two sloops under the command of Vice Admiral Sir George Elphinstone (later Admiral Lord Keith), and

carrying some 800 soldiers under Major General Sir James Craig. Backed by an equal number of sailors from the squadron, the troops stormed the Dutch encampment on August 7th. After further British troops arrived from India, the Dutch surrendered the colony on September 14th. As well as securing the East Indiamen's trade, the Cape provided an important base for British squadrons operating against the French at Mauritius and the Bourbon Islands.

Above: *Command of the sea gave the British great scope for amphibious operations, such as this that led to the capture of Martinique in the West Indies. The British took the island twice during the French Revolutionary and Napoleonic Wars, in 1794 and 1809.*

Right: Seen as a captain in 1807, Thomas Cochrane was an extraordinary man possessing great flair as a frigate captain but also an amazing ability to irritate his superiors. This fascinating figure, who featured strongly in the independence wars of South America, was the single most important conceptual source for the creation of Jack Aubrey.

Similar conquests quickly followed, and for similar reasons. Dutch territories in the West Indies, vital for trade with the Americas, and East Indies were taken in 1796; Trinidad and Madagascar in 1797; Minorca in 1798, in the process giving the British an invaluable base at Port Mahon; Surinam in 1799; Curaçao, Goree (Senegal), and Malta in 1800; Danish and Swedish possessions in the West Indies in 1801. Although most of these prizes were restored to their former possessors under the terms of the Peace of Amiens in 1801-02—Malta, Ceylon, Trinidad, and large areas of India seized from native rulers thought to favor the French were the exceptions—most were swiftly reconquered after the Peace was broken in 1803. Considering that at the

Through Aubrey's Eyes

Jack Aubrey has an ambivalent attitude toward the Admiralty, its functionaries, and its systems. This becomes clear at an early stage of Aubrey's relationship with this body (*H.M.S. Surprise* Chapter 1). On the one hand Aubrey is a strong believer in the importance of established authority and the value of passed-down tradition, both evident in the nature and workings of the Admiralty. On the other hand he is a thinking man, and therefore sees the Admiralty's machinations as sometimes too slow to cope with the nature of the war. As essentially a man of action, Aubrey also chafes at the involvement of civilians in the workings of the Admiralty, the ponderous nature of this body's decision-making processes, and the slow implementation of decisions. As his progress up the Navy List brings Aubrey into more frequent involvement with the Admiralty, his fundamental opinions do not change, although he is still impressed by capabilities of the senior officers controlling the professional naval aspects of the Admiralty's responsibilities.

Above: The British took Gibraltar from the Spanish in 1704, thereby securing a significant base for control of the western end of the Mediterranean and its exit into the Atlantic Ocean.

beginning of 1793 the Royal Navy had had only four overseas bases—Gibraltar, Jamaica, Antigua, and Halifax, Nova Scotia—its international expansion had been remarkable.

Returning to Jack Aubrey's adventures, we can deduce from his reminiscences that at various times after 1792, in addition to his commission in HMS *Queen* mentioned above,

he served as a lieutenant in HMS *Agamemnon* (again), *Arethusa* (38), *Bellerophon* (74) (in which he had once been a midshipman), *Colossus* (74) and *Orion* (74) (in both of which, he says at different times, he took part in the Battle of Cape St. Vincent in February 1797) and *Ardent* (64), in which he says, in *Desolation Island*, he was present at the Battle of Camperdown in October 1797, and several other ships. All these appointments must have been brief, for we know that on August 1st, 1798 he took part in the Battle of the Nile as a lieutenant in HMS *Leander* (50). It was certainly not unusual for an officer to move quite frequently from ship to ship for a variety of reasons. Sometimes a commander would ask for a favored officer to be transferred to his ship; sometimes an officer might exchange ships to avoid an "unhealthy" posting like the West Indies, or to move from home to foreign waters for personal reasons (in Jack's case, if we are to judge from the troubles that afflict him from time to time throughout the canon, to escape from financial embarrassments). A commission seldom lasted more than two years in any case, and to avoid a period on half-pay most officers would quickly seek a new ship: Nelson served in eight ships before he became a post captain, and held that rank in five more before becoming a rear admiral.

Leander Under Fire

HMS *Leander*, like Jack himself, emerged with no great harm from the Battle of the Nile, where the ship suffered 14 wounded. As a fourth-rate of only 50 guns it had been most unusual for her to stand in the line of battle, and she had spent most of the fight attempting to help the grounded *Culloden* off a reef. Within three weeks, however, she was engaged in a much bloodier fight, from which Jack, by his own account in *Master and Commander*, emerged as the only surviving lieutenant. (It should be noted here that Patrick O'Brian, as he states in an Author's Note in *Master and Commander*, based all the naval actions in his books on real conflicts. Thus, although there was no "Jack Aubrey" aboard the *Leander* at the Nile, or anywhere else, and although O'Brian may invent a warship or adapt a real one for fictional purposes, or change dates for the purpose of his narrative, the battles he mentions or describes are real.)

Immediately after the victory in Aboukir Bay, the *Leander*, having lost a further 50 men to man a prize and being left with a complement of about 280, was chosen (as the fleet's weakest ship, and because of Nelson's shortage of frigates) to carry Nelson's dispatches to England. On August 18th, west of Candia, Crete, she encountered the *Généreux* (74), one of two French line-of-battle ships that survived the Nile battle. With the wind in her favor, the *Généreux* engaged. Heavily outgunned and vastly outnumbered (the *Généreux* carried more than 900 men), Captain Thomas Thompson fought his ship most gallantly. Early French attempts to board were beaten off, and in light airs a gun duel raged for some six hours. Even with his mizzen and fore topmasts shot away, Thompson managed to bring the *Leander* across the French warship's stern and rake her.

At last, however, with *Leander's* fore and mainmasts and bowsprit shattered, and 23 men killed and 58 wounded,

Thompson, himself badly wounded, struck his colors to prevent further useless slaughter. The *Généreux* had lost 100 killed and 188 wounded; all the boats of both ships had been destroyed, and a French midshipman had to swim to the British ship to accept her surrender. Captain Lejoille and his men showed little chivalry: the *Leander*, which was retaken by a Russo-Turkish squadron at Corfu in the following year and later rejoined the Royal Navy, was thoroughly looted to the extent of even the surgeon's instruments with the result that he could not attend to the wounded. When Lejoille offered to take any captured seaman

into the Revolutionary navy, he was resoundingly rebuffed by a maintop-man, George Bannister: "No, you damned French rascal! Give us back our little ship and we'll fight you again until we sink!" Paroled with his officers later in the year, Captain Thompson returned to face the inevitable court-martial for giving up his ship. The court praised his conduct and acquitted with him honor; he and his officers were cheered round the fleet at Sheerness, and he shortly received a knighthood. In *Master and Commander*, Jack ascribes his step to commander to his service in the *Leander*.

Above: The capture of the Leander (50) by the Généreux (74), one of the Nile's two French survivors, on August 18th, 1798. The Leander was carrying the Nile dispatches, and struck after fighting for more than six hours.

Above, top: Peter Downes was the Leander's senior midshipman, and was killed in the battle.

Aubrey's England

Although Jack Aubrey is a man of the sea, and nowhere happier than out of sight of land and higher authority other than the Articles of War, the naval world in which he finds himself was, of course, just one facet of a pan-European and, to a certain extent, global situation.

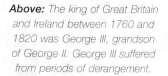

Aubrey is aware of the fact, even though he tries at times to ignore it, but the presence of his "particular friend," Stephen Maturin the doctor, naturalist, and secret agent, is a constant reminder of the fact. Maturin is an altogether more political creature than Aubrey, and his undertakings on behalf of the British intelligence apparatus serve to embroil Aubrey in European and increasingly in world events.

Aubrey and Maturin swim metaphorically in a sea of social, economic, political, and nationalist factors that had been developing since the end of the Middle Ages. After early setbacks caused by plague and famine, the population of Europe nearly doubled in overall terms, and while this growth was considerable in rural areas, it was even faster in towns and cities. In 1500 only Paris, Milan, Naples, and Venice had a population of 100,000 or more, but by 1700 the number of cities that could boast such a population had trebled, and London and Paris each contained more than 500,000 inhabitants.

Above: The king of Great Britain and Ireland between 1760 and 1820 was George III, grandson of George II. George III suffered from periods of derangement.

Above right: By the outbreak of the French Revolutionary and Napoleonic Wars, London (seen here from the Tower to London Bridge) was a great mercantile, as well as political, capital.

Urban Growth

Factors that promoted this spurt in urbanization were the steadily more complex nature of national governments, the rapid development and growth of national and international trade and finance, the enlargement of the monied class (now including a substantial middle class to complement the existing upper class), and the understated but nonetheless real belief that existence was better in cities. This urbanization offered new chances for development and change. Most notably, they generated a massive demand for eastern Europe's wheat and rye. In the period of 100 years to 1650, for example, exports of these commodities swept into western Europe as far as Italy, Spain, and Portugal. This was one of the major reasons for the fast-growing

financial strength of Holland, which had a virtual monopoly of the Baltic trade. With powerful shipbuilders, merchants, and manufacturers, the Netherlands was the cardinal point of a slow but very important shift in commercial power.

At the beginning of the 16th century, industries had been compressed largely into the corridor running in the north from Antwerp and Bruges, through Ulm and Augsburg in the center, to Florence and Milan in the south. By the beginning of the 18th century the north/south corridor had been replaced by a west/east corridor. At the western end were England and Holland, which were the most important textile producers, the homes of the largest fleets of merchant ships and the most aggressive and capable traders, and rapidly expanding centers of shipbuilding and the manufacture of metal goods. The corridor extended to the east via the lower Rhine to Saxony, Bohemia, and Silesia.

In this period industrial expansion had been achieved not by the exploitation of new technology, but rather by an

expansion of the numbers of workers in traditional indus- trial occupations. Even so, the enlargement of the indus- trial base in terms of manpower if not technology opened the way to an important organizational improvement in industry: production processes were split up, allowing the expansion of industry into hitherto purely agricultural and craft areas in the country and exploiting the cheap part- time labor of peasant families. At much the same time, this spasmodic intensification and diversification of national industries was mirrored and partially overtaken by the striking development of international trade. This was no longer limited to the countries of Europe, but now extended increasingly to other parts of the world. The major powers, which had the steadily growing tonnage of shipping to allow the establishment of colonies and trading ports all over Asia and the Americas as well as southern Africa, now bent their efforts to creating and boosting the trade in very expensive luxury commodities.

Above: Although published in 1825, 10 years after the end of the Napoleonic Wars, Cruikshank's "Sailors Carousing or a Peep in the Long Room" reflects the public image, and indeed much of the reality, of how the sailor behaved on release from the rigors of his ship to the freedoms of the shore.

66 ...but the decisive factor in this colonial war was not land power but sea power. 99

The nature of any country's national industries and international trade was inevitably reflected in the wars to which governments committed their countries. Thus England and Holland fought wars to protect and expand their shipping and trading interests. What could not be denied, however, was that war was becoming increasingly costly to wage. Thus the wars of the period ruined Spain, and severely damaged France and several smaller countries. Only England and Holland had the financial acumen to limit their military operations within the bounds of sensible financing.

18th-Century Conflict

The Treaty of Utrecht was signed in 1713 and it signalled the effective end of the War of the Spanish Succession (1701-14). The treaty left the Spanish empire and its trading monopolies basically unaltered, and was intended to create a balance of power that would ensure the stability of Europe and its overseas possessions. What resulted, however, was the continuation of colonial conflict. Territorial expansion continued throughout the 18th century. These colonial conflicts were only part of the continued friction in international affairs, though, for trade monopolies became a still greater source of difficulty. Such overseas problems inevitably spread back to the parent countries in Europe, where decisions were inevitably taken.

In 1739-40 European peace ended, yet again, as Great Britain and Spain went to war (the War of Jenkins's Ear, 1739-48) in defense of their trading rights, and Frederick the Great's Prussian invasion of Silesia triggered the events that became the War of the Austrian Succession (1740-48). Then the start of hostilities between Great Britain and France in 1744 linked together the war over Caribbean trade and the war for Silesia in a conflict characterized by fighting on a global basis extending from North America to India, and from the West Indies to Russia. The Seven Years' War marked only the beginning of a struggle that lasted, with breaks, to 1815 and soon became a contest between France and Great Britain for global supremacy.

In 1748 the Treaty of Aix-la-Chapelle that ended the War of the Austrian Succession settled none of the problems that had led to the war in the first place, and this resulted in a resumption of fighting in North America during 1754. Just two years later France had achieved a local advantage in this French and Indian War (1754-63), but the decisive factor in this colonial war was not land power but sea power, for it was control of the lines of communication to North America that was decisive. So while France was handicapped by its continental commitments after the French and Indian War had become merely the North American aspect of the Seven Years' War, Great Britain took advantage of its freedom from continental obligations to seize complete control of the Atlantic and thus to sunder the French forces in North America from sources of supply and reinforcement in France. Thus the British were able to take France's possessions in North America.

Above: The capture of Puerto Bello in 1739 during the "War of Jenkins's Ear." This war reflected growing trade and imperial differences between Spain and Great Britain in the Americas, and the first major British success was the seizure of Puerto Bello by forces under Admiral Vernon.

The nature of trade and the demands of war also generated a huge demand for "hard" money, which took the form of bullion (gold and silver). This was available in adequate quantities from Spain (silver from Mexico and Peru after 1550) and Portugal (gold from Brazil from the 1690s). After arrival in the Iberian peninsula, the bullion found its war into the European economy through trade and Spanish government transactions, much of it then being used to finance trade deficits with the East Indies and the Levant.

But between the end of the Seven Years' War in 1763 and the start of the War of American Independence in 1776, France made a huge effort to rebuild her navy and create a new web of alliances. Faced with the possibility of war with an alliance of France, Spain, and the Dutch Republic, the threat of the "armed neutrality" of the Baltic powers, and the financial and military strains of defending what was now an empire stretching from Canada to India, Great Britain lost control of the waters off North America in 1781. Admiral Rodney's victory over the French in the Battle of the Saintes in April 1782 ensured that Great Britain kept her islands in the Caribbean, but North American reverses on land and sea cost Great Britain the 13 colonies that secured their formal independence as the United States of America by the Treaty of Versailles in 1783. Despite the lingering animosities of the war, trade between Great Britain and North America was soon resumed.

Yet in the same period Great Britain came into possession of a new empire, this time on the other side of the world in India. Here the emergence out of the ruins of the Mogul empire of independent kingdoms made it necessary for both the British and French East India Companies to protect their commercial interests by interference in local affairs. British and French interests were soon at war with each other, and again sea power was to prove itself the arbiter of affairs. Despite early French gains on land, the British maritime capacity to send in reinforcements but deny the same advantage to the French opened the way for the halting of French ambitions and the first stages of the establishment of a British empire in India with Robert Clive's victory in the decisive Battle of Plassey (1757). In combination with the victory of an invading Afghan army over the Marathas at the Battle of Panipat (1761), this yielded command of the rich province of Bengal to the British.

Above: *One of the great figures of the later 18th century was Admiral Lord Rodney, seen here in an 1787 portrait by Joshua Reynolds. With the French Admiral Suffren and British Admiral Jervis, Rodney shattered the old order of naval tactics.*

Left: *The Royal Navy generally dominated at sea in the War of American Independence. Here a British squadron destroys an inept American effort to seize Penobscot Bay in August 1779.*

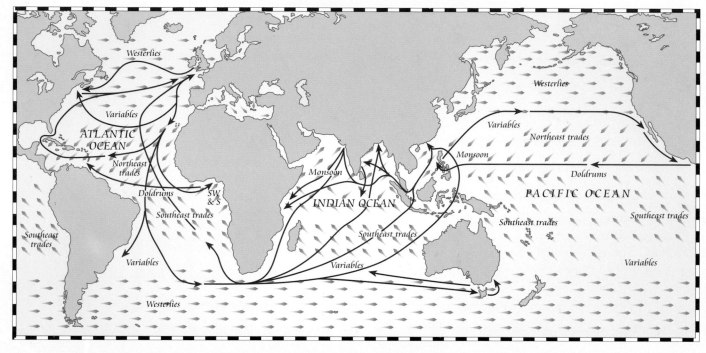

Right: The driving forces behind the European race to empire were the need for raw materials (especially bullion) and, increasingly, trade. These were entirely dependent on the sea lanes between the major European powers and their overseas possessions and trading partners, and these sea lanes were naturally dictated by the prevailing winds.

> ❝ ...there had been a huge enlargement in both the volume and the physical extent of world trade, even before these two elements began to be magnified by the effects of the Industrial Revolution that started in about 1750. ❞

Far right: The heart of British trade with India was the Honourable East India Company, which had its headquarters at East India House in London, depicted here in 1817. The growth of British trade with and power in India was one of the primary driving forces of the British economy.

In overall terms, trading and commercial links with the Americas and with Asia had already started to make a significant contribution to European wealth. The two markets constituted major outlets for the manufactured goods of the "home countries" in return for the exotic foods and materials that were otherwise not obtainable in Europe. Europe's links with the Americas and Asia were radically different from each other, but the commercial completeness of the trading circle was provided by the movement of South and Central American silver via Europe to Asia.

The Industrial Revolution

Up to 1775 there had been a huge enlargement in both the volume and the physical extent of world trade, even before these two elements began to be magnified by the effects of the Industrial Revolution that started in about 1750. In the first three-quarters of the 18th century Great Britain almost trebled its overseas commerce, while in a slightly shorter time France, starting from a smaller base, multiplied the value of its export trade more than eight times and in the process nearly reached the British level. More importantly, perhaps, whereas most British trade at the beginning of the 18th century was with countries of the European mainland, by the start of the century's last quarter, about two-thirds

of British trade was with customers outside Europe.

In the pattern of world trade linking the Americas, Europe, and Asia, the commodity most frequently used to settle accounts, after the coarse details had been eliminated by bills of exchange, was Spanish silver. Silver was thus the fuel of the engine of trade between East and West.

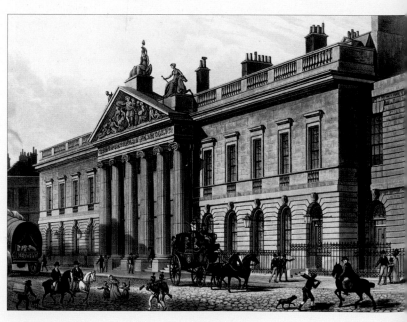

And this world trade enriched several European cities (most importantly London, Liverpool, Glasgow, Bordeaux, Amsterdam, Hamburg, Lisbon, and Cadiz). For most of the 18th century, the merchant class had dominated the British economy. It was only when the Industrial Revolution got fully into its stride that the importance of this class was reduced in relation to the new manufacturers whose efforts effected a radical change in the economical and social natures of Great Britain.

The Industrial Revolution marked the switch from an agrarian to an industrial society, first in Great Britain, then in Europe, and finally all over the world. Although it can be said to have started in about 1750, and was therefore under way even as Jack Aubrey was fighting Great Britain's enemies in the Revolutionary and Napoleonic Wars, the Industrial Revolution began to become a dominant factor only in about 1820, making Great Britain the "workshop of the world." The beginnings of the Industrial Revolution lay in the reign of George III (1760-1820), and entailed major shifts in the nature of the British economy and the structure of British society as production of coal, pig iron, engineering products, and textiles rose dramatically.

Moreover, while the nations of continental Europe were periodically beset by the wars of the 18th century, Great Britain suffered only two relatively small campaigns fought on British soil, namely the Jacobite risings of 1715 and 1745. This did not mean that Great Britain was not involved in wars, but merely that she fought her wars at sea or on other people's territory. Wars with France opened the way for an expansion of the British empire and its trade, especially in Canada and India, while the loss of the 13 colonies in North America had no major short-term impact on trade. Even after the start of the French Revolutionary and Napoleonic Wars, the loss of European markets was more than offset by the expansion of British trade with South America. Moreover, the wars in which Great Britain became involved in fact helped to spur the growth of industries such as iron making, engineering, shipbuilding, and textile manufacturing.

Thus were laid the foundations of the global economy and the international situation in which Jack Aubrey finds his far-flung and varied involvement in the French Revolutionary and Napoleonic Wars. Aubrey understands the basic outline of the global situation, but has the invaluable advantage of being able to draw on the rich knowledge base located in the retentive and astute mind of Stephen Maturin. While Maturin can be described as a man who is content to live in the current world situation while trying to effect changes, Aubrey has a deep love of the Royal Navy and its traditions, but yet has the wit and skill to see where things are wrong and need to be changed. This extends from basics —such as how to fight battles—to the desirability of treating his men as human beings rather than as dehumanized creatures who can only work the ship under direct supervision and under the threat of harsh treatment or brutal punishment. These are factors directly related to the nature of Great Britain and its navy at the end of the 18th and beginning of the 19th centuries.

Above: *King George III presents a sword of honor to Admiral Howe after his great victory over the French in the Battle of the Glorious First of June in 1794. As depicted by Henry Perronet Briggs, the event took place on board Howe's flagship, the 2,286-ton Queen Charlotte. The ship was named for Queen Charlotte, wife of King George III, who is seen at his side.*

The Navy of Aubrey's Time

One of the most serious difficulties in which the Royal Navy of Aubrey's time found itself, at a time of ever-increasing commitments and the construction of large numbers of ships, was the perpetual shortage of manpower. In 1740 the navy had a strength of 36,000 men, and this total rose to 55,000 men in 1757, 65,000 men in 1794, and 140,000 men in 1815, the final year of the Napoleonic War. The need for men was boosted not only by the enlargement of the navy,

Eyewitness

"People may talk of Negro slavery and the whip, but let them look nearer to home and see a poor sailor arrived from a long voyage exulting in the pleasure of being among his dearest fr iends and relations. Behold him just entering the door, when a press gang seizes him like a felon, drags him away and puts him into a tender's hold, and from thence he is sent on board a man-o'-war ready to sail for some foreign station, without either seeing his wife, friends or relations; if he complains, he is likely to be seized up and flogged with a cat, and if he deserts he is flogged round the fleet nearly to death. Surely they had better shoot a man at once; it would be greater lenity."

W. Richardson, *A Mariner of England*

Above: *"Manning the Navy" by Collings depicts a naval press gang rounding up men, of pretty poor quality by the look of them, on Tower Hill in London. Such methods were the only way to ensure that ships were adeqately, if not well, manned.*

was impressment, which was a right of the state to seize men for service in the defense of the realm. Even at the time, the practice was acknowledged as both brutal and inefficient. In an effort to overcome the worst excesses of impressments, which could decimate ports and leave them virtually destitute after its source of income had been taken into navy service, there developed a system of "protections:" seamen in government employ, City of London watermen, fishermen, apprentices, tradesmen, and those under 18 or over 55 years old were in theory exempt from impressment. There was also the right of an impressed man to provide a substitute if he could.

The process of seizing a man for impressment was often violent and bloody, but this was not the exclusive preserve of the press gang, for the men of these gangs were often fought off. Moreover, if a press gang impressed an exempt man, there could follow legal proceedings (although the man in question had often disappeared to sea in the meantime) and even a rebuke from the Lords of the Admiralty for the officer in command.

Among the restrictions imposed on the press gangs was the inviolability of a merchant ship's master or officers. However, the requirement for prime seamen meant that merchant ships returning to Great Britain were often

but also by the necessity of replacing those lost in action or maimed and therefore put ashore, or alternatively lost to the active strength through non-combat reasons, such as disease and desertion.

Conditions on board British warships were so bad that there was never a sufficient number of voluntary enlistments to make good losses and provide the additional manpower needed for new construction. The only solution stopped and stripped of many of their sailors. Indeed, there was an incident in 1802 when a Royal Navy ship stopped a homeward-bound East Indiaman, carrying an extremely valuable cargo, in the Bay of Biscay and so denuded her of able-bodied men that she was forced to surrender without a fight when she fell in with a French privateer only a short time later. Another source of bodies was boys at the establishments of philanthropic societies created to find employment for waifs and orphans.

Thus genuine volunteer enlistments accounted for perhaps as little as a quarter of the ship's company. Such men were sometimes drawn by the bounty, which varied from £1 10s (£1.50, about $2.20) to £10 ($15), or by the desire for a change, or to escape events on land, or even

the possibility of bettering themselves by working their way up the navy's promotion ladder to a responsible position, such as a ship's master with an Admiralty warrant, or perhaps even to commissioned rank.

The Royal Navy's lack of manpower was so desperate in the early part of the French Revolutionary War that two Quota Acts were passed by Parliament in March 1795. By the terms of these acts each borough and inland county had to provide a quota of men: the borough of Dartmouth had to produce 394 men, while the quotas for counties included 1,081 from Yorkshire, 589 from Lancashire, 593 from Devon, and so on: London's quota was 5,704. The fruits of the Quota Acts were known as "Billy Pitt's men"

after the prime minister responsible for the acts. Each man was theoretically entitled to a bounty of up to £70. In the absence of sufficient men to fulfil the demands of the Quota Acts, magistrates were told to use the provisions of the Vagrancy Acts to impress those languishing in jail. Inevitably its was the rotten apples of the jails who were the first that were sent to sea, and this had serious effects on the Royal Navy's discipline as evidenced in the mutinies at Spithead and the Nore.

Quite apart from the requirements of discipline, it took harsh treatment to help train these "landmen" and weld them with genuine seamen into an efficient and capable crew that could be of use at sea without delay. Even so, not all ships were characterized by the brutal treatment of its crew. Other than the "great mutinies" of 1797, there were relatively few mutinies on board individual ships. That on the *Hermione* stands out as the bloodiest ever to take place on a ship of the Royal Navy: the crew rebelled against the tyranny of her captain, Hugh Pigot, who was one of nine officers who were murdered. The men then sailed to ship to South America and handed her over to the Spanish, In the next 10 years 20 of the mutineers were captured by the British and hanged (see Chapter 7).

Above: *As seen by Thomas Rowlandson in "Portsmouth Point," life ashore in a naval port was bustling with debauchery as well as industry. This is a scene that might have greeted Jack Aubrey's eyes as he made his way to The Crown for bread and cheese and a quart of beer.*

Left: *Men crowd the yards of the line-of-battle ship Queen Charlotte as Lord Howe comes aboard his flagship in 1796. The scene was repeated in the following year at the end of the "great mutiny" at Spithead as the much respected admiral was once again rowed out to his flagship.*

Naval Administration

So far as the administration of the navy was concerned, it should be remembered that a cabinet of senior government ministers, including the First Lord of the Admiralty, supervised the business of running Great Britain. The cabinet at the time of the French Revolutionary and Napoleonic Wars had a great interest in maritime affairs and as such exercised control of naval strategy, including the annual budget that should be requested from Parliament. This latter comprised the largely dominant House of Lords, the upper chamber composed mainly of large landowners,

Through Aubrey's Eyes

Because of his father's vociferous but ill-informed political opposition to the government, his own financial problems, and unfortunate episodes with senior officers, Jack Aubrey is somewhat wary of close encounters with officialdom at the Admiralty. Here he has several times been forced to wait on officials and sometimes given bad news. The Admiralty has only a small staff, however, and much of its work is effected by word of mouth and in social gatherings in other parts of London. It is in such a situation that Aubrey, in Chapter 4 of *The Thirteen-Gun Salute*, learns of his reinstatement in the navy. All the more gratifyingly, this news comes from the lips of Lord Melville, the First Lord and brother of Aubrey's great friend Heneage Dundas.

and the House of Commons, the lower chamber whose members were elected by a decidedly undemocratic arrangement, of which Jack Aubrey himself is able to take advantage in *The Thirteen-Gun Salute*.

Each year the Parliament voted a sum for naval affairs, this being divided into three parts—the ordinary estimate for maintenance of ships and dockyard facilities, the extra estimate to allow the boosting of the navy's strength by new construction or the reduction in any failures of maintenance, and the manpower estimate for a specific number of seamen and marines.

The professional administration of the navy was the responsibility of the Board of Admiralty under the First Lord of the Admiralty. The First Lord was sometimes an officer of the Royal Navy, but was more generally a politician. The Board of Admiralty had another five or six members, of whom about half were serving officers. The Board was responsible for promotions and appointments, the disposition of fleets and ships, and the best use of resources. It also supervised the Navy Board in matters of the navy's equipment, and met every day at the Admiralty, which from 1796 was in touch by telegraph semaphore with the main dockyards and naval bases. The Admiralty also

> **The professional administration of the navy was the responsibility of the Board of Admiralty under the First Lord of the Admiralty.**

First Lords of the Admiralty in Aubrey's Time

John Pitt, Earl of Chatham	1788-1794
George Spencer, Earl Spencer	1794-1801
Admiral John Jervis, Earl of St. Vincent	1801-1804
Henry Dundas, Viscount Melville	1804-1805
Admiral Charles Middleton, Lord Barham	1805-1806
Hon. Charles Grey, Viscount Howick	1806
Thomas Grenville	1806-1807
Henry Phipps, Lord Mulgrave	1807-1810
Charles Yorke	1810-1812
Robert Saunders Dundas, Viscount Melville	1812-1827

accommodated a small staff that was responsible for the implementation of the Board's instructions. This staff included the Marine Department, Naval Works Department, and Admiralty Court, as well as messengers and porters.

Responsibile for the technical and financial aspects of naval administration, the Navy Board comprised naval officers, shipwright officers, and civilian administrators. The Navy Board was responsible for most of the warrant officers. It examined and posted boatswains, carpenters, and cooks, and appointed without examination other warrant officers, such as masters, surgeons, and pursers. The Navy Board also watched over the dockyards, was responsible for the maintenance of ships and buildings, and also supervised two subordinate Boards, the Victualling and the Sick and Hurt. The head of the Navy Board was the Controller of the Navy, an experienced naval captain, and included two (from 1813 three) Surveyors of the Navy entrusted with control of ship design, building, and maintenance.

Far left: The waiting room of the Admiralty as seen by George Cruikshank. Here officers, both junior and senior, had to await the pleasure of their Lordships of the Admiralty, often for very lengthy periods, with regard to postings and promotions. Jack Aubrey was no exception to this rule.

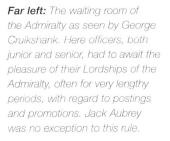

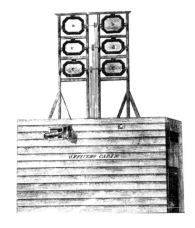

Above: Linking the Admiralty in London with major ports and vantage points was a series of telegraph semaphores that could relay information quickly and accurately except in adverse weather. This is the station erected on the roof of the Admiralty building in the course of February 1796.

Left: Drawn by Thomas Rowlandson and Auguste-Charles Pugin for publication in 1808, this is the Board Room of the Admiralty. Here the most senior figures involved in the operation of the Royal Navy met regularly to plan the course of events with the aid of items such as the rolled maps on the wall.

Unlike other elements of naval administration, the Ordnance Board was a government department in its own right and therefore not under the control of the Admiralty because it was responsible for the supply of guns, ammunition, and associated equipment to the army as well as the navy. The Ordnance Board undertook experimental work, contracted with private foundries for the manufacture of guns, ran the Woolwich Arsenal which received and tested guns before they entered service via the ordnance depots near the main dockyards, supervised the Faversham and Waltham Abbey gunpowder mills, and appointed gunners.

The troop- and equipment-carrying demands of the War of American Independence had been met by the hire of merchant shipping under the auspices of the Navy Board, but in 1794 there appeared the Transport Board to assume this task. The board acquired a good reputation, and in 1796 the task of looking over prisoners of war was transferred from the Sick and Hurt Board to the Transport Board.

Of altogether longer establishment was the Victualling Board, tasked with supplying food and drink to ships together with the pursers who supervised shipboard storage and distribution. The board was headquartered in London, had its primary depot at Deptford, and operated naval victualling yards at the main dockyards as well as other points round the world. The board supervised several breweries, and a large bakery at Portsmouth. The Sick and Hurt Board, sometimes known as the Sick and Wounded Board, was responsible for surgeons and their supplies, the administration of naval hospitals, and supervision of prisoners of war until these last were transferred to the Transport Board.

Above: As well as fighting its own particular type of maritime war, the Royal Navy was also responsible through the Transport Board for conveying and escorting elements of the British army dispatched for service abroad. Seen here at Blackwall on the lower Thames in April 1793, in a painting by William Anderson, cavalry embark in their transport ships.

The Royal Dockyards

The task of maintaining the navy's ships was entrusted to the royal dockyards. Designed to service ships, the dockyard was part of a naval base complex that also included a victualling yard, ordnance depot, hospital, and Marine barracks. The dockyard was responsible in some cases for building ships or in other cases for supervising their construction in nearby yards. The dockyard undertook the repair work on nearly all naval vessels, and supplied the vast number of items needed to keep the vessels seaworthy and serviceable. The dockyard also looked after ships "laid up in ordinary," (i.e. mothballed) and made equipment such as anchors and blocks.

Although private enterprise had been deemed inadequate for the building of naval vessels through much of the 18th century, the outbreak of the French Revolutionary and Napoleonic Wars forced a change as the royal dockyards could not handle the demand. The building of all three-deckers was undertaken in the royal dockyards, while the construction of two-deckers was divided about equally between state and private enterprise. Most frigates came from privately owned yards. In the period of the French Revolutionary and Napoleonic Wars, private yards built all but 78 of the 627 ships of the fourth rate and smaller. Even so, the royal dockyards supervised the building work of the private yards, and all ships emerging from private yards were delivered to royal dockyards for coppering of their lower hulls and for fitting out.

Life On Board

The subject of how a warship was manned and run is considered in detail in Chapter 4. Suffice it to say here that on board their ship the members of the crew, or the "people" as they were generally called, were quartered into divisions under the command of a lieutenant, and further subdivided into messes and gun crews. The quartermaster and boatswain's mates, who were the warrant officers with the more direct authority over the men, had considerable powers of minor punishment that in the event were frequently exceeded, while more serious offenders were brought up before the captain.

The "people" were classified into fo'c'sle (forecastle) men (able seamen stationed in the fore part of the ship with the older men responsible for the lower part of the rigging, the lead and the stowage of stores, and the younger so-called topmen who worked aloft on the masts, yards, and rigging), the afterguard attending the quarterdeck, manning the helm, trimming the sails, and other such tasks, and the waisters. These were generally the landmen used for brute manual tasks such as manning the capstan and drudge jobs such as swabbing the decks with pumice "holy-stones"—so called as they looked like bibles—and the idlers who did not stand watches and served as barbers, cooks, clerks, etc.

After one year at sea a man was rated an Ordinary Seaman, rising to Able Seaman after three years. He messed at tables hooked to the beams of the deck above him, slept in a hammock slung in the same volume and aired by being rolled up and stowed in the hammock nettings along the sides of the upper deck and along the break of the poop, where they created a breast-work for the Marines at action stations. The man had to change his linen twice a week, ports were opened and sail ventilators were rigged when-

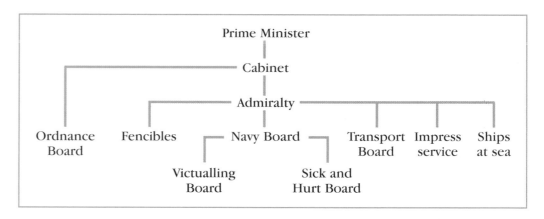

ever possible as an aid to ventilation, cleanliness was promoted by the use of sand (dry rather than wet to reduce damp) to scrub the lower decks, and light was provided by candles that had to be burned in lanterns to reduce the chances of fire. Smoking was permitted only in the galley and on the forecastle, and this led to the sailors' habit of chewing their tobacco.

Below: *Although it preferred to have its vessels built in royal dockyards to a high standard, the Royal Navy's pressing need for ships meant that many of them were built in private yards such as Blackwall, shown here.*

Below: An illustration from Cruikshank's "Midshipman Blockhead" series, entitled "Master B Finding Things Not Exactly What He Expected," reveals something of the extremely cramped nature of the midshipmen's berth on a warship. In fact the artist depicted the scene as being considerably roomier than it was in reality.

The highlight of the sailors' day was the twice-daily rum ration, although enjoyment also attended the drinking of beer (sometimes replaced by wine if the ship's victualling dictated the fact) with food. Drunkenness had been a major problem until Admiral Vernon, commanding in the West Indies in 1740, ordered that the rum ration be mixed with water (in the ratio of half a pint of rum to one quart of water) before issue to the men: this mixture became known as grog from the admiral's nickname "Old Grogram." When ships were in port women were allowed on board, often from the bumboats which surrounded the ships selling fruit and other delicacies not available at sea.

The poor rates of pay for all who served in the ships of the Royal Navy were a constant and justified grievance, but this should not be taken to mean that great windfalls did not sometimes fall to ships. This windfall was prize money, a matter in which Jack Aubrey was at times considered to be very lucky, especially in the earlier part of his career. The basic system whereby prizes were condemned by the Court of Admiralty was laid down in the Cruizers and Convoy Act of 1708 "for the better and more effectual encouragement of the Sea Service," and in this the Crown also gave up its

enter one of the professions, at that time deemed to include the army and now the Royal Navy. It is revealing that at the age of 14 Prince William, son of George III and later William IV, entered the Royal Navy. Many of these scions of the aristocracy rose to some seniority, and unlike the situation prevailing in the army, this seniority was generally gained by merit of a high degree of professional skill.

A boy wishing to embark on a career as a naval officer in the 18th century joined the service either as a Volunteer-per-Order or, more frequently when there was a relative or family friend who would accept him, as a Captain's Servant. In 1794 all—rather than just a part of them as had been the case up to this time—became known as Volunteers, First Class, the second- and third-class entrants being boys prepared to train as seamen. In 1815 the custom of allowing "followers" was abolished. With a few years at sea under his belt, the young man was rated a midshipman, a breed of non-commissioned officer falling into two distinctive parts characterized as "youngsters" and "oldsters." The latter were youngsters who had failed their lieutenant's examinations and were often extremely embittered, vicious, and notable for the quantities of drink they consumed. Although they might not be flogged, midshipmen were often "cobbed" by their seniors (laid over a gun barrel and beaten with a wooden plank or, until banned at the end of the 19th century, a hammock clew with 22 cords) or "mast-headed" by a lieutenant (dispatched to the main topmast crosstrees). An unusual punishment, but one which Jack Aubrey suffers, was being disrated, which meant being demoted to seaman and sent "before the mast" to mess with the ship's crew.

Although some young officers spent a short time at the largely ineffectual Royal Naval Academy, Portsmouth, most young officers completed their educations, such as they were, at sea under the tutelage of the ship's schoolmaster or chaplain, who received extra pay for giving the "young gentlemen" one or two hours of tutoring per day. Jack Aubrey often calls in his midshipmen to check on the progress of their education and, in the case of the more able of them, to further their education in mathematics and the skills of navigation.

rights to any part of the prize money. The exact proportions in which prize money for the capture of enemy ships (merchant and naval) was distributed varied from time to time, but an extended and successful cruise could result in considerable riches for the men of the ship involved as well as for the flag officers under whose orders they sailed.

A Naval Career

By the beginning of the 19th century, the Royal Navy had for the first time reached an equality with the British army in terms of the respect in which it was held. This was reflected by the fact that a naval career was deemed fitting for a son of the aristocracy. Since the eldest son inherited the family estate, it was customary for the younger sons to

Far left: A Rowlandson drawing of 1799 provides a good impression of the type of uniform worn by a lieutenant of the Royal Navy during the period of the French Revolutionary War.

Above: This engraving by Benjamin West shows Prince William as midshipman in 1782 at the age of 17. Third son of George III, William later became the Duke of Clarence and then King William IV. He was also the last Lord High Admiral.

> 66 ...hence the current toast of "A bloody war and a sickly season"... 99

Admirals' Ladder of Promotion Post-Trafalgar

Admiral of the Fleet

⬆

Admiral of the Red

⬆

Admiral of the White

⬆

Admiral of the Blue

⬆

Vice Admiral of the Red

⬆

Vice Admiral of the White

⬆

Vice Admiral of the Blue

⬆

Rear Admiral of the Red

⬆

Rear Admiral of the White

⬆

Rear Admiral of the Blue

Right: *Here seen as a vice admiral, Cuthbert Collingwod was second-in-command of the British fleet in the Battle of Trafalgar in 1805, the year in which he became commander-in-chief in the Mediterranean. Note the red flag behind him.*

After at least six years at sea and at an age of 20 or more, a midshipman sat the lieutenant's examination which, if passed, secured his promotion to commissioned rank and opened the way to progress up the promotion ladder (see Chapter 4). This could be an exceptionally slow process that could be speeded by losses in action or to disease (hence the current toast of "A bloody war and a sickly season") or "interest," as the patronage of important persons was called. Interest could allow the name of the boy to be entered on the books of two or more ships so that sea time could be amassed very quickly. However, the Royal Navy was unlike the army in forbidding the purchase of commissions.

Command of the Fleet

Command of a squadron or fleet of ships at sea demanded a great deal of planning and previous preparation in the days before radio equipment was available. An early method of subdividing the English fleet into squadrons is said to have been introduced in the time of Elizabeth I, although the earliest surviving instructions for the wearing of colored flags to denote the three squadrons into which the fleet was divided dated from 1617. In this system the admiral's squadron wore a red flag, the vice admiral's squadron a white flag, and the rear admiral's squadron a blue flag. However, as fleets grew in size and their three organic squadrons became correspondingly larger, it was realized that it was impossible for a single admiral to exercise efficient control of his squadron's evolutions from his position in its center. Thus there emerged the concept of allocating three admirals to each squadron in the form of a full admiral in command, a vice admiral as his second-in-command, and a rear admiral as his third-in-command.

In this theoretically perfect command structure, the white squadron was commanded by an Admiral of the White, with a Vice Admiral of the White, and a Rear Admiral of the White as his subordinates. Within the fleet, the squadrons were ranked in the order red, white, and blue, and admirals took rank according to the color of their squadron. Promotion of admirals also took place in this order, a Rear Admiral of the Blue on promotion becoming a Rear Admiral of the White as his first step in flag rank, and a Rear Admiral of the Red becoming a Vice Admiral of the Blue when he received promotion. This system was not followed at first in the red (senior) squadron: there was no Admiral of the Red since he was in overall command of the whole fleet and thus the Admiral of the Fleet. It was only after the Battle of Trafalgar in 1805 that the rank of Admiral of the Red was introduced, largely as a means of rewarding the most successful admirals. It was not until 1864 that the organization of the fleet into colored squadrons was finally ended: at this time the red, or senior, ensign was allocated to the merchant navy, the white ensign to the Royal Navy, and the blue ensign to the auxiliary vessels of the Royal Navy.

This then was the navy that Jack Aubrey loved. It was a service possessed of very significant flaws, especially in the brutality with which it could treat men who were very often unwilling, desperately poorly paid, badly fed, and granted little or no leave of absence for fear that they would desert, or "run." It was also a service that performed operational miracles and, when led by the capable and humane officers of which it had surprisingly large numbers, had many happy ships.

Jack Ashore

Although he loves the sea and everything to do with it, Aubrey is not wholly a nautical man. At times he is without a command, or between commands, or indeed on occasion attempting to dodge from the law as a result of his financial problems. At such times he is a man of the land. This is not a milieu to which Aubrey is ideally suited, but it is one in which he can rub along as a member of the gentry rather than of the aristocracy.

Right: "Men of War Bound for the Port of Pleasure," a mezzotint of 1791, reveals the pleasures and dangers awaiting Jack ashore. It was an inevitable consequence of keeping warships at sea for many months without a break, and shows why most captains were loath to free their men from the discipline of shipboard life for the riotous debauchery of a run in port.

Above: *This caricature of Lady Hamilton, the mistress of Horatio Nelson, by James Gillray, provides evidence of the Georgians' distrust of the woman who had "ruined" their hero, and also reveals the age's penchant for biting satirical cartoons.*

Aubrey's existence away from the sea is typical of the gentry as a whole, for he enjoys the country rather than the town, is concerned to acquire and develop land, and concentrates on the development of his family and friends as well as providing employment for his followers when no ship is available. After his election to the House of Commons he generally eschews the dubious delights of party politics in favor of expressing his concerns about matters of which he considers himself knowledgeable, namely the Royal Navy and the conduct of the war against France.

As a gentleman with land—his success in the matter of prize money allows him to buy land in increasing quantities and build his home, Ashgrove Cottage—Aubrey is very much a man typical of his time and class. Although he is not an urban creature to the extent that Stephen Maturin is, Aubrey does on occasion travel to London, but it is a city that he generally associates with problems of one sort of another, most generally financial. Aubrey is a poor

economist, and as well as being defrauded in several ways, in *The Reverse of the Medal* he finds himself for a time in the Marshalsea, one of London's notorious prisons, after being convicted of fraudulent dealings as a result of his own impetuous and trusting nature. Here prisoners were held on civil rather than criminal charges, and therefore permitted quite a lot of personal autonomy and, when they could pay for it or have it bought by a third party, comfortable accommodation and adequate food. The occasional privilege was allowed of making trips from the prison on a day-release basis or, in more limited instances, permission was granted to live in the immediate environs of the prison under a system known as "living within the rules."

On the whole, therefore, Aubrey is happier away from London and enjoying the company of his family and friends in the country from his home at Ashgrove Cottage. Aubrey loves to ride and is an enthusiastic member of the local hunt, becomes involved in cricket matches (described in a

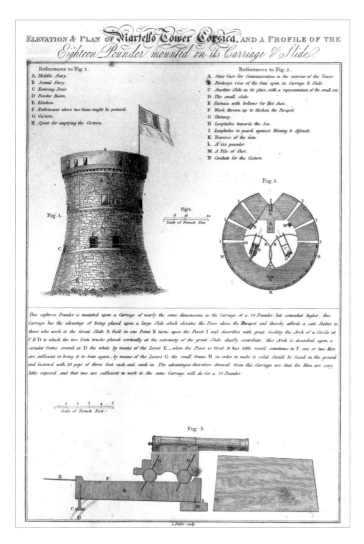

ELEVATION & PLAN OF Martello Tower Corsica, AND A PROFILE OF THE Eighteen Pounder mounted on its Carriage & Slide

maritime militia raised in Great Britain for limited service over a limited period during the course of the French Revolutionary and Napoleonic Wars. The Sea Fencibles were comprised largely of fisherman and the residents of coastal areas, and service in it was popular as it conferred an immunity from impressments. Such was the importance attached to the defense of Great Britain's coast, thought to be in

Far left: Fixed defenses have the edge over naval firepower, and provided a strong deterrent to attacks on naval bases. A cornerstone of British shore defenses was the so-called Martello tower. Aubrey speaks approvingly of them in The Surgeon's Mate.

Above: French plans for an invasion were based on securing at least temporary command of the English Channel for the French troops to make their crossing in craft such as this flat-bottomed transport.

imminent danger of French invasion for much of the period between 1793 and 1815, that the Sea Fencibles were junior to line regiments of the British army and to the Marines, but senior to yeomanry and volunteer units. The Sea Fencibles were raised in 1798 and reached their numerical peak in 1810, when they had a strength of 23,000 men.

It is worth noting that several references are also made in the Aubrey canon to those other landmarks of British coastal defense, the Martello tower and the coastal canal. The former was constructed in significant numbers at strategic locations to serve as artillery fortresses and as bases for local defense in the event of a French descent on the British coast. The latter were constructed inside various parts of the south coast of England to provide major lateral lines of communication so that supplies could be moved swiftly in an area lacking much in the way of road transport, and so that places under attack by the French could be reinforced as quickly as possible.

vastly amusing East Indies' episode in *The Reverse of the Medal* among other places), takes great pleasure in racketing around the countryside in a coach driven at great speed although not with the élan displayed by Maturin's wife Diana as depicted in *The Yellow Admiral* and other books, and watching prize fights. These bouts were the origins of modern boxing, although they were considerably more brutal, as is described in *The Yellow Admiral.*

The Sea Fencibles

Even though he takes a great delight in such country pursuits, Aubrey is always aware of the threat lurking on the other side of the English Channel from the French, and for a time he holds a position in the Sea Fencibles. This was a

> ❝ The Sea Fencibles were raised in 1798 and reached their numerical peak in 1810, when they had a strength of 23,000 men. ❞

❝ ...a force of 43 warships and transports, carrying 13,000 French troops, sailed from Brest to make a landing in Ireland. ❞

Below: *The destruction of the French frigate* Droits de l'Homme *in Hodierne Bay near Brest on January 17th, 1797 by the British frigate* Indefatigable, *which is firing signal rockets. The Droits de l'Homme was part of force that that had attempted an abortive invasion of Ireland in late 1796.*

The Irish Question

Another aspect of Aubrey's day-to-day life is brought to light by Maturin's feelings about Ireland. Maturin is a man of Irish and Catalan origins, and if so complex a matter can be compressed into a single phrase, his loyalties lie not with the British crown as such but rather with the concept of liberty as a means to self-determination. This means that Maturin opposes Napoleon with his whole being, and so supports the British as the cornerstone of European resistance to Napoleon. Nevertheless he looks for means eventually to throw off what he sees as the British yoke from the shoulders of the Irish. Maturin favors the United Irishmen.

The core of the movement for Irish independence from Britain in this period was the United Irishmen. They were the members of the United Irish Society that was formed in 1791 as one of the most advanced associations for reform of the relationship between Britain and Ireland. Initially led by Protestant merchants and professionals from Belfast and Dublin, the United Irishmen included both Protestant and Catholic adherents. Soon the movement became militantly anti-English and pro-republican, and in 1795 was driven underground as its objectives were seen as blatantly treasonable. In the period 1795-98 United Irishmen helped to organize a movement of the politically disaffected in England as the so-called "United Englishmen." The United Irishmen also negotiated for foreign military support, but the United Irish Society dissolved as an organization in the aftermath of the suppression of the Irish Rebellion of 1798. The 1798 Banishment Act excluded them from Ireland, and from this time onward they operated in exile in England, France, and Hamburg, while many of its members sailed for the United States of America.

The Irish Rebellion came about as a result of the socioeconomic and sectarian discontent that had already found expression in the Whiteboy, Defender, and other movements but was now focussed into a campaign for radical constitutional change. It was promoted by the United Irishmen in an effort to generate widespread politically motivated unrest in the Protestant as well as Catholic populations of Ireland. Such was the threat of this unrest that legislation, notably the Insurrection Act of 1796, was enacted locally, as well as in England, to strengthen the position of the government. In this same year a yeomanry force was formed to provide the Irish authorities with a means of checking local risings. An effort by Wolf Tone of the United Irishmen to secure support from the French revolutionary government led to an abortive invasion attempt in December of that year, when a force of 43 warships and transports, carrying 13,000 French troops, sailed from Brest to make a landing in Ireland. However, it was largely defeated by the weather and French command incompetence. Although a portion of the French force reached Bantry Bay, the effort was abandoned, and the French lost five ships to the weather and another six to the British.

In 1797, alarmed by the rising swell of Protestant dissent in parallel with that of the Catholic majority, the British government ordered the disarming of Ulster, a largely Protestant area where the population had traditionally been allowed to bear

arms. The British then turned their attention to Leinster, in the east of Ireland, and early in 1798 tried to arrest leaders. This achieved little other than the mortal wounding of Lord Edward Fitzgerald, the radical son of a leading Whig family. In May and June there was a series of uncoordinated risings, most widely in the south-east of Ireland, where a final stand was made at Vinegar Hill on June 21st after a mob without effective leadership had stormed and burned Enniscorthy in County Wexford, and then camped on the hill overlooking the camp. Troops under General Gerard Lake surrounded the Irish who, after as short resistance, surrendered.

Risings in Ulster subsided after a major battle at Bally-nahinch. French forces dispatched in the late summer and fall were speedily repelled after 1,200 French troops had landed at Killala Bay but were forced to surrender. The revolutionary and separatist movement then went underground. In overall terms, some 30,000 to 50,000 men had been involved in risings in over 18 counties, and the total death toll (mainly rebels) may have been as high as 20,000. Many of the survivors were convicted of involvement in the rising or of other seditious activity, and sentenced to transportation to the new penal colonies in Australia, which Aubrey reaches in *The Nutmeg of Consolation*.

Above: A painting by Nicholas Pocock reveals the capture of the French Résistance and Constance by the British San Fiorenzo and Nymphe on March 9th, 1797. This event followed a French landing in west Wales of a motley collection of ill-trained troops embarked in these ships that was timed to coincide with a planned invasion of Ireland. Both enterprises were undone by adverse weather.

CHAPTER THREE

Hearts of Oak

Jack Aubrey is the complete seaman and also the complete naval man. As such, the very essence of his being is to be found in the sea and the ships (especially the warships) that sail on it. Of course, Jack also has entanglements on land, notably his family and his complex and often disarrayed financial situation, but in overall terms it can be said that it is only as his ship weighs anchor and sets sail out of harbor that Jack really becomes alive.

Opposite page: *Although the greatest power was offered by a few first- and second-rate ships, such as the 100-gun Queen Charlotte seen here during the bombardment of Algiers in 1816, the main strength of the British and French fleets was provided by a larger number of third-rate ships, generally of 74 guns.*

Below: *Ships of Admiral Howe's Channel Fleet bring captured French vessels into Spithead after the Battle of the Glorious First of June, 1794. Wherever possible, captured ships were repaired and brought into British service.*

On land Jack is constrained by all manner of events largely outside his control, but at sea he is in command of his own destiny. Even in this milieu there are natural constraints on him, most notably the weather and the mathematics of navigation, and those man-made shackles, the Articles of War and the "customs and usages of the sea," which Jack is nonetheless happy to place upon himself. It is ships in general, and the beautiful *Surprise* in particular, that exercise the strongest hold on Jack's heart and imagination, so a basic understanding of the ships of the Georgian navy is essential to any understanding of the core of Jack Aubrey's being.

Jack Aubrey's Ships

The vessels with which Jack is most associated are the *Sophie*, a sloop of war captured from the Spanish; the "horrible" *Polychrest*, a double-ended monstrosity of no

fixed classification and designed originally to carry a secret weapon; the *Lively*, a comparatively large frigate; the *Surprise*, a small frigate captured from the French; the *Boadicea*, essentially a large frigate; the *Leopard*, a fourth-rate ship; the *Ariel*, a sloop; and the *Worcester*, a third-rate line-of-battle ship. As far as can be gleaned from Jack's various comments about the ships, the *Sophie* was of 150 tons displacement with a gundeck 70ft long, and carried an armament of 14 4-pounder guns and two 12-pounder bow chasers. The *Polychrest* was a shallow-draft vessel without a hold, and carried an armament of 24 32-pounder carronades. The *Lively* was launched at Woolwich Dockyard in July 1804 and was of 1,076 tons with a length of 154ft 1in on the gundeck and carrying an armament of 28 18-pounder guns, 14 32-pounder carronades, two long 12-pounder guns, and 2 long 9-pounder guns.

The *Surprise* was built at Le Havre and completed in 1794 with a displacement of 579 tons and a gundeck length of 126ft, and she carried an armament of 32 32-pounder carronades and two long 6-pounder guns. The *Boadicea* was launched in 1797 from the yard of Adams at Bucklers Hard, and carried an armament of 38 guns. The *Leopard* was launched at Sheerness in 1790 and carried an armament of 50 guns. The *Ariel* was built in 1806 and carried an armament of 16 32-pounder carronades and two 9-pounder guns. The *Worcester* carried 74 guns.

In the strict sense, it should be noted, a ship is a vessel with a bowsprit and three masts, each carrying a topmast and a topgallant mast, and yards on each of these masts. Even in the days of sail, though, this definition did not prevent the general use of the word "ships" to cover the full range of seagoing vessels. Up to the middle of the 16th century ships were generally regarded as male entities, but from this time onward it became almost universal to regard ships as female.

Right: *Taken from a Phillips print of 1690, these two images reveal the British warship of the late 17th century but are still relevant to the warship of 100 years later, which differed in detail rather than concept from those seen here. The upper plan reveals the rigging and sail plan of a typical third-rate line-of-battle ship, while the lower plan highlights the internal arrangements of a first-rate line-of-battle ship.*

> 66 The general practice in the early days of sail, before the advent of gunpowder weapons, had been to hire merchant ships for service as warships in times of war. The introduction of gunpowder meant that the ship as used for warlike purposes could now carry its own intrinsic armament. 99

Vessels that could not properly be designated as ships were barques, barquentines, brigs, brigantines, sloops, and cutters. A barque has three masts but is square-rigged only on the fore and mainmasts, and fore-and-aft rigged on the mizzenmast; the barquentine is also three-masted, but square-rigged only on the foremast and fore-and-aft rigged on the main and mizzenmasts; the brig is two-masted and square-rigged on both these masts; the brigantine is also two-masted and square-rigged on the foremast but fore-and-aft rigged on the main mast. Although formally a single-masted vessel with a fore-and-aft rig, the sloop in naval service was any vessel too small to be rated. By the beginning of the 19th century, the designation had become slightly more formalized to recognize the three-masted ship sloop and two-masted brig sloop, both of them square-rigged on all their masts.

The cutter, which first appeared in about 1740, was a small but decked vessel with a bowsprit and a single mast, generally rigged with one of two headsails (two jibs or a jib and a staysail), a square yard and topsail, and a gaff mainsail with a boom. The cutter was notably fast, especially upwind, and although first used almost exclusively for the carrying of dispatches, was later developed into a minor warship carrying up to 10 4-pounder guns.

Warship Development

It is worth noting that the development of the sailing ship as a dedicated warship had been comparatively slow. The general practice in the early days of sail, before the advent of gunpowder weapons, had been to hire merchant ships for service as warships in times of war. The introduction of gunpowder meant that the ship as used for warlike purposes could now carry its own intrinsic armament. Previously ships had served merely to carrying the fighting men who fought at sea with what were basically land weapons in melee battles—the object was to come alongside an enemy ship and board it with a view to effecting its capture. Shipboard guns led directly to the development in various seafaring nations of ships created for war purposes and therefore with no real role in times of peace. The first such ships were wall-sided vessels characterized by a low freeboard and guns mounted on their poops and forecastles.

As guns developed in size and numbers, however, the increase in hull stability problems meant that it became necessary for the guns to be mounted as low as possible in the ship. This led to the evolution of the warship with a revised hull cross-section providing greater freeboard and a pronounced tumblehome above a maximum beam set as low as possible to keep the great guns as low to the water as possible. However, the gundeck had to be sufficiently wide to allow both the port and starboard batteries to be run in when necessary. High castles were erected at the bow and the stern to give a better field of fire for small (and therefore light) anti-personnel guns and muskets, and also to provide the "higher ground" from which the ship's crew could mount an effective defense against boarders entering the ship by the waist portion of the ship between the two castles. These ships were poor performers when sailing on a wind, though, for their high forecastle meant that their bows were blown down to leeward.

The warships of these early years of development were of about 500 tons maximum displacement, but in the first part of the 15th century some English shipwrights produced ships of perhaps twice this displacement. During the second half of the 16th century, and once again in England, the high forecastle was abandoned in warships to allow the creation of faster and more weatherly ships. This English innovation was soon emulated by the shipbuilders of the European mainland, and the general design of sailing warships became very similar, differing only in size and number of guns mounted. During the 17th and 18th centuries, and the first few years of the 19th, there was virtually no significant advance in the core concept of the sailing warship. Ships merely increased in overall size up to a final displacement, by the mid-19th century, of about 3,000 tons with an armament of up to some 130 guns disposed on three gundecks.

Above: *The launch of the Cambridge at Deptford Dockyard in 1755. This was one of the last 80-gun three-deckers, a type poorly suited to all-weather operations.*

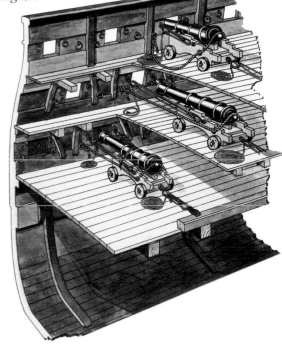

Right: *The three positions of a heavy gun on a three-decker are seen here: run-out through an open gun port ready for firing on the upper deck, in the recoiled position for reloading on the middle deck, and secured with the gun port closed on the gun deck. Control of these heavy and cumbersome weapons was effected by ropes and tackles, limited traverse being achieved with the aid of hand spikes.*

> 66   The fleet to windward was less affected by smoke from the guns, which blew downwind... 99

The Rating System

From the middle of the 18th century most European navies opted to classify their sailing warships into six rates based on the number of guns they mounted. Vessels of the first three rates, and occasionally the fourth, were recognized as line-of-battle ships (ships with an armament powerful enough to lie in the line of battle). Fifth- and sixth-rate ships were known as frigates, whose tasks in times of war varied from active participation in battles as signal-repeating ships for the main fleets to convoy escort duty (see also Chapter 5). The ships of these six rates had the standard arrangement of three square-rigged masts. Lesser warship types, not classified as ships in the proper sense of the world, included types such as brigs and sloops, whose numbers swelled considerably as tasks such as the delivery of dispatches and high-value personnel became more important to navies.

The system of dividing ships into rates was based on the concept of the line of battle. This was the line formed by the ships of any fleet before they entered battle against those of an enemy fleet. Since sailing warships were able to bring the maximum weight of fire to bear on the enemy only when they were able to fire on the beam or quarter, the line of battle that had become standard in the time of Jack Aubrey was either line ahead or quarter-line. In the days of sail, the admiral commanding a fleet had to take only the wind and the sea conditions into account when he ordered his ships into line of battle, the most important single factor being whether he wished to be to windward or to leeward of the enemy's line when battle was joined. As fleet actions were generally battled out at ranges of 100 yards or even less, factors such as the visibility and the relative position of the sun were of only secondary importance.

Both the windward and leeward positions had their tactical

advantages. The fleet to windward was less affected by smoke from the guns, which blew downwind toward the enemy (and could sometimes obscure his ships), and it could easily make out the signal flags hoisted by the repeating frigates. In the event that the line of the windward fleet overlapped that of the enemy, the windward position also made it possible for the admiral to order the ships of his van or rear to "double the enemy's line," i.e. to come up on the other side of the line so that the enemy's van or rear was sandwiched between the fire of the opposing ships.

The advantages offered by the leeward position were that enemy ships, if disabled, would fall downwind and could thus be captured. Ships in the leeward line could also bear away from the enemy before the wind, and in the process leave room for ships not already caught up in the fighting to take their place. Another major factor was that the ships of a leeward line, heeling away from the enemy in the prevailing wind, could keep their lower-deck gunports open in a seaway much longer than could the ships to windward, in the process bringing a heavier and more sustained weight of fire to bear on the enemy.

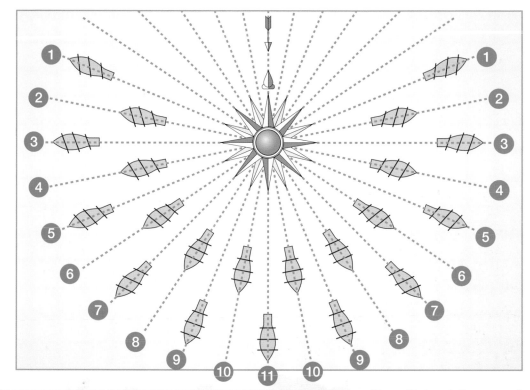

Above: *Under sail, the course of the vessel in relation to the wind is measured in "points," each describing $\frac{1}{32}$nd of a compass card's circumference (11 degrees 15 minutes). For a square-rigged ship, the points of sailing between 1 and 10 on the port and starboard tacks (with the wind over the port or starboard sides respectively) are 1) close-hauled, 2) one point large, 3) two points large (wind on the beam), 4) three points large 5) four points large, 6) five points large, 7) six points large (wind on the quarter), 8) three points on the quarter, 9) two points on the quarter, and 10) one point on the quarter. 11) is before the wind.*

Left: *At the Battle of the Nile the French were moored in line, and the British attacked in two columns to fire on the French from port and starboard.*

The Six Rates

The six rates into which the warships of navies of Jack Aubrey's day were classified were based on the number of guns carried. Although virtually every navy of the period later used the rating system, it was introduced in Britain by Admiral Lord Anson during his first years as First Lord of the Admiralty, an office he held from 1744 to 1762. The first rating system, based on the number of the crew, had been pioneered in 1653, but in 1746 Anson changed this to the more realistic basis of the number of guns carried.

The first-rate ships were those that carried 100 (later 110) or more guns on three decks, the change from 100 to 110 taking place in 1810. First-rate ships generally carried a crew of 850 or more men. Second-rate ships carried from 84 to 100 (later 90 to 110) guns also on three decks, and generally had a crew in the order of 750 men. Third-rate ships carried 70 to 84 (later 80 to 90) guns on two decks, and generally had a crew in the order of 500 to 720 men. Fourth-rate ships carried 50 to 70 (later 60 to 80) guns on two decks, and generally had a crew in the order of 350 to 420 men. Fifth-rate ships carried 32 to 50 (later 60) guns on one deck, and generally had a crew in the order of 215 to 295 men. If commanded by a post captain, sixth-rate ships carried 20 to 32 guns on one deck, and generally had a crew in the order of 120 to 195 men; when captained by an officer of the rank of commander rather than post captain, however, such ships were rated as sloops. It was not until 1817 that carronades, which had first been introduced into ships of the Royal Navy in 1779, were not included in the number of guns which decided a ship's rating.

Only the ships of the first three rates were generally considered powerful enough to lie in the line of battle in actions between main fleets. Fourth-rate ships, which were notably rare, did not lie in the line of battle among larger navies, but occasionally did so in smaller navies. Ships of the fifth- and sixth-rates were generally known as frigates.

Up to the 1st Anglo-Dutch War (1652-54), warships had not fought in formation, each ship sailing into battle with the purpose of finding an enemy vessel to tackle in one-on-

Left: *Published in 1804 and dedicated to the Duke of Clarence, Admiral of the White, this print reveals something of the rating system and numbers the guns and crew of most major ships. Included in the total of 726 vessels are 10 first-, 21 second-, 138 third-, 27 fourth-, 164 fifth-, and 192 sixth-rate ships.*

one combat. The first effort to make a fleet fight in formation was made by Robert Blake in the Battle of Portland (1653), but the line of battle proper did not become a reality until the 2nd Anglo-Dutch War (1665-67), by which time fleets were altogether more tightly controlled by their admirals. Moreover, because at that period a ship's guns lacked any traverse capability, being limited to firing through their gunports at right angles to the ship's keel line, the line of battle had necessarily to be of the line-ahead type in which each ship followed in the track of her next ahead. This formation was rigidly laid down in the *Fighting Instructions* issued to all fleet and ship commanders, and wholly governed the fighting dispositions of British ships.

As the 18th century dawned, the British became increasingly concerned to regularize the design and construction of their warships, and this was one of the factors that opened the way for the classification of warships into six rates. As it was only the first three rates that were deemed adequate to lie in the line of battle, these became known as line-of-battle ships, or alternatively as ships of the line.

The fifth- and sixth-rate ships, or frigates, never fought in the line of battle, but in fleet actions were stationed separately with primary duties other than fighting. The frigate sailed considerably better than its larger brethren, and this

Warship Rates

	Number of guns (1746-1810)	Number of guns (after 1810)	Number of decks	Crew
First-rate	more than 100	more than 110	Three	850 or more
Second-rate	84 to 100	90 to 110	Three	750 to 850
Third-rate	70 to 84	80 to 90	Two	500 to 720
Fourth-rate	50 to 70	60 to 80	Two	350 to 420
Fifth-rate	32 to 50	32 to 60	One	215 to 295
Sixth-rate	up to 32	up to 32	One	120 to 195

capability was exploited for carrying out such tasks as providing reconnaissance for a main fleet and, in battle, serving as a repeating ship to fly the admiral's signals so that other ships in the line, possibly denied any direct line of sight to the admiral's ship by gun smoke or intervening ships, could read his signals. The frigate could also operate independently of a fleet for the escort of convoys or, as the converse of this task, finding and attacking the enemy's convoys or independently routed merchantmen, a role in which the frigate was generally known as the cruiser.

In the era of fighting sail there was an unspoken convention that line-of-battle ships did not fire on frigates during any fleet action unless the frigate opened fire first. It was not unknown for frigates to engage line-of-battle ships on occasion. This convention applied only in a general fleet engagement, so a frigate caught alone while cruising, for example, was "fair game" for any larger ship.

During the War of the French Revolution and the Napoleonic Wars, covering the period between 1793 and 1815, the British introduced a fourth-rate frigate. Carrying around 50 guns on two gundecks, these ships were not successful, for they were still too small to lie in the line of battle, and by frigate standards were too large and cumbersome to catch and destroy a smaller frigate that had the sea-room to exploit her superior sailing characteristics.

Above: *First published in 1781, this print reveals the London, a second-rate three-decker of 90 guns, sailing before the wind off Rame Head, the western headland of Plymouth Sound.*

Left: *A drawing by L. Francis reveals the nearly complete construction of the Nelson three-decker at Woolwich Dockyard, probably in 1810. The building of major warships was labor- and capital-intensive, and generally undertaken in a royal dockyard.*

Right: *A model of the Bellona, a 74-gun two-decker, reveals structural details such as the vertical full frames rising from the keel and braced longitudinally by the port sills. Between the full frames are the filling frames, and, yet to be added, the outer planking and copper sheathing on the lower hull. The Bellona was completed well before the French Revolutionary and Napoleonic Wars as the pioneer of the 168-foot third-rate ship, and served right through these conflicts.*

Ship Construction

The ships in which Jack Aubrey and every other seaman of the period sailed were made almost entirely of wood, with iron used only for bolts and pieces to strengthen joints, and copper employed for nails and the sheathing with which the outer surface of the lower hull was covered to prevent the attacks of boring beetles. The preferred timber for the primary structural members was English oak, although oak from the Baltic region had to be used later because there was insufficient quantities of the domestic type, which required 100 years or more to grow to the right dimensions. Elm was employed for the keel and sternpost as this was available in the straight lengths that were needed for these two members, and was also used for planking.

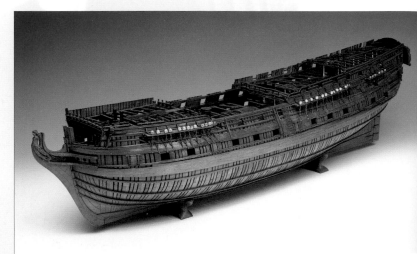

keel rose the multi-piece frames that provided the hull with the desired cross-section at every point along its length. These frames were held in alignment at this stage by ribbands (long strips of flexible timber) except at the bow and stern, where there were the more complex and acute curvatures that would most affect the ship's sailing qualities. Here harpins (pre-determined and cut to exactly the right shape) were used.

Over the skeleton thus created was laid the interior and exterior planking, which was of the carvel type, i.e. with the planks laid edge to edge and, like the deck planks, caulked to prevent water getting in. The hull planking had to be pierced and braced at the relevant places for the gunports and other necessary openings. Into the hull thus created were added the timbers that supported the various decks, and then the deck planks that were themselves pierced by hatches and other openings.

The process of caulking the decks' sides and decks was extremely laborious, and required large quantities of oakum or rope junk. This was driven into the seams between the planks with a hot caulking iron and a heavy hammer to a level below the surface of the planks, and was then covered by hot pitch or some other compound that would prevent water from reaching the oakum or rope junk and causing it to rot. Oakum and rope junk comprised tarred manila or hemp fibers that had been produced by unpicking old ropes, an extraordinarily tedious process to which the inhabitants of workhouses were assigned. Naval malingerers were often condemned to this task also.

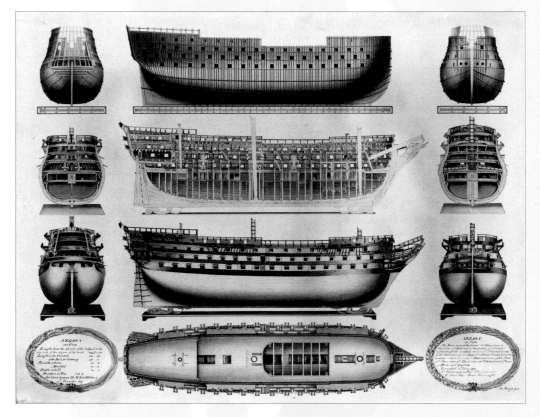

Above: *The configuration of the Nelson, a 120-gun three-decker of the "Surveyors of the Navy" class launched in 1814, is fully revealed in these excellent drawings of the period. The ships were not notably successful.*

Although the timber skeleton of the warship in the era of sail was extremely complex, and required the utmost skill of the yard workers to create successfully, the essence of the structure was simple. The structural heart of the ship was the keel, which ran from the stem to the sternpost and was crossed a right angles by the floor timbers. Above this

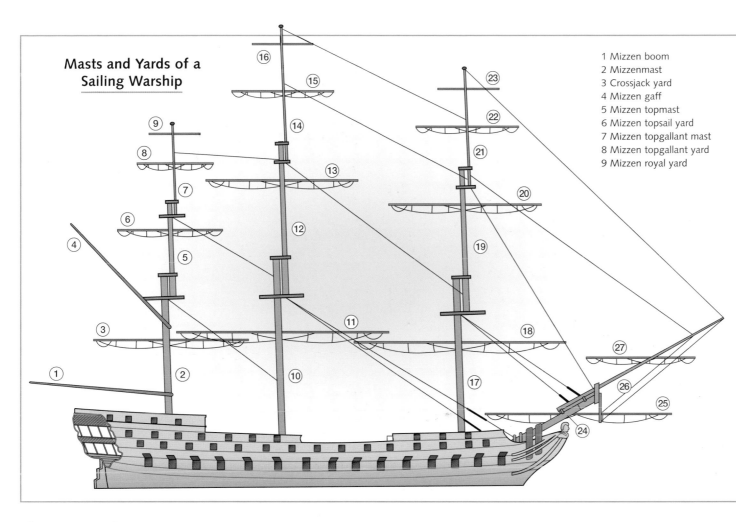

Masts and Yards of a Sailing Warship

1 Mizzen boom
2 Mizzenmast
3 Crossjack yard
4 Mizzen gaff
5 Mizzen topmast
6 Mizzen topsail yard
7 Mizzen topgallant mast
8 Mizzen topgallant yard
9 Mizzen royal yard
10 Mainmast
11 Main yard
12 Main topmast
13 Main topsail yard
14 Main topgallant mast
15 Main topgallant yard
16 Main royal yard
17 Foremast
18 Fore yard
19 Fore topmast
20 Fore topsail yard
21 Fore topgallant mast
22 Fore topgallant yard
23 Fore royal yard
24 Bowsprit
25 Spritsail yard
26 Jib boom
27 Sprit topsail yard

The Masts and Rigging

From the main deck emerged the ship's masts. The mast is a vertical spar whose primary function in a sailing ship is, of course, to carry the sails. In sailing ships the circular-section masts normally emerged through holes in the deck and their squared-off heels fitted into steps in the ship's keelson (interior keel). In larger ships they were held firm in the holes through which they emerged from the deck by means of wedges, and were secured laterally by shrouds extending from the masthead or the hounds to chainplates on the sides of the ship, and longitudinally by stays extending from the masthead to deck level forward and aft of the mast. In square-rigged vessels, such as rated warships, the yards were crossed on the masts, from which they were held in position by lifts, with the sails set on the yards. In fore-and-aft rigged vessels the sails were set on the masts,

almost invariably by hoops attached to the luff of the sail and left free to slide up and down the mast as the sail was hoisted or lowered.

Before the growth in the size of ships during the 17th century, ships' masts were single spars, created from the trunk of a fir tree, but as the size of ships increased dramatically during the 17th and 18th centuries, the need arose to carry more sail. Additional masts were thus needed to carry their yards. The original type of pole mast fashioned from a single trunk was no longer strong or long enough to support the quantity of yards and sails now needed. The result was the made mast, i.e. one fabricated of several pieces of timber in order to get the height and strength that was now needed. In most ships of the 17th century onward, the lower masts were all made masts, while the topmast and topgallant mast were pole masts.

Above: To keep sea water from entering through the gaps in the planking, these were caulked with oakum and then covered with pitch. These are some of the tools of the caulker's trade.

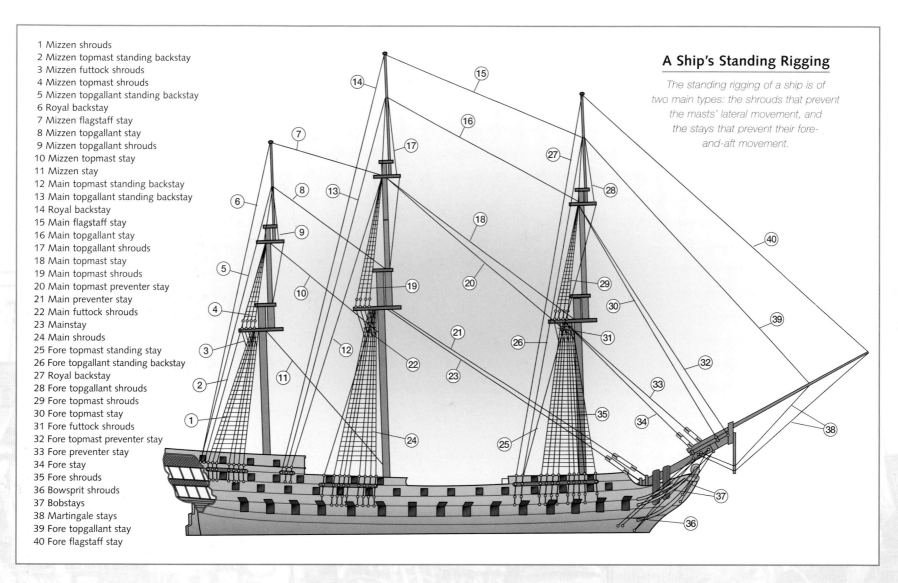

1 Mizzen shrouds
2 Mizzen topmast standing backstay
3 Mizzen futtock shrouds
4 Mizzen topmast shrouds
5 Mizzen topgallant standing backstay
6 Royal backstay
7 Mizzen flagstaff stay
8 Mizzen topgallant stay
9 Mizzen topgallant shrouds
10 Mizzen topmast stay
11 Mizzen stay
12 Main topmast standing backstay
13 Main topgallant standing backstay
14 Royal backstay
15 Main flagstaff stay
16 Main topgallant stay
17 Main topgallant shrouds
18 Main topmast stay
19 Main topmast shrouds
20 Main topmast preventer stay
21 Main preventer stay
22 Main futtock shrouds
23 Mainstay
24 Main shrouds
25 Fore topmast standing stay
26 Fore topgallant standing backstay
27 Royal backstay
28 Fore topgallant shrouds
29 Fore topmast shrouds
30 Fore topmast stay
31 Fore futtock shrouds
32 Fore topmast preventer stay
33 Fore preventer stay
34 Fore stay
35 Fore shrouds
36 Bowsprit shrouds
37 Bobstays
38 Martingale stays
39 Fore topgallant stay
40 Fore flagstaff stay

A Ship's Standing Rigging

The standing rigging of a ship is of two main types: the shrouds that prevent the masts' lateral movement, and the stays that prevent their fore- and-aft movement.

> 66 ...the standing rigging was vast in extent and complexity... 99

The term that comprises all ropes, wires, or chains used in ships (as well as smaller vessels) to support the masts and yards, and for hoisting, lowering, and trimming sails to the wind, is rigging. This falls into two basic subdivisions, which are standing rigging for the support of the bowsprit, masts, and yards, and running rigging for the control of the yards and sails.

Standing Rigging

In the square-rigged ship the standing rigging was vast in extent and complexity, for it had to support the bowsprit and three masts, each of the latter comprising three or, if a royal mast was employed, four separate parts, each needing its own support. In addition each mast had up to five yards crossed on it and each of these, too, had its own complement of standing rigging. As noted above, lateral or athwartship support was provided by the shrouds extending from upper attachments on the hounds or, in place of the hounds, a stayband just under the top of the mast to the chainplates on the outer side of the hull abreast the mast. The shrouds were made from special four-stranded rope, and were adjusted for tension at their lower ends by lanyards threaded through deadeyes. In large ships multiple shrouds spaced two feet apart at the chainplate were needed to carry the strains exerted on the mast by large sails, and these were controlled across their width by ratlines which helped to maintain and equalize the tension in each shroud, and also formed a rope ladder by which the men ascended or descended the mast.

When topmasts and topgallant masts were fitted, their shrouds were led from their hounds or staybands to the "top" of the mast below: this top was a platform carried by crosstrees and trestle-trees and it provided sufficient width to spread the shrouds so that the topmast or topgallant mast was supported against lateral loads. The trestle-trees were correctly positioned cheeks bolted to each side of the mast, and the tops were fixed to the crosstrees and trestle-trees as well as being braced by futtock shrouds extending from the outer ends of the top downward to a futtock stave secured to the shrouds or alternatively to a stayband round the mast.

Support of the masts against fore-and-aft loads was provided by the stays. For the foremast (especially in large ships with both top and topgallant masts) the necessary support base was lengthened forward by use of the bowsprit and, when fitted, the jib-boom which had themselves to be braced before they could support any load. This was provided in the lateral plane by pairs of shrouds led from the end of the bowsprit and the jib-boom and secured to plates at the widest part of the bows, and in the vertical plane by a bobstay from the end of the bowsprit to a fitting on the ship's stem near the waterline, and by martingales from the end of the jib-boom and similarly secured to the stem.

In order to give a wider angle of support for the jib-boom, a dolphin striker was fitted to lead the martingales down at a more oblique angle than would otherwise be possible. The foremast was braced by a forestay secured at its bottom to the stem (or the deck just inside the stem) and its top to the stayband. In exactly the same way the fore topmast was stayed from the bowsprit end to its topmast stayband, and the fore topgallant mast from the end of the jib-boom to its stayband. These stays supported the relevant masts against rearward movement, and the mainmast and mizzenmast were supported similarly by stays led from the mast ahead of them.

Forward movement of the masts was checked by backstays. These were led aft in pairs from the tops of the various masts to the sides of the ship. Stays were much beloved by

Jack Aubrey, who in heavy weather dearly loved to set up "double preventer backstays" so that he could press on with a mass of canvas that might otherwise have carried away a mast: this concept is vital to the *Leopard* managing to keep ahead of a pursuing Dutch warship, which is eventually driven under, in the magnificent *Desolation Island*.

Above: *The topmen were elite seamen. "A Storm Coming On," which commemorates the loss of Admiral Thomas Graves's squadron in a hurricane during 1782, shows how the topmen had to go aloft in all conditions.*

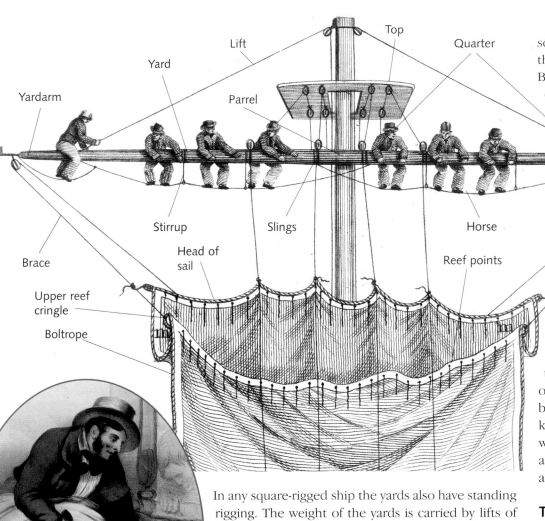

Labels on diagram: Yardarm, Yard, Lift, Top, Quarter, Parrel, Stirrup, Slings, Horse, Brace, Head of sail, Reef points, Upper reef cringle, Boltrope

square sails were bundled up to their yards by jiggers and then laced to the yards ready for spreading when required. Being large and made of heavy canvas, the square sails were equipped with small lines or purchases (buntlines) from the yard down to the foot of the sail as a means of offering greater lifting power when the sails were being furled or reefed. As was the case with the standing rigging, individual halyards took their names from the mast and sail they served, such as main staysail halyard.

Unlike fore-and-aft sails, square sails were not directly trimmed to the wind. In the case of these sails, their yards were trimmed by braces attached to each yardarm and led aft: the sail, which was laced to the yard along its complete head, had of necessity to conform. However, when it was close-hauled to the wind, the individual sails could be trimmed in a little harder by bowlines attached to bridles on the leeches of the sail and led forward toward the ship's bow. Hauled hard in, the bowlines on the weather leeches kept the leech taut to the wind so that a better leading edge was obtained. A forward-led tack and aft-led sheet were attached to the clews of all the square sails in order to get a better trim of the sail.

The Sails

The whole beautiful and magnificently complex arrangement of masts and rigging was provided for the purpose of carrying the sails, which gave the ship its motive power. The sails themselves were made of canvas, a material properly made from hemp. Supplied in bolts that were then cut and sewn by the sailmaker, either at a shore establishment or on board a ship, the nature of the canvas's thickness and weave was denoted by a number, the lowest number denoting the coarsest and strongest canvas, and the highest number indicating the finest and lightest canvas. The canvas was cut to the required length and shaped in the fashion needed to catch the wind and so impart movement to the ship on which the sail was set. The various cloths that were necessary to create any particular sail were seamed together with a double seam, and the sail's leech was shaped with gores to give it the required belly.

Above: A colored lithograph published by William Spooner reveals something of the labor of handling a heavy canvas sail, but omits the dangers of doing so in heavy weather.

In any square-rigged ship the yards also have standing rigging. The weight of the yards is carried by lifts of chain, one on each side of the mast running from a band round the mast above the yard to each quarter of the yard. The center of the yard is secured to the mast itself by a truss or parrel loose enough to allow the yard to turn on the mast when braced round to the wind. At intervals along the yard, short perpendicular ropes, known as stirrups, support the horse (footrope) held parallel to—but some three feet below—the yard to provide a secure foothold for men handling the sails.

Running Rigging

The running rigging was used in hoisting or striking the yards, and in hoisting, lowering, and trimming the sails. The purchases for hoisting sails were the halyards, those for hoisting the yards the jeers. In square-rigged ships only the triangular sails (jibs and staysails) had halyards, for the

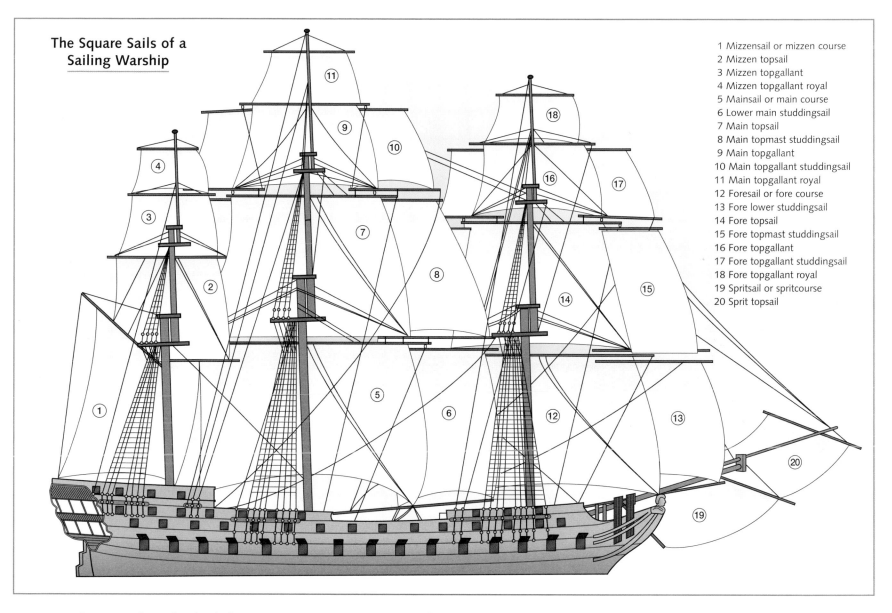

The Square Sails of a Sailing Warship

1 Mizzensail or mizzen course
2 Mizzen topsail
3 Mizzen topgallant
4 Mizzen topgallant royal
5 Mainsail or main course
6 Lower main studdingsail
7 Main topsail
8 Main topmast studdingsail
9 Main topgallant
10 Main topgallant studdingsail
11 Main topgallant royal
12 Foresail or fore course
13 Fore lower studdingsail
14 Fore topsail
15 Fore topmast studdingsail
16 Fore topgallant
17 Fore topgallant studdingsail
18 Fore topgallant royal
19 Spritsail or spritcourse
20 Sprit topsail

In general terms, sails can be divided into two categories: those for square-rigged ships, which are set on horizontal yards crossing the masts; and those for fore-and-aft rigged ships which are set from their luffs on masts or stays. It should be remembered, though, that the two types of sail were to be found on the same ship—for instance, the jibs, staysails, and spanker (or driver) of a square-rigged ship, and, more infrequently, a square sail set from a yard when running before the wind in a fore-and-aft rigged ship.

With all plain sail set, square-rigged ships were charac-terized by four square sails on each mast, although a fifth sail was sometimes set on the main mast. From bottom to top, the ladder of sails so created were the course, topsail, topgallant, and royal; the fifth sail sometimes set on the main mast was the skysail. Moreover, in good conditions without too much of a sea and with a modest wind abaft the beam, special sails, known by the overall term kites, could be set to make the most of the wind. A short royal mast was sometimes fixed above the topgallant masts to set moonrakers above the royals and skysails.

Above: *With all its canvas set, studdingsails as well as plain sails, the line-of-battle ship was a hugely impressive sight. The handling of all the sail required a very large and well-trained crew.*

Below: This print of Sir Richard Strachan's action of November 4th, 1805 reveals that the Royal Navy preferred to enter action with the courses of its ships clewed up to keep the flammable canvas well clear of the flash and burning wads emerging from the muzzles of the ships' guns.

Studdingsails (pronounced stunsails) could be set from booms rigged out from both yardarms of the topsail and topgallant yards of the fore and mainmasts to serve as quickly removable enlargements of the topsails and topgallants. Moreover, in Jack Aubrey's period another method, considered somewhat old fashioned, was occasionally used to enlarge the area of a course by lacing a strip of canvas, known as a bonnet, to its foot. The use of the bonnet generally ceased during the first decade of the 19th century.

Eyewitness

"It was afternoon, and shortly before the time the Fleet generally reefed topsails for the night, and as I was stationed in that duty next to the man at the earing in the starboard fore-topsail yardarm…just as I got upon the sail, about four feet below the yard (a dangerous position at any time), the signal was made by the Admiral to form the line of battle; our ship was in her station and the *Superb* (74) was…bearing down athwart our hawse…as our Lieutenant thought we might come in contact with each other…he ordered the topsail to be shivered (that is shook) to cause our ship to drop astern, the topsail shook, and I was hanging by it, with nothing to support me…I was first thrown one way and then another, till I gave up every hope of life…my ship-mates advised me to throw myself clear of the ship, into the sea as my only resource for safety, for if I fell by the fluttering of the sail, I might fall on deck and be instantly killed; at that awful moment, a rope called the sliding sail halliard flapped close to me and knowing an opportunity like it might not occur again, I let go my doubtful hold, and risked the seizure of it, which I providentially accomplished, and rapidly descended until safely upon the fore yardarm."

George Watson, *The Adventures of a Greenwich Pensioner*

> ❝ Every ship of the Royal Navy included among its complement a sailmaker as one of the essential members of the crew along with men such as the boatswain, carpenter, and gunner. ❞

When the wind rose and it became time to shorten sail, the sails were struck in order from the top of the masts, and eventually the ship would be sailing with only its courses and topsails set. Only these of the square sails had reef points. On a square sail, a reef was taken in on the head of the sail, not on the foot as in the sails of fore-and-aft rigged vessels. Square sails took their names from the mast on which they were set—for example, the fore topsail, main course, and mizzen topgallant.

Square sails were always cut from canvas delivered to the ships in bolts. The bolt was a roll of canvas 39 yards long. There was no standard width, the canvas normally coming in widths between 22 and 30 inches. The standard "working" sails were sewn of heavier canvas, while the lighter canvas was reserved for the kites. Every ship of the Royal Navy included among its complement a sailmaker as one of the essential members of the crew along with men such as the boatswain, carpenter, and gunner. Such men and their mates and assistants were vital to the success of any long-lasting passage or mission, when the ship might be out of touch with shore facilities for months on end and had therefore to be as self-reliant as possible.

The four sides of a square sail were known as the head at the top, the foot at the bottom, and the two leeches at the sides, the last being classified as the weather and lee leeches depending on their location relative to the wind (weather was the side on which the wind hit the sail, and lee that away from the wind) or port and starboard. The two top corners were called the earing cringles, while the bottom corners were the clews (sometimes rendered clues), which were again distinguished as the weather and lee, or port and starboard, clews. The central part of a square sail was normally cut and sewn with a full belly to hold the wind, and was known as the bunt.

Fore-and-aft Sails

Fore-and-aft sails on a ship of the Royal Navy were either three- or four-sided. The three-sided sails were the jibs occupying the triangle formed by the foremast, bowsprit, and various fore stays, and the staysails set between the masts. The sides of a triangular sail were called the luff, leech, and foot at the front, rear, and bottom respectively; their corners were called the tack (lower front), head (upper front), and clew (rear) respectively. The only four-sided fore-and-aft sail

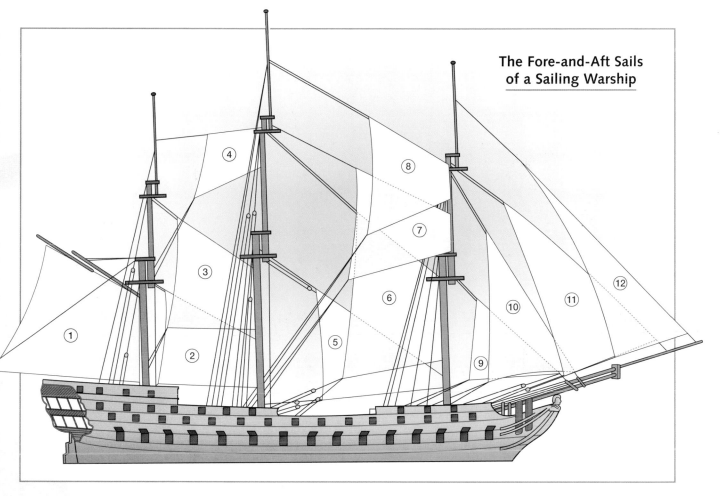

The Fore-and-Aft Sails of a Sailing Warship

attached to a mast (staysails were attached to stays) was the spanker (originally driver) set on the lower part of the mizzenmast as an alternative to a mizzen course. The sides of such a gaff sail were known as the head at the top, the foot at the bottom, the luff at the forward edge, and the leech at the rear edge. The sail's corners were the throat at the leading edge of the top, the peak at the trailing edge of the top, the tack at the leading edge of the bottom, and the clew at the trailing edge of the bottom. A spanker was sometimes extended by setting a topsail above it to fill the area between the mast and the gaff: the two types of topsail were the jib-headed topsail extending from the jaws of the gaff to the masthead, and the jackyard topsail extending above the top of the mast to provide a greater area of sail in winds of light or moderate strength.

There were many terms associated with sails, which were of course wholly vital to the operation of any ship before

the introduction of powered propulsion. Setting sail was, in the purist sense, the hoisting or loosing of the sails to start the ship moving, but the phrase was frequently used figuratively for the departure of a ship at the beginning of a voyage. Making sail was the spreading of additional canvas to increase the ship's speed. Shortening sail was the taking in or reefing of sails to reduce the speed of a ship. Striking sail was a sudden lowering of sails.

Jack Aubrey is a true connoisseur of sails and knows just how to extract the best possible performance from his ship by constant attention to the setting of the sails under any and all weather conditions after the ship had been properly trimmed by the movement of ballast and the fore-and-aft rake of the masts had been adjusted. The love of the man for the art of seamanship is all too evident throughout the canon of novels, which display an excellent understanding of how a square-rigged ship handled and was sailed.

1 Spanker or driver
2 Mizzen staysail
3 Mizzen topmast staysail
4 Mizzen topgallant staysail
5 Main staysail
6 Main topmast staysail
7 Middle staysail
8 Main topgallant staysail
9 Fore staysail
10 Fore topmast staysail
11 Jib
12 Flying jib

Naval Supremacy

The largest line-of-battle ships built in Great Britain were the 120-gun ships that came off the slips in the later stages of the Napoleonic War and after its conclusion. They included ships such as the *Hibernia, Howe, Caledonia,* and *Queen Charlotte*. However, the only surviving example of a first-rate British line-of-battle ship is the smaller *Victory*, a 100-gun three-decker, which is still technically in commission and as such flies the flag of the Commander-in-Chief, Portsmouth. The *Victory* was on active service from her completion in 1765 right up to the end of the Napoleonic War in 1815, and was the flagship of Jack Aubrey's hero, Admiral Lord Nelson, at the decisive Battle of Trafalgar during October 1805. The ship was in the water as late as 1924, when she was restored and placed in dry dock.

Left: *The most striking survivor of the naval warfare of the French Revolutionary and Napoleonic Wars that Jack Aubrey knew is HMS Victory, preserved at Portsmouth.*

Below: *Jack Aubrey's hero is Horatio Nelson. This illustration reveals part of Nelson's success: 26 line-of-battle ships in the capture of which he had a hand between 1793 and 1801.*

As a typical British first-rate of the Napoleonic War, *Victory* represents the type of ship which played so decisive a part in maintaining Britain's command of the sea which allowed the implementation of a blockade of France and her allies, and at the same time ensured the continuity of the trade on which Britain was reliant for her survival as a nation. The 2,164-ton *Victory* has a length of 186ft and beam of 52ft, carried a broadside of 100 guns, and was sailed and fought by a crew of 900. Toward the other end of the size scale, frigates were built in much greater numbers than the line-of-battle ships, and a good example of the larger type of frigate is the *Imperieuse* of Captain Thomas Cochrane, another officer to whom there are frequent references in the Aubrey novels. A 38-gun ship, the 1,046-ton *Imperieuse* was sailed and fought by a complement of 284 men including 35 Marines.

The ship had been built in France, and was captured in 1804 and then placed in British service. This was a common practice at the time, and many of the best British warships of the time were in fact of French origin. It was firmly believed, with some justification, that ships of French design were better sailers than those of British build. Jack Aubrey greatly prizes the ability of French-built ships to point up into the wind (sail closer to the wind), which offered the possibility of escape to windward when challenged by a more powerful ship, or to dictate to a lower-pointing ship whether or not battle was joined.

The need for captured ships to be repaired and placed in British service is indicated by the extent to which the Royal Navy grew in size in the period between the War of American Independence (1776-83) and the end of the Napoleonic War. In 1776 the strength of the Royal Navy was 373 ships, of which 256 (58 line-of-battle ships and 198 frigates) were nominally in commission and the other 117 were laid up in ordinary. By 1805 this total had increased to 570 ships manned by 117,304 men, and by 1813 the strength of the Royal Navy stood at 606 ships manned by 130,127 men.

Shipbuilding Materials

Impressive as the first-rate line-of-battle ship undoubtedly was, it was in fact the smaller second- and third-rate ships that bore the brunt of the British naval effort in both the humdrum routine of blockade work and the occasional fury of battle. It is really the third-rate line-of-battle ship that

should be seen as the lynchpin of Britain's success at sea, which made the country the world's most important power for a century. The typical third-rate was a 74-gun ship of about 1,800 tons. Such a ship could be built more cheaply, more quickly, and in a larger number of yards than the larger second- and first-rate ships. Even so, the construction of a third-rate line-of-battle ship required 3,000 loads of oak and 400 loads of elm for planking below the waterline. As domestic supplies of timber that was of suitable dimensions and adequate seasoning had fallen below demand by the beginning of the 19th century, the Royal Navy was forced to look elsewhere for at least part of the materials needed for its ships.

Fir for masts and yards was acquired in North America, oak for hulls came from the Baltic, and it was the same region that also supplied flax for sail cloth, hemp for rope, and tar for caulking and painting. It is worth noting that after the United States of America had secured its independence during 1783, there was a switch in British procurement tendencies toward greater reliance on the Baltic. However, French military successes in that region made it more difficult to secure raw materials from this source, and in 1811 Britain imported 125,000 loads from the Baltic but almost 155,000 loads from North America. The declining availability of suitable oak and the rise in the availability of teak meant that some large

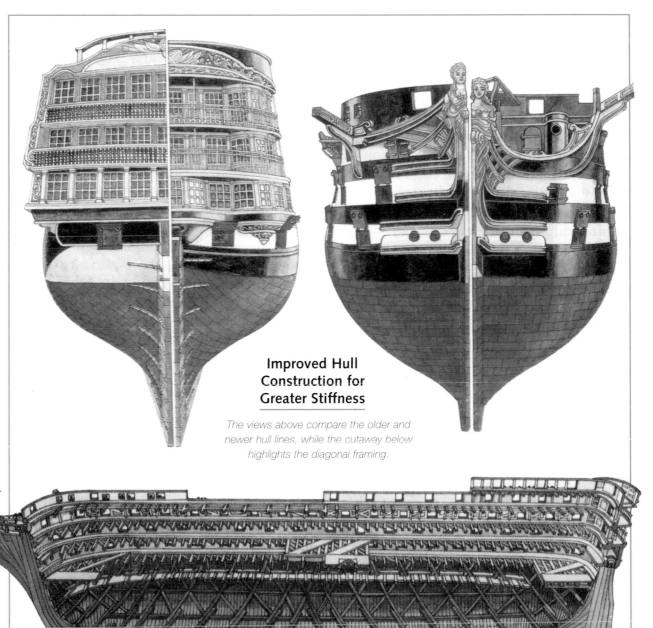

Improved Hull Construction for Greater Stiffness

The views above compare the older and newer hull lines, while the cutaway below highlights the diagonal framing.

ships were built of teak in India before the end of the Napoleonic War. In Europe shortages of oak and other premium timbers meant that a number of frigates were built of fir, but these were of so little real use that they were generally known as "pasteboard frigates"—probably quite

an accurate estimation of their strength for naval purposes.

It should be stressed that the shortages of suitable timber reflected not only a national situation in which demand had risen beyond the figures that growers of oak and elm had estimated at least a century earlier, but also the fact that the

Above: *Late in the Napoleonic War, British shipbuilders introduced a more rounded bow and stern, and diagonal framing for greater hull stiffness.*

Below: The poop (right) and quarterdeck of the Canopus reveal the areas from which the ship was controlled, and below which was much of the accommodation for the officers. The quarterdeck was reserved largely for the officers, the starboard side generally being used only by the captain.

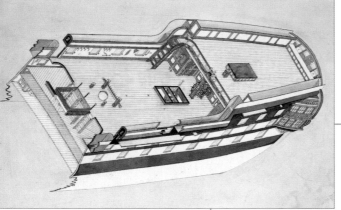

available timber often did not reach the hands of the shipwrights in the country's yards. This resulted from a combination of contractors who were notably corrupt in an era in which modest corruption seems to have been accepted as part of everyday life, and of dockyard authorities who were at best wholly inefficient and at worst notably corrupt in their own right. This situation resulted in the widespread perpetration of frauds on the public purse. The position was equally dire with regard to all aspects of equipping ships with everything needed for their operation, from primary items such as cordage and sailcloth to the victualling supplies that the ships needed for sustained operation at sea.

Perhaps the most classic example of how the increase in the use of inadequate materials,

in this instance unseasoned timber, affected ships of the Royal Navy is the August 29th, 1782 loss at Spithead of the 100-gun *Royal George* first-rate line-of-battle ship. The ship had been launched in 1756, but only 26 years later was so rotten in her planks that the sheathing pins fell out: as the ship was being heeled for repair, her bottom fell out and the ship went down with some 900 men, women, and children. Some of the right lessons were learned, however, and it was decided that the bottoms of all ships should be coppered. The first British warship with a coppered bottom had been the frigate *Alarm*, which was so fitted in 1761.

The Decks of a Warship

Standing by the ensign staff at the aftermost part of the ship's highest deck, the poop deck, a person looking forward along the length of the ship would descry, after only a short distance, the steps leading down to the quar-

> 66 **The first British warship with a coppered bottom had been the frigate *Alarm*, which was so fitted in 1761.** 99

Right: This cutaway illustration details the decks of a British line-of-battle ship of the late 18th century. Pierced by hatches and connected by companionways, the decks helped divide the interior of the hull into the maximum usable area for the mounting of the broadside guns above the waterline and all manner of stores, as well as the powder, below the waterline.

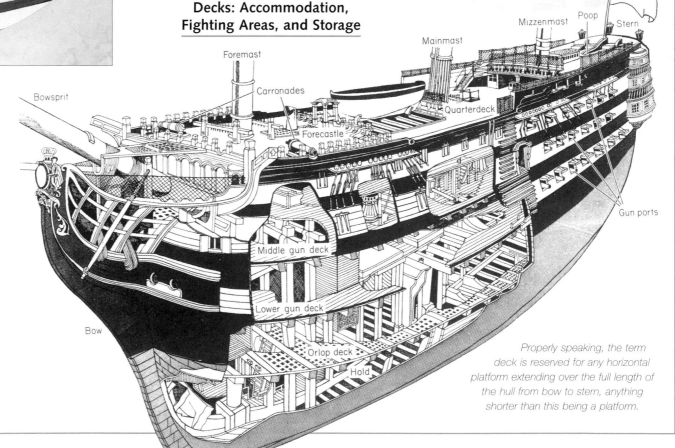

Decks: Accommodation, Fighting Areas, and Storage

Foremast

Bowsprit

Carronades

Forecastle

Mainmast

Quarterdeck

Mizzenmast

Poop

Stern

Gun ports

Middle gun deck

Lower gun deck

Bow

Orlop deck

Hold

Properly speaking, the term deck is reserved for any horizontal platform extending over the full length of the hull from bow to stern, anything shorter than this being a platform.

terdeck, where the most important features were the binnacle and wheel close to the entrance to the captain's cabin. The quarterdeck continued forward to the break in the waist just abaft the main mast. To each side of the well that constituted the waist were the gangways and spardecks that extended forward to the forecastle, and here were the sick bays and, on the beakheads, the heads.

The highest deck running along the full length of the ship was the main deck, on which were mounted the lighter 18-pounder guns of the broadside batteries. The entry port provided access through the side onto this deck, which also accommodated the admiral's cabin and, right aft, the stern and quarter-galleries. From the main deck a ladder descended to the middle deck (if the ship was a three-decker) and the lower deck, on which the heaviest element of the broadside, the 32-pounder guns, were mounted. The middle and lower decks were also the men's primary mess decks with the lieutenants' wardroom abaft them and the galley and manger (livestock accommodation) forward of them by the hawse holes for the anchor cables. Descending farther, to the levels below the water line, one reached the orlop deck on which were located the midshipmen's berth, the surgeon's cockpit, and the spirit room. Still farther down was the hold accommodating the felt-lined magazines and also the stores in which sailcloth, ropes, water casks, and provisions were kept.

Above: The lower decks could be regions of rough and tumble, as seen in this Cruikshank engraving revealing the treatment meted out to an unpopular man. He is being tipped down a hatch as a grating is pulled out from under him. The illustration also serves to reveal the cramped nature of the men's living and working spaces. Note also the Marine by the mast, the woman on the right, the powder monkey, and the shot around the hatch.

Right: This illustration of the Venerable, a 74-gun two-decker, cleared for action reveals how the officers' cabins were cleared away to provide the maximum possible fighting area on the upper deck. Also evident is the netting set in the rigging in an effort to prevent shot-away rigging and other debris, including blocks and broken spars, from falling on the crews working the ship's guns.

> On being called to action by drums beating "Hearts of Oak," the crew cleared away cabin screens.

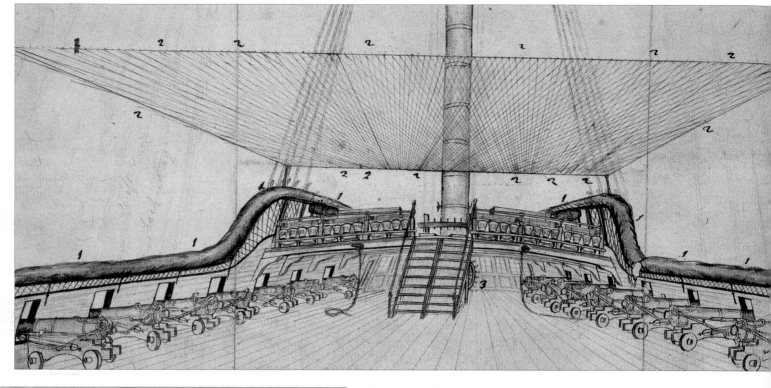

Above: 32-pounder guns on the gun deck on the Bellerophon, a 74-gun ship known to her crew as the "Billy Ruffian." The upper-deck guns were 18-pounders.

Action Stations

On being called for action by drums beating "Hearts of Oak," the crew cleared away cabin screens and partitions (replaced by wet canvas cloths) to create a clear length along the deck over its full length, and the guns were readied for action: cloth-covered charges and priming powder were brought up from the magazines by the "powder monkeys," and oiled shot (chipped to remove rust and so ensure a shape that was as nearly spherical as possible) was available in the racks beside the guns. The Marines took position on the upper deck and in the tops to provide musketry fire and man the carronades.

Named for the Carron Iron Founding and Shipping Company near Glasgow, the carronade was a murderous short-range weapon called a "smasher" by the British. Less accurate than a cannon as a result of its short barrel, the carronade was carried on a slide rather than a wheeled carriage. It originally fired case or grape shot to clear the deck of an enemy ship, but because of its lower manufacturing cost it was used increasingly as part of the primary armament firing solid shot. As conceived and first used, however, the carronade was a very useful addition to the armament of a navy that opted to fight at very close range rather than copy the French practice of firing on the up-roll of the ship to try to carry away or otherwise wreck the enemy ship's rigging, spars, and sails, so immobilizing her and leaving her vulnerable to subsequent boarding.

Through Aubrey's Eyes

In common with many of the other Royal Navy officers, Jack Aubrey is a man of strong mathematical bent. This expresses itself at an intellectual level in Aubrey's fascination with maritime navigation and the development of this as a science, and at a practical level in his fascination with naval gunnery. His concern with gunnery takes two forms. The first of these is the standard naval preoccupation with firing broadsides as rapidly and decisively as possible at short range to hull the enemy and so cause him to sink or strike his colors. The second is the use of the chasers, the long cannon mounted in the bow and at the stern of his ships, for aimed long-range fire. Designed to carry away a key part of an enemy's rigging or damage the hull at or near the waterline, this type of gunnery was more properly mathematical in its need for an understanding of ballistics and the effect of the wind on flying shot. Aubrey often involves himself in loading, laying, and firing his special chasers, for which he provides the best possible powder out of his own pocket. His dedication to gunnery is particularly evident in *The Fortune of War* when Aubrey, a passenger on HMS *Java* when she meets the American frigate USS *Constitution*, fights the forecastle battery of the British frigate as she is battered into defeat and captured in Chapter 3.

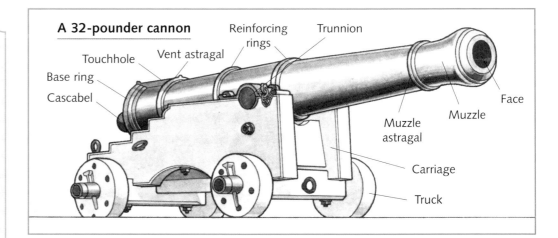

A 32-pounder cannon

Touchhole · Vent astragal · Reinforcing rings · Trunnion · Base ring · Cascabel · Muzzle astragal · Muzzle · Face · Carriage · Truck

Above: *The standard gun of line-of-battle ships, the 32-pounder cannon, was 9ft 6in long and weighed some 6,160lb. Broadside firing generally took place at very short range.*

Gunnery improvements that had been introduced by the time of Jack Aubrey's heyday included the use of flannel rather than silk cartridge cases as flannel left less deposit in the barrel and so made possible a higher rate of fire, and an increase in the guns' traverse to 45 degrees left and right. This made it possible for a captain to have his ship's gun crews fire obliquely, and so not to have to position his ship exactly parallel to the enemy.

Firing The Guns

Practiced endlessly, but often without actually firing live as powder and shot were expensive, a ship's gunnery was all-important in battle. British short-range tactics generally demanded the highest possible rate of fire. The sequence in which the gun was loaded and fired was as follows: the tompion was removed from the muzzle, a powder-filled cartridge was inserted and rammed down to the breech end of this muzzle-loading weapon, then followed the ball and the wad that prevented it from rolling back toward the muzzle. The gun crew then used the tackles to run out the gun on its carriage so that the gun's muzzle emerged from the opened gun port in the side of the ship. The touch hole above the cartridge was primed with a quill of black powder, and finally the priming powder was ignited by a slow-burning match or, in later guns, a flintlock mechanism operated by a lanyard.

Once fired, the gun recoiled inboard and was secured by ropes (breeched home) to prevent any movement as the ship rolled. It was sponged out to wet—and thereby render safe—any fragments of cartridge case or other hot residues, reloaded, and run out once more. A well-trained crew could fire three rounds in two minutes, and although the cannon's effective range was as much as one mile, battles were generally slugged out at very much shorter range.

Jack Aubrey was noted for his enthusiasm for gunnery, and he ensured that the crews of his ships had plenty of training, including live firing, to ensure rapid and accurate fire. Aubrey was also a devotee of the use of smaller guns known as chasers. Located in the bows and on the poop deck, these chasers were lighter but longer than the main guns and generally of brass rather than iron construction as this offered greater accuracy. The object of the chasers was generally to knock about the rigging, spars, and sails, or alternatively to hull the enemy close to the waterline.

Above: *Under the eye of an officer and direct supervision of the gun captain, members of a gun crew lever the rear part of their gun's carriage to alter its training relative to the ship's beam. Most fighting took place at very short range, the British preferring to fire broadsides low into the enemy ship's hull.*

CHAPTER FOUR

A Life on the Ocean Wave

In the early 19th century the square-rigged warship was the most complicated machine in existence and its efficient operation required the individual and collective skills of a large number of people. The absolute responsibility for this rested entirely upon one man—the captain—but he depended in his turn upon the unswerving support of many specialists.

Recruitment and Wages

Below: Despite bounties, such as the two pounds two shillings offered here, there were never enough volunteers for service in the Royal Navy.

TWO GUINEAS BOUNTY

Will be Given Immediately by the Corporation of **PORTSMOUTH**

To Volunteers who shall enter the Service of the **ROYAL NAVY** March 10th 1796

Right: Life aboard a warship, even for the officers, was probably far less attractive than the scene depicted here of young officers in the steerage of a British frigate. It was painted by Augustus Earle.

Officers and warrant officers were posted to a ship through a mixture of applications from individuals, influence, and straightforward filling vacancies by the Admiralty. Attempts to join a particular ship were frequently based on the known reputation of the captain or of the ship, although more venal motives could also come into play, such as the possibility of prize money or the fact that, as shown in the table, in most grades the larger the ship, the better the pay.

Sailors had less influence on the choice of ship, and were frequently simply sent where the needs of the Service required. Rather more sailors were volunteers than is generally acknowledged, and these joined from the usual motives of adventure, patriotism, love of the sea, a career, or an escape from some aspect of domestic life. Where there were shortages, however, they were impressed. The reasons for impressment were quite simple: neither the politicians nor the British electorate were prepared to pay and provide the men for a sizeable standing navy in peacetime, nor were they prepared to support conscription in wartime, but the men had to be provided somehow.

The first target of the press gangs were merchant seamen, since, as trained mariners, they could be put straight to work. These could be rounded up in ports or even lifted (hijacked would be the modern term) from British merchant ships at sea. Having been "pressed," most reluctant recruits were taken to a receiving ship, a foul, dank, worn-out hulk, where they were held pending allocation to a ship. Later the Quota Acts were introduced, which ran in parallel with impressment, in which the country was divided into geographical areas, the annual quota being set each year according to the perceived needs of the navy,

and it was then left to the local authorities to find the men as best they could. The large non-volunteer element was one of the causes of the harsh disciplinary system which was necessary to ensure control.

At the start of the wars in 1793 the pay in the navy had not changed for many years, but it was slowly improved until by 1815 the men were earning the amounts shown in the table (right), although the net sum paid was reduced by stoppages for items such as clothing.

Pay Rates for Selected Sea-Going People in the Royal Navy in 1815			
Rank or Rating	Pay per Lunar Month		Remarks
	First-rate	Sixth-rate and under	Notes 1,2
Captain	£32.4.6	£16.6.0	
Lieutenant	£8.8.0		Note 3
Chaplain	£11.10.9		Note 4
Surgeon	£14.0.0		Note 5
Master	£12.12.0	£7.7.0	Note 6
Carpenter	£5.16.0	£3.1.0	
Boatswain; gunner; purser	£4.16.0	£3.1.0	
Master's mate	£3.16.6	£2.12.6	
Midshipman	£2.15.6	£2.0.6	
Captain's clerk	£4.7.0	£2.18.6	
Schoolmaster; master-at-arms; armorer	£2.15.6	£2.0.6	Note 7
Carpenter's mate; caulker, ropemaker	£2.10.6	£2.0.6	
QM, boatswain's/gunner's mates; yeoman of powder room; corporal; armorer's mate	£2.5.6	£1.16.6	
Sailmaker	£2.5.6	£2.0.6	
Caulker's mate	£2.6.6		Note 8
Yeoman of sheets; coxswain	£2.2.6	£1.16.6	
Quartermaster's mate; captains of forecastle, foretop, main top, afterguard, and mast	£2.0.6	£1.15.6	
Trumpeter	£2.0.6	£1.14.6	
Quarter gunner; carpenter's crew	£1.16.6	£1.15.6	
Gunsmith; steward	£1.15.6	£1.9.6	Note 9
Cook	£1.15.6	£1.14.6	
Able seaman	£1.13.6		
Ordinary seaman	£1.5.6		
Landman	£1.2.6		

(Source: *A Social History of the Navy 1793-1815*, M.A. Lewis, 1960)
Notes: 1. In many cases the rate of pay varied in a decreasing scale according to the rating of the ship from first-rate (maximum) to sixth-rate and below (minimum). The second and third columns therefore represent the maximum and minimum for each rank. Where there is a figure in the second column and none in the third, this indicates that the rate of pay was standard, regardless of the ship's rating.
2. Amounts are expressed in 19th century English money, where the figures represent pounds (£), shillings (s), and pence (d); i.e., £3.14.6 = three pounds, fourteen shillings, and sixpence. The system was that 12 pence = 1 shilling (s); 20 shillings = 1 pound (£).
3. Pay of lieutenant in a flagship was enhanced by 14s.0d per month.
4. Chaplains on first- to fifth-rates only. Could also act as schoolmaster, in which case he earned the appropriate bonus and capitation rate (see Note 7).
5. Surgeons' rates depended upon length of service: 6 years: £14.0.0; 7-9 years: £15.8.0; 10-19 years: £19.12.6; 20 years: £25.4.0.
6. £6.6.0 for second masters in brigs, sloops, and cutters.
7. Schoolmasters also earned an annual bonus of £20 plus capitation rate of £5 per pupil.
8. Caulker's mate in first- to fourth-rates only. 9. Gunsmith in first- to third-rates rates only.

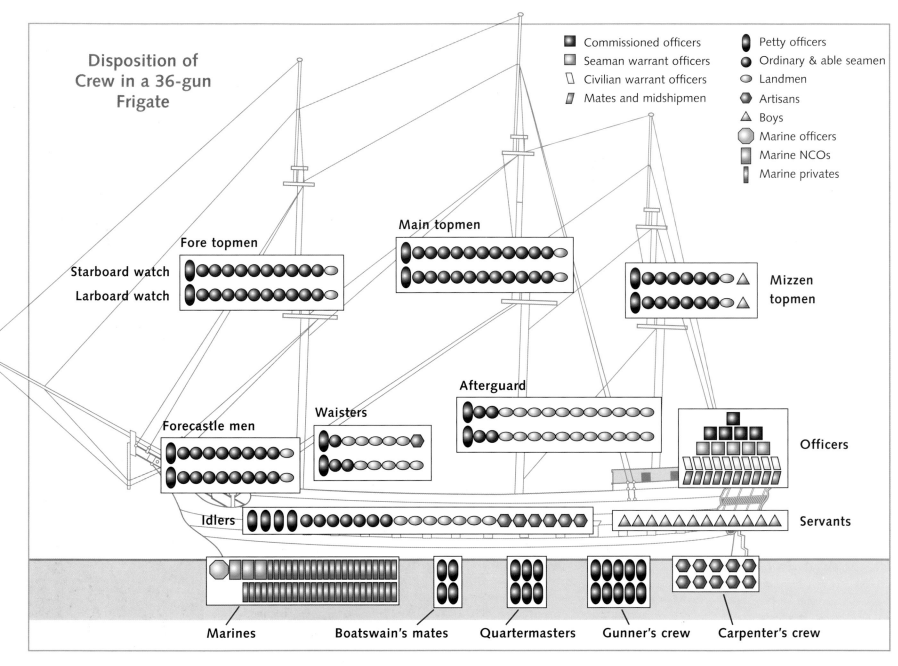

Disposition of Crew in a 36-gun Frigate

Commissioned officers
Seaman warrant officers
Civilian warrant officers
Mates and midshipmen

Petty officers
Ordinary & able seamen
Landmen
Artisans
Boys
Marine officers
Marine NCOs
Marine privates

Fore topmen

Starboard watch
Larboard watch

Main topmen

Mizzen topmen

Afterguard

Forecastle men

Waisters

Officers

Idlers

Servants

Marines   Boatswain's mates   Quartermasters   Gunner's crew   Carpenter's crew

Above: The disposition of the crew of a 36-gun frigate based on a two-watch system. Note that most officers and warrant officers would also have been watchkeepers. The large proportion of Marines is also apparent.

The number of men in the ship's complement and their specializations was authorized by the Admiralty and depended primarily upon the size (i.e. the rating) of the ship (see Chapter 3). Within the ship, the organization of the crew was the general responsibility of the captain. However, the detailed work, such as the allocation of every man in the ship to watchbills and quarterbills, was programmed by the first lieutenant, who based his system on a mixture of Admiralty regulations, the captain's wishes, his personal experience, and the key ingredient, which could be variously described as "tradition" or "the custom of the Service."

The commanding officer of any ship, regardless of its size and his naval rank, was the captain, who was responsible for the control, fighting, and safety of his ship, and the organization, sustenance, and discipline of its crew. Rated ships were known as "post ships" and their commanding officers were post captains, that is to say, they were captains in naval rank as well as being captains of a seagoing ship. Aubrey achieves the rank of post captain in the novel of the same name accepting temporary command of HMS *Lively*. Commanding officers of warships smaller than sixth-rates— sloops, brigs, etc.—were lieutenants in naval rank, but were usually designated "master and commander," had a special commission to this effect, and wore certain distinctions on their uniform. However, they reverted to their normal rank of lieutenant if they returned to a larger ship.

SHIP ORGANIZATION

The ship was organized into a number of parallel hierarchies. First, there was the naval rank structure, with each man holding a designated rank, or its equivalent. At the top of the tree were those holding a Commission signed by the King, a small number of Royal Navy and Royal Marine officers, whose status as both officers *and* gentlemen was indicated by their dress, their accommodation in the wardroom, and the allocation of a servant. Next were warrant officers, who held a warrant issued by various boards, and of which there were three types: those with wardroom status (i.e. they shared the facilities of the wardroom), the standing officers, and the cockpit mates. The petty officers led groups of seamen, of which there were four grades: able seaman, ordinary seaman, landman, and boys (also known as volunteers). The midshipmen were slotted into this structure, but, although their tasks were plain to see, their actual status was somewhat ill-defined, as will be described below.

Secondly, many of the crew were organized into departments, each with a specialized function, such as gunners, carpenters, and sailmakers. Thus, for example, the gunner's department consisted of the armorer, plus his armorer's mates and the gunsmith; the gunner's mate and quarter gunners; and the yeoman of the powder room.

Thirdly, in order to provide 24-hour coverage of the ship's essential functions, most of the crew was then divided into two watches in which they had a specific duty relating to a "part-of-ship," such as topman, forecastle hand, waistman, or afterguard. Each such party was led by an able seaman with the title of "captain" (e.g. captain of the

maintop) or yeoman (e.g. yeoman of the sheets). With only a very few exceptions, ships worked a two-watch system over the course of a ship's day, although some adopted a three-watch system, which was much more popular with the crew since it gave them the occasional opportunity of a full night's sleep.

Those men who were not part of a watch and whose tasks were predominantly performed during daylight hours, were collectively described as idlers. This meant that they could sleep through the night, but they were, of course, liable to answer each and every "all the hands" call.

Men in larger ships also belonged to a division, an administrative structure which in modern terms was responsible for man management and welfare. Each lieutenant in the wardroom headed a division, which was sub-divided into sections, each under a master's mate or midshipman.

Watches, Quarters, and Stations

A watch consisted of a balanced proportion of the crew necessary for maneuvering and general evolutions during routine cruising. One watch was always on duty. For major evolutions "all the hands" was piped and every man had an assigned station, relative to the handling of the ship and the evolution to be performed. But, when "action stations" were piped, they had a different "action station" or quarter, the great majority of them acting as gun crew.

Above: A sailor "catting the anchor" to secure it to the cathead.

Below: Master (with trumpet), quartermaster (at wheel), officer of the watch (by cannon) and lookout in cold-weather gear, but the midshipman (foreground) and servant shiver.

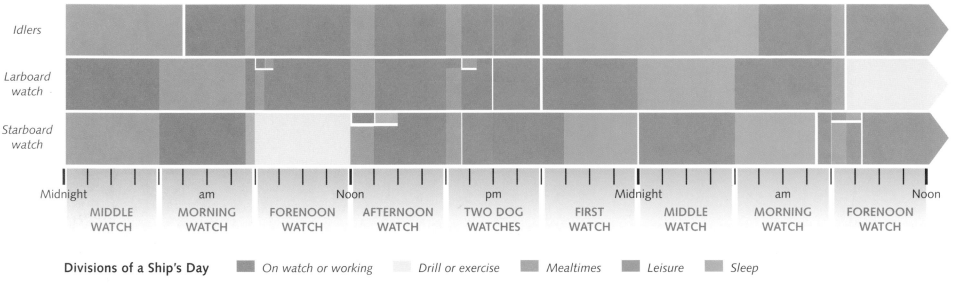

	Midnight		am		Noon		pm		Midnight		am		Noon

Idlers

Larboard watch

Starboard watch

MIDDLE WATCH	MORNING WATCH	FORENOON WATCH	AFTERNOON WATCH	TWO DOG WATCHES	FIRST WATCH	MIDDLE WATCH	MORNING WATCH	FORENOON WATCH

Divisions of a Ship's Day   ■ *On watch or working*   ■ *Drill or exercise*   ■ *Mealtimes*   ■ *Leisure*   ■ *Sleep*

Notes: • Watch timings and names were universal throughout the Navy, but there were minor variations in times of reveille, meals, leisure time depending upon the captain's preference, and factors like the season, climate, etc.
• The ship's "day" ran from noon to noon, but in practice began with rousing the idlers.
• The length of the meal breaks depended upon the captain, but they were usually either 30 or 45 minutes long. Lunch, the main meal, might be longer. Once fixed, they were considered sacrosanct and captains were very reluctant to invade them without very good reason. If forced to do so, they would do their best to make up for it as soon as possible thereafter.
• The progress of each watch was marked by a series of bells sounded at 30-minute intervals, increasing from "one bell" half-an-hour after the start of the watch to "eight bells" at the end of that watch.

Right: A gun crew in action, with a Marine (foreground) moving the carriage bodily using a "spike" according to the orders of the gun captain (right). Despite reports to the contrary, many captains, such as Broke of HMS Shannon, trained their gun crews to take careful aim at the target. Jack Aubrey is a keen devotee of gunnery and seizes every opportunity to train his gun crews.

Action Stations

In action, by far the largest proportion of the crew were allocated to the guns in a "quarter bill" prepared by the first lieutenant. Admiralty regulations stipulated the crew required by each type of gun, based on a rule-of-thumb of one man per 5cwt of gun, which worked out as 14 men for a 32-pounder, 11 men for an 18-pounder, and so on. These were the absolute minimum required and if, as generally happened, only one side of the ship was engaged with the enemy, then the crews on the unengaged side crossed the deck to assist the crew of the gun directly opposite them. The crew of each gun was led by a gun captain but most of his crew had another designated task and when called for by the pipe had to leave the gun. Such tasks included trimming the sails, manning a boarding party, fetching powder, acting as boat's crew, and so on. Gun crews frequently also included at least one Royal Marine.

On the call "action stations" other men were allocated to various essential tasks. Those Marines not serving in gun crews were employed as sharpshooters or held in reserve

as the nucleus of a boarding party. The surgeon, assistant surgeon (if appointed), surgeon's mates, purser, and chaplain set up a medical treatment center in the cockpit, while the captain's clerk was on the quarterdeck, keeping a written record of the engagement. Most midshipmen were placed in charge of a section of two to three guns, while others acted as captain's messengers, or in smaller ships were in charge of signaling.

Above: Stylized depiction of raising the anchor, an operation requiring some 200 men on the forecastle (top right), at the capstan (top left), through the gundeck (center) to the orlop (below). For those who lived on the orlop deck, the smell of a newly raised cable must have been overpowering.

Wardroom Officers, Midshipmen, and Total Crews of Selected Ships c.1812

Ship Rating	1	2	3	4	5	6	Brig
Guns	100	98	74	50	36	24	10
Captain	1	1	1	1	1	1	0
Lieutenant	8	8	6	4	3	2	1
Master	1	1	1	1	1	1	0
2nd Master	0	0	0	0	0	0	1
Surgeon	1	1	1	1	1	1	0
Asst surgeon	0	0	0	0	0	0	1
Purser	1	1	1	1	1	1	0
Midshipmen	24	24	16	10	6	4	2
Lower deck	801	702	614	325	253	155	37
TOTAL	837	738	640	343	264	145	42

(Source: Adapted from *Nelson's Navy*, Brian Lavery, 1989)

Other Tasks

In addition to all these, there were many domestic tasks to be performed around the ship. For example, each wardroom officer had a servant, some of whom were permanently assigned, while others were sailors or Marines who took it on as an additional duty. Officers also performed tasks such as wardroom caterer, while sailors were selected for messing duties for their particular group.

Above: A seaman swings the lead to measure the depth of the water beneath the ship. The lead line varied in length from around 25 fathoms for shallow water to more than 100 fathoms for deeper water.

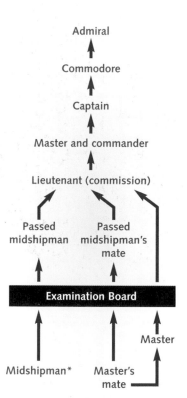

Admiral
↑
Commodore
↑
Captain
↑
Master and commander
↑
Lieutenant (commission)
↑   ↑
Passed   Passed
midshipman   midshipman's
              mate
↑   ↑   ↑
Examination Board
↑   ↑   ↑
                       Master
Midshipman*   Master's
              mate

* after minimum six years' sea service, three as a midshipman

Right: *The scene in the ship's wardroom, with the officers relaxing over a glass of wine. Note the cutlasses and pistols above the stern windows, and the stand of muskets on the right.*

RANKS AND APPOINTMENTS

Captain

The captain was, quite simply, absolutely responsible for everything and everybody in his ship: the "first after God." His status was enhanced by the fact that he lived alone in the grandest accommodation at the stern of the ship and he usually kept to himself, although he would generally eat with some of the officers on one or two occasions each week. As is usual in any walk-of-life, captains had different personalities and exerted their authority in different ways: some were austere and distant, others cheerful and direct; some brutal, others comparatively benign (at least, by the standards of the day); some imposed their authority by frequent application of the lash, others led by courage and personal example. Jack Aubrey falls very much into the latter category.

Lieutenants

The only other commissioned naval rank aboard a ship was lieutenant, the numbers serving on board depending upon the size of the ship; for instance, a first-rate had eight and a fifth-rate three. All such lieutenants were watchkeepers, but they all also had other tasks, including commanding a

section of guns, being in charge of an administrative division, signals officer, or treasurer or caterer in the wardroom. A minimum of six years' previous service as a midshipman was essential before appearing before the mandatory lieutenants' promotion examination board. This board was formed of captains, but they were not always particularly thorough in their quizzing of the candidate, especially if he was known to have "influence." Passing the board was not the end of the matter, however. Being selected for a seagoing appointment was of even greater importance, and, once again, previous distinction and influence could be of considerable assistance here. Promotion to captain was, in theory, by merit, although, yet again, "interest" could play a role. It also helped if the officer distinguished himself in action and the captain then included his name in the "record of proceedings."

Temporary Ranks

There were three types of officers' appointment which carried a temporary rank, which was relinquished when the particular appointment came to an end. A post captain could be given a temporary appointment in command of a small number of ships and be designated commodore, with a special pennant to indicate his status. Aubrey gains

more officers, particularly for watch-keeping. Thus, he was given a second master, who was responsible for navigation, and a meritorious senior midshipman who was given the temporary rank of sub-lieutenant.

Warrant Officers

Warrant officers were so called because they (and their mates) received a formal warrant from the appropriate government department: the master from the Navy Board, the purser from the Victualling Board, and the surgeon from the Sick and Hurt Board. At the top were the warrant officers with wardroom status who messed in the wardroom and walked on the quarterdeck, although their cabins were not usually alongside those of the commissioned officers. Their position, at least by implication, was that of being officers but not quite gentlemen.

The sailing master was responsible for the navigation and pilotage of the ship on the course and to the destinations ordered by the captain; he was the best-paid man aboard after the captain, while his accommodation was on a par with that of the first lieutenant. His other responsibilities included calculating the ship's position and taking the noon sightings, supervision of the midshipmen; stowing the hold (since this had a major effect on the sailing qualities of the ship), and the provision and condition of the sails, rigging, and anchors. One of his most important tasks was to maintain the Master's Log—which was the ship's official record. The master was assisted by master's mates. Larger ships also had a second master. Smaller, unrated ships had a second master, but no master.

The surgeon had to be qualified by an examination held by the Barber-Surgeon's Company and there was only one per ship. Like the master, he was assisted by one or more mates, and, again, smaller ships such as brigs and sloops had only an assistant surgeon.

The purser was given wardroom status in 1808. He had control of all ship's stores, clothing, and provisions. A unique requirement demanded that he had to place a bond with the Victualling Board, whose value depended on the rating of ship, ranging from £400 for a sixth-rate to £1200 for a first-rate. The purser was assisted by the ship's steward and his mates (who issued the daily provisions), plus the cooper and his mate. Unlike his modern descendants, the purser was not responsible for paying the crew.

this distinction in *The Mauritius Command*. At a lower level, the captain of a vessel smaller than a sixth-rate, particularly sloops and brigs, was a lieutenant in rank but in view of his special responsibility was designated a "master and commander," usually shortened to "commander." This was a greatly sought after appointment since it gave a deserving officer the opportunity to prove himself in independent command, but the title was relinquished if the officer subsequently moved back to a ship-of-the-line or was placed on half-pay. The commander wore a different uniform to an ordinary lieutenant (see below). The third of these temporary ranks was that of sub-lieutenant, which was introduced in 1804 when it was found that the lieutenant in command of a sloop or brig needed the assistance of

Below: *Humorous depiction by Thomas Rowlandson of a purser (c.1800) consulting his accounts. His well-fed appearance suggests that his activities have not been without personal profit.*

Left: *The quarterdeck of HMS Deal Castle, a sixth-rate frigate. The quarterdeck was hallowed ground, restricted to officers and those who had to work there, such as the quartermasters. Even so, space was found for animals, such as the goat seen here, which formed an essential supplement to the navy-supplied rations.*

The chaplain also enjoyed wardroom status. By midway through the Napoleonic wars there was one established in fifth-rate ships and above, although, due to lack of applicants, it was rare to find a chaplain in any ship smaller than a third-rate. By regulation, only Church of England chaplains were allowed, and they were supposed to hold religious services at least once every week. A great deal depended upon the individual chaplain's personality and behavior, but they were generally regarded with benign tolerance by the officers, and with a mixture of derision and suspicion by the lower deck.

The three "standing officers," so-called because they stayed with the ship, were not of wardroom status, but had great prestige, not least because they could only be disrated by the Admiralty and not by the commanding officer. The first-among-equals was the gunner, who was in charge of the main guns and the ammunition, small arms and hand weapons such as cutlasses, the powder room, and gunnery tools such as rammers. Depending upon the size of the ship, his crew consisted of one or more mates, an armorer, a quarter gunner for each four guns, and the yeoman of the powder room.

The second in this group was the boatswain (bosun), whose responsibilities included maintenance of the sails, rigging, and cordage, and the securing of boats, anchors, and booms. He, too, was assisted by his bosun's mates, and also supervised the sailmaker and ropemaker. He and his team were also responsible for discipline, which included getting the crew on deck on "all the hands" being piped, and encouraging recalcitrant members of the crew by use of starters (short knotted ropes).

Third of the standing officers was the carpenter, who usually started his career as an apprentice carpenter in a naval dockyard and then obtained his warrant from the Navy Board for service at sea. His tasks, assisted by his carpenter's mates, mainly concerned the maintenance of the hull, masts, and yards. He also oversaw the work of the caulker and his mate.

Three other crew members deserve mention. The ship's cook was normally a long-service seaman, usually either elderly or disabled in some way; he was rarely either trained or skilled in his trade. Many ships had a schoolmaster, whose primary task was to teach navigation and mathematics to the midshipmen, although some also taught the younger seamen and boys to read and write. The precise status of the schoolmaster was somewhat nebulous, but he messed with his charges, the midshipmen, which was not a recipe for success. The third of these was a petty officer, the master-at-arms, who was assisted by one or more ship's corporals, and provided the police force.

Midshipmen

Midshipmen found themselves in a curious position between the lower deck and the quarterdeck. They had a uniform and were clearly intended as candidates for commissions, but they lived in the cockpit—well outside "officer country." They were expected in many respects to behave like officers but were often treated like children—and naughty ones at that. Sometimes they were put in charge a gang of sailors, a few of whom could be two or three times their age. On other occasions they were made to look foolish in front of the same men by being forced to spend hours at the masthead or "seized" (tied) to the rigging as a punishment for some very minor misdemeanor.

The Marines

Every ship had a detachment of Marines—*Royal* Marines from 1804—who formed a surprisingly large proportion of the total ship's company; about one-fifth in large ships and

Left: *The cutting-out party from HMS* Surprise *retakes HMS* Hermione, *which had been surrendered to the Spanish Navy by mutineers in 1797. The Marines use their muskets, while the sailors attack with cutlasses.*

> **66** Midshipmen were expected in many respects to behave like officers but were often treated like children—and naughty ones at that. **99**

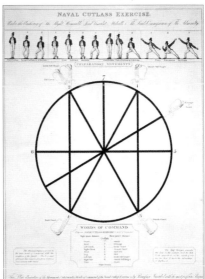

Above: *A formalized system of naval cutlass exercises (c.1814). It is doubtful whether real combat would have allowed for such precise and graceful movements.*

Royal Marine Complements of Selected Ships-of-the-Line 1808-1815

Rating	1	2	3	4	5	6	Brig
Guns	100	98	74	50	36	24	10
Captain	1	1	1	0	0	0	0
Lieutenant	3	3	2	2	2	1	0
Sergeant	4	3	3	2	2	1	1
Corporal	4	3	2	2	2	1	1
Drummer	2	2	2	1	1	1	0
Private	156	138	115	52	41	26	13
TOTAL	**170**	**150**	**125**	**59**	**48**	**30**	**15**

(Source: Adapted from *Nelson's Navy*, Brian Lavery, 1989)

about one-sixth in smaller ships. Between 1806 and 1815 the corps was some 31,400 strong with most serving afloat, where larger detachments were commanded by a captain, medium-sized detachments by a first lieutenant, and by a sergeant in smaller ships such as sloops and brigs. On board ship the Marines' duties included serving as sharpshooters, boarders, and guncrews, and they also served as naval infantry during cutting-out and land operations. One of their most important duties, however, was the prevention of mutiny, for which they provided a number of sentries (for instance, outside the door of the captain's cabin). They were accommodated between the crew and the officers. They also stood guard when punishments such as the lash were being inflicted.

NAVAL UNIFORMS 1795-1815

Officers

Naval officers did not have uniforms until 1748, when, following requests from the fleet, standard forms of dress were introduced. There were minor changes over the next 40 years, but new patterns were introduced in 1787 and these were being worn when the war started in 1793. The patterns for lieutenants and above were changed again in 1795, the reason being, as far as can be established, to reduce unnecessary expense in wartime, although the simplifications in civilian dress may also have played a part.

The next major change came as a result of the Prince of Wales, who had harbored plans to alter the uniforms of the Army and Navy for some time. His opportunity came when he was appointed Prince Regent in 1811. He then acted quickly, the new naval regulations being promulgated in March 1812, and

Eyewitness

"Our first lieutenant was a very droll and strange personage, in dress as well as in manners…A red waistcoat, nankin breeches, and black worsted stockings, with great yellow buckles, on round-toed shoes, a hat that had been cocked, but cut round, with a very low crown, so that he was obliged to keep his hand to his head to prevent it blowing off in the lightest breeze."

From The Recollections of James Anthony Gardner

these remained in force for the rest of the Napoleonic Wars. Officers were not always dressed uniformly, partly due to personal idiosyncrasies—always a failing among certain types of British officer—but also due to the usual permission to allow superseded patterns to be worn out. In addi-

Above: Captain (over three years' service), 1795-1812. Note the two epaulettes, blue frock with high collar and buttoned cuffs, white stock, cocked hat, sword, and white pantaloons.

Right: Family and servants gather round to admire a newly-commissioned lieutenant trying on his uniform for the first time. Note the single epaulette on his right shoulder and the fore-and-aft hat (worn by his admiring younger brother).

"frock." The major changes over the period effected the design of the coat and its facings, the amount and quality of the braid, and the style of the hat. The cocked hat, which had evolved from the early 18th-century tricorne, had a rear brim higher than the front, and was originally worn "athwartships" (with the points above the shoulders). This changed, however, to a hat with equal sized brims, which was worn "fore-and-aft" although admirals in full dress persisted with the older athwartships fashion until 1825.

> **"** Officers had two patterns of dress: full dress, worn for ceremonial occasions; and undress usually known as a "frock." **"**

Royal Navy Officers: Undress Uniform Distinctions under the 1795-1812 Regulations

	Lapel	Cuff	Collar	Epaulettes
Captain; over three years	Blue unlined	Plain with three buttons	Blue unlined	Two
Captain; under three years				One—right shoulder
Commander				One—left shoulder
Lieutenant	Blue with white piping	Three buttons with one row of white piping	Blue with white piping	None
Sub-Lieutenant (from 1804)	As lieutenant			
Midshipman	None	Three buttons	Blue with white collar patch	None

The use of epaulettes had started in Europe but they were not authorized for the navy until 1795. Thereafter two were worn by admirals and post captains with over three years seniority, while junior captains wore one on their right shoulder, commanders one on the left. Lieutenants wore none. In 1812 this changed yet again, in order to allow lieutenants to wear them. Thus, the single plain epaulette was now worn by lieutenants (right shoulder), while commanders wore two, also plain, but all with bullion around the edges. All captains now wore two, but with an additional embellishment on the shoulder-board: an anchor for newly-appointed captains, and a crown and anchor for those with over three years' seniority.

tion, officers on long overseas cruises—some of which lasted two years or more—might be unaware of changes until they returned to their home port.

Officers had two patterns of dress: full dress, worn for ceremonial occasions; and undress usually known as a

Left: Vice Admiral Sir James Saumarez. The admiral's frock was cut-away to reveal the white waistcoat, while the insignia of Orders, such as the Bath, were embroidered. Note the white pantaloons and silk stockings, sash, twin epaulettes, and turned-back cuffs. The character of Saumarez appears in Chapter 7 of The Surgeon's Mate—both Aubrey and Maturin have a high regard for his abilities.

Above: *A warship's master dressed in the uniform of the 1787-1807 period. The blue civilian pattern frock was "navalized" by the addition of lapels with buttons and turned-back cuffs.*

was designated for boatswains, carpenters, and gunners. From 1787 to 1805 naval surgeons wore the same uniform as other warrant officers, but in that year they were given equal status with Army surgeons and the uniform was altered to mark this change. This was a better quality blue coat with a stand-up collar, white waistcoat and breeches, and with buttons bearing the crest of the Sick and Hurt Board. Naval physicians, of whom there were a few, but all shore-based, wore a similar uniform to the surgeons, but with a considerable amount of gold braid to indicate their superior status.

Midshipmen's dress reflected their position, being similar to, but much less grand, than that of officers, and it changed remarkably little over the period. The uniform consisted of a single-breasted blue cloth coat with an upright collar carrying the badge of his position, a large white patch with a blue decorative hole and a small naval pattern button at the upper end (which remains in use today). At the start of the period midshipmen wore a cocked hat, but they were one of the first to adopt the top hat.

Sailors

For the sailors, the position was quite simple; there was no such thing as uniform, although in general they wore a short jacket, loose, wide-bottomed trousers, and some form of headgear. Many captains tried to exercise some degree of uniformity among their own crew, and a few even imposed it, with their entire crew wearing identical outfits. The purser carried a stock of clothing issued to him by the dockyard storekeeper, which he sold on, such standardization as there was being achieved through bulk purchasing rather than as a result of a deliberate policy. Sailors of the time were, perforce, adept with needle and thread, and many purchased material from the purser and then made their own clothes. Some captains made their crews wear a standard form of headgear and the practice of carrying the ship's name on the sailor's hat appeared during the Napoleonic wars, being either painted on to a hard hat, or embroidered on a ribbon.

Warrant Officers

The Dress Regulations of 1787 introduced uniforms for warrant officers and master's mates. This was essentially a civilian pattern coat, but of naval blue cloth, with lapels, turned-back cuffs with three buttons, and white waistcoat and breeches. The major naval distinctions were the gold buttons with an anchor, which were, in fact, of the same design as that used by captains under the earlier regulations. Master's mates wore a very similar uniform, but without lapels.

In 1807 the cut of the coat was altered slightly, and new buttons introduced, with a Navy Board crest for masters and the Victualling Office crest for pursers. At the same time the old pattern coat with the previous pattern buttons

Royal Marines

Up to 1802 Marines' officers wore scarlet jackets with white facings and collar, silver epaulettes, and a cocked hat worn athwartships. In 1802, however, the corps was granted the title "Royal" which meant that, in line with Army regiments with a similar honor, the facings were changed to blue, while metallic items such as epaulettes, buttons, and lace changed from silver to gold. As with naval officers, the style of the cocked hat changed during the early 1800s and it became worn fore-and-aft rather than athwartships.

Royal Marine officers also wore a cockade in their hats, a variety of colors being used, which appear to have indicated the detachment's base port: Chatham, Plymouth, or Portsmouth. All officers wore a red sash and an old-fashioned metal gorget, which hung around the neck. All officers also wore epaulettes which were used to indicate rank, one on each shoulder for captains and just one (on the right shoulder) for lieutenants. Until 1802 these epaulettes were on a scarlet cloth base with looped braid and fringe of silver, which changed to gold in 1802. The design for these junior officers was changed again in 1810 when the shoulder board was entirely covered in gold lace and fringed with gold.

Unlike the unfortunate sailors, Marine non-commissioned officers and privates not only had a standard uniform but were issued with a new one every year by the Navy Board. As with the officers, this uniform was based on that of the army and when the Royal title was conferred in 1802 the king specifically instructed that the Marines' uniform was to be based on that of the First Footguards (later re-designated Grenadier Guards after the Battle of Waterloo). Until 1807 the corporals' rank was indicated by a shoulder knot, while sergeants wore both a knot and lace trimmings on their jackets. In 1807 this was brought into line with changes implemented a few years earlier in the Army, with three large white cloth chevrons for a sergeant, and two for a corporal.

At sea, Marines wore their full uniform for guard duties, parades, formal occasions, and battle, but they also had a working dress which, like the sailors, usually consisted of items purchased from the purser's slop room, although some ship's captains insisted on a standardized outfit.

Left: Marine officers in 1797. Note the scarlet jacket with white facings, cocked hat worn athwartships, red waist sash, and twin epaulettes.

Below: Royal Marines private in 1805. The top hat was later also adopted by the officers.

Bottom: A sailor in 1805 in typical nautical garb.

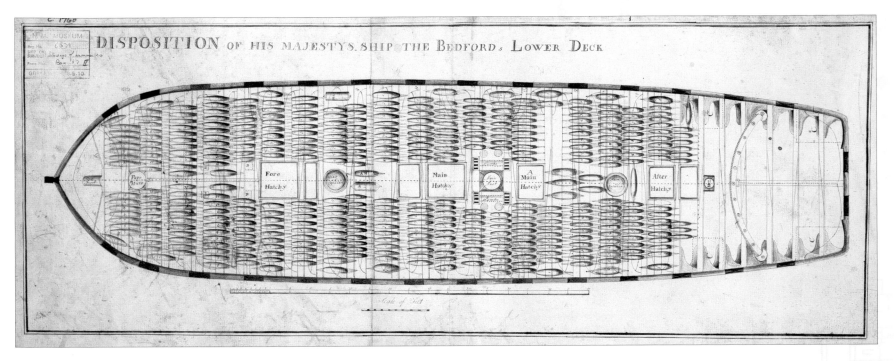

Above: The hammock plan for HMS Bedford (74). Preparing the sleeping arrangements was one of the administrative tasks of the first lieutenant.

> ❝ Every warship fulfilled two basic functions: it was a fighting platform and it was the home of its crew, who lived aboard for months— and sometimes years— at a time. ❞

Right: Cartoonists found endless amusement in the hammock, Rowlandson here showing how to enter and leave one in a single, easy movement.

LIVING CONDITIONS

Every warship fulfilled two basic functions: it was a fighting platform and it was the home of its crew, who lived aboard for months—and sometimes years—at a time. The disposition and comforts of all aboard depended upon three factors: the size of the ship in which they served, their rank, and the status of their appointments, the two latter not necessarily being synonymous.

The Lower Deck

Petty officers and seamen formed the vast majority of the ship's company and these were accommodated below decks, and amidships and forward. Every man received a government-issue hammock, measuring 6 feet in length and 3 feet in width, with cords at either end for slinging. The size of these hammocks determined his living space, which was laid down in an elaborate plan devised by the first lieutenant. Able-bodied and ordinary seamen, landmen, and boys were allowed a space 14 inches wide, although efforts were made to ease the strain by placing men on opposite watches in adjacent berths. For petty officers one of the perks of promotion was that they were given outer berths and allowed 28 inches apiece.

The hammocks were made of strong cloth and were slung from two iron hooks in the underside of the overhead deck beams, but, contrary to popular belief, the occupant did not sleep directly in the hammock but used it to accommodate his bed which was composed of a flock- or wool-filled mattress, blankets, and a pillow, all of which had to be provided by the sailor himself. The hammock was, in fact, large enough to contain two, since sailors shared them with their women when in harbor. The sailors had few personal

Eyewitness

"On the same deck with me…slept between five and six hundred men; and the ports being necessarily closed from evening to morning, the heat in this cavern of only six feet high, and so entirely filled with human bodies, was overpowering."

Unnamed sailor quoted in *Five Naval Journals 1789-1817*

possessions, but were allowed a sea-chest, usually shared with several others, and all had a cloth bag for their clothing which was slung from a hook beside their hammocks.

Such a large space, containing several hundred bodies, many of them neither washed nor sober and some inevitably suffering from seasickness, was not the most pleasant nor healthiest place to live. Conditions were made worse by the poor lighting and lack of natural ventilation, but efforts were made to improve matters. All hammocks and bedding had to be rolled up every day and stowed in netting along the ship's sides (or below decks in bad weather). Ventilation was poor at the best of times, and in bad weather was almost non-existent, but some ships used manually-operated air pumps to pass air to the lower decks, while others used wind-sails for this purpose.

The lower decks were very poorly-lit although lanterns were provided by the purser. However, in view of the ever-present danger of fire, they had to be extinguished when the night watch went on duty. No heating was permitted, although with such a large number of bodies, this generally proved to be unnecessary.

Conditions for the Royal Marines were no different, although they were always accommodated at the after end, between the crew and the officers. Some petty officers and sailors slung their hammocks on the orlop deck, which may have provided more space, but was notorious as the main home of the ship's rat population.

Officers

Accommodation for commissioned and warrant officers differed according to the size of ship and could be broadly divided into ships-of-the-line and frigates and below. It should also be noted that in some cases people slept in one place but ate and socialized in another.

The captain's accommodation reflected his unique position and he lived in solitary splendor in a large cabin on the uppermost deck level at the stern of the ship. In most cases the cabin was sub-divided by canvas screens into a suite of

rooms, consisting of a day cabin, sleeping cabin, and dining area. He also had direct access to two quarter galleries, one of which was his private toilet and the other for contemplation and watching the sails. There was only one entrance to the captain's area, which was guarded by a Royal Marine sentry at all times. The captain also had a small retinue of servants, the number depending upon the size of the ship.

Below: The captain's cabin was spacious and nicely lit by the stern windows, but it also housed a number of guns and was dismantled ready for battle before going into action.

Below: Typical cabin plan for a sixth-rate in the early 1800s. All dividing "walls" were made of canvas and they had to be dismantled every time the ship went into action.

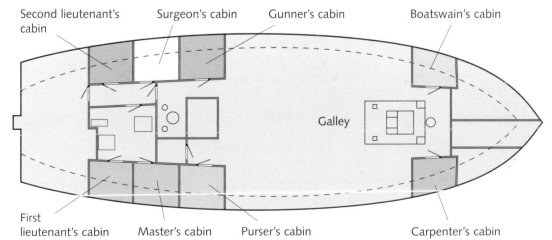

Second lieutenant's cabin   Surgeon's cabin   Gunner's cabin   Boatswain's cabin

Galley

First lieutenant's cabin   Master's cabin   Purser's cabin   Carpenter's cabin

Below: *A master's cabin (note his speaking trumpet lying on the deck and the sextant case sitting on the bulkhead), painted in 1825 by Rev. Thomas Streatfield, a ship's chaplain. Although the master had a large cabin, this watercolor greatly exaggerates the amount of space available. But even these cramped conditions did allow the officer some welcome privacy.*

In third-rates and above there was a wardroom located aft beneath the captain's cabin, which was on the lower deck of a three-decker (the admiral's cabin was on the upper deck), or the upper deck of a two-decker. All the commissioned officers and warrant officers with wardroom status ate and socialized here, but their cabin arrangements differed. The naval lieutenants, the master, the senior Royal Marine officer and the chaplain had cabins on either side of the wardroom, the first lieutenant's being slightly larger and with access to one of the quarter gallerys for his personal toilet, the remaining officers using the other quarter gallery. Several officers had cabins one deck lower adjacent to the

gunroom, while the purser and the surgeon were further below still, with cabins on the orlop, where their stores and sick-bay were located.

Frigates and smaller vessels did not have a wardroom as such, the officers other than the captain occupying the gunroom on the lower deck, again finding accommodation in cabins disposed on either side.

The captain and wardroom officers had to share their cabins with guns and on action stations being called, their cabins' walls were dismantled and their property stowed away so that the crews could fight their guns. To facilitate this, the regulations were that cabin walls (officially designated curtains) were to be made of canvas, although in some ships this canvas was mounted on a wooden frame.

Fifth-rates and above had an orlop deck, which was the lowest true deck in the ship, and below which were the holds and ballast. This orlop was used for stowage and on fourth-rates and above also for accommodation. The surgeon and purser had cabins aft on this deck and further aft still was the cockpit which was the home of the midshipmen, the master's and surgeon's mates, and the schoolmaster (if one was carried).

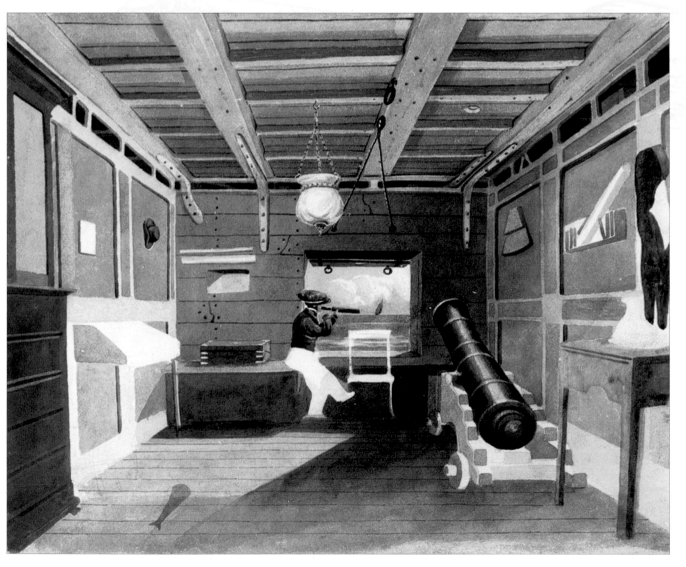

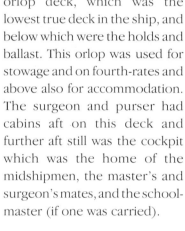

Food

Eating was one of only two legal pleasures aboard a warship (the other was drinking) and captains treated the crew's mealtimes with great respect, going to considerable lengths to avoid disturbing this part of the sailors' routine, or, if there was no alternative, making full restitution as soon as possible thereafter. All food was prepared in the galley, usually sited under the fore-

Sanitation

The officers had access to private toilets, but for the main part of the crew these facilities were provided in the bows, immediately abaft the figurehead with seats and chutes to carry the waste cleanly into the sea. (These were in a position known as the "heads" which remains the Royal Navy term for all toilets to this day.) A number of urinals were positioned around the ship, which simply consisted of a funnel and tube in the side of the ship

> ❝ ...regulations were that cabin walls were to be made of canvas, although in some ships this canvas was mounted on a wooden frame. ❞

CRIMES AND PUNISHMENTS

By Admiralty regulation, the Articles of War had to be read aloud to the assembled ship's company at the commissioning of a ship and thereafter once a month, usually on a Sunday. This was an essential requirement in an era when few on the lower deck were able to read. Indeed, even for those who could read, the full legal terminology made the articles difficult for the less educated to understand, while for the unintelligent they must have been incomprehensible. But these Articles were the laws by which the business of the navy was conducted, where transgressions were identified and punishments laid down. They were originally documented in the 1650s, with later amendments in 1749 and 1757, by which time they had the status of an Act of Parliament.

Article 1 differed from the remainder in that it was simply a general exhortation that commanding officers were to ensure that church services were held and Sunday observed "according to law" but no penalty was stated for failure to observe this article. The remaining 34 articles set out the offenses, identified who was subject to them, and then laid down the punishments available to a court-martial. Most offenses were applicable to all serving men, sometimes spelt out as "any officer, mariner, soldier or other person of the fleet," while others referred more generally to "all

castle, which was the home for a large Admiralty-pattern iron stove. This could be used to boil, stew, grill, or bake, with one side being used to prepare unsophisticated meals for the lower deck and the other the more elaborate dishes for officers. The officers and warrant were, in fact, issued with the same rations as the sailors, but they chose to supplement them with agreed "mess subscriptions."

Above: *Chaplain Edward Mangin's cabin, HMS Gloucester (74). He described it as being about eight feet square and six feet tall.*

Far left: *Cooking in the galley aboard a warship. Sailors inevitably grumbled about their food, but most received more regular and larger meals than would have been their lot ashore, and undernourishment was not a common problem.*

> 66 ...the worst was being "flogged around the fleet" where the victim was rowed to every ship in harbor where he was given the appropriate number of strokes. 99

Opposite page, top: Augustus Earle's painting of divine service led by the captain. Note that the Marines sit separately, one of them accompanied by his wife.

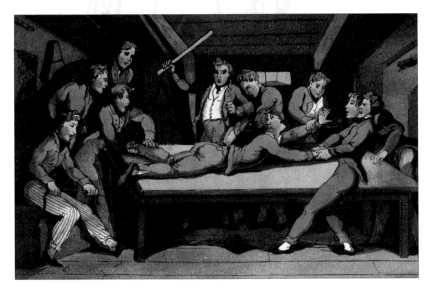

Above: Midshipmen had their own code of conduct and punishments. The latter included caning, or "cobbing," which, fortunately for them, was usually administered within the privacy of the gunroom.

persons in the fleet," although a few referred only to officers, such as Article 32, which concerned scandalous behavior. There was, however, one—spying—which could be applied to anybody, including civilians, even if they were otherwise not subject to naval discipline. The most infamous of the provisions, particularly among the sailors, was the last, Number 35, a "catch-all" which stated that: "All other crimes not capital committed by any person or persons in the fleet, which are not mentioned in this act, or for which no punishment is hereby directed to be inflicted, shall be punished by the laws and customs in such cases used at sea." That could mean anything to anybody!

Other Rules and Regulations

Like any bureaucracy, the Admiralty issued many volumes of written directives, the main one affecting the fleet being *Regulations and Instructions to His Majesty's Service at Sea*, which were involved in ship administration, storekeeping, accounting and the like. The captain also produced instructions

Summary of The Articles of War—1757

Article	Subject	Those Affected	Punishment (see notes)
2	Swearing, drunkenness	All	Suitable
3	Communicating with enemy	All	Death
4	Communication from enemy	All	Death/Suitable
5	Spying or delivering messages from enemy	Spies, etc.	Death/Suitable
6	Sustenance to enemy	All	Death/Suitable
7	Captured papers not sent to higher authority	All	Forfeit prize money, plus Suitable
8	Removing contents from prize	All	Forfeit prize money, plus Suitable
9	Ill treating captives	All	Suitable
10	Cowardice	Commanders	Death/Suitable
11	Failure to obey orders	All	Death/Suitable
12	Failure to fight	All	Death
13	Failure to pursue enemy	All	Death
14	Delay/discourage action against enemy	All	Death/Suitable
15	i. Desertion (actual/promoting)	All	Death/Suitable
	ii. Receiving a deserter	Commanding officer	Cashiered
16	Protection/treatment of convoys	All	Reparation, plus Death/Suitable
17	Unauthorized receiving of property	Officers	Cashiered
18	i. Sedition or mutiny	All	Death
	ii. Contempt of superior	All	Suitable
19	i. Concealing treachery or mutiny	All	Death/Suitable
	ii. Failing to report treachery/mutiny	All	Suitable
20	Stirring up disturbance to right a grievance	All	Suitable
21	Violence to or disobedience of superior.	All	Death/Suitable
22	Quarrelling or fighting	All	Suitable
23	Waste or embezzlement of stores	Offenders, abetters, buyers, receivers	Suitable
24	Burning ship, boat, or magazine	All	Death
25	Allowing a ship to ground or be wrecked	All	Death/Suitable
26	Sleeping on watch or negligence on duty	All	Death/Suitable
27	Murder	All	Death
28	Buggery or sodomy of man or beast	All	Death
29	Robbery	All	Death/Suitable
30	Falsification of muster book	All	Cashiered
31	Failure to arrest or hold a criminal	Provost martial	Suitable
	Failure to charge an offender	Captains, officers	Suitable
32	Scandalous, infamous behavior	Officers	Dismissed from service
33	Mutiny, desertion or disobedience ashore	All	As if aboard ship
34	Other offenses ashore	All	As if aboard ship
35	All other crimes not capital	All	According to laws and customs of the sea

Notes: 1. "Suitable" covers a variety of phrases including "such punishment as a Court Martial shall think fit to impose, and as the nature and degree of their offence shall deserve" and "such punishment as a Court Martial shall think fit to inflict."
2. In this table, "Death/Suitable" means that a court-martial had an alternative to a death sentence; while "Death" means that, on being found guilty, there was no alternative to a death sentence.

reflecting his own views on how the ship's business should be conducted, which would today be known as Standard Operating Procedures.

Transgressions and Punishments

Minor breaches were dealt with immediately—and by no means always fairly—by an officer or petty officer on the spot. This could take the form of hitting with a "starter" or cane, or being seized (tied spreadeagled) to the shrouds. Midshipmen and other young boys could also be dealt with by a caning on the backside, exactly as if they were in school. More serious offenses were referred to the captain, some of whom were very fair and open in hearing the cases, including allowing the accused to state a defense and officers to speak on the man's behalf. Others were much less fair. Punishments started with disrating and graduated through stopping grog to flogging, the theoretical maximum

allowable to a captain being 12 lashes (see also Chapter 7). For the more serious offenses men had to be referred to a court-martial, but if a ship was on a lengthy detachment, as was often the case in the Royal Navy, then it could be many months before more ships could be found to convene such a court. As a result, the 12 lashes limit was often breached.

Members of the lower deck charged with more serious offenses and all warrant and commissioned officers were tried by a court-martial which consisted of between five and 13 members. The procedure was generally similar to that of a civil court, except that the members, who took the place of a jury, were all officers. The proceedings were probably as fair as those in contemporary civil courts, but the punishments were draconian. Hanging was not uncommon nor was flogging, the worst of the latter being "flogged around the fleet" where the victim was rowed to every ship in harbor where he was given the appropriate number of strokes.

Above: *A more public punishment for midshipmen was being seized to the shrouds for a specified time— most unpleasant in a rough sea.*

HAZARDS OF LIFE AT SEA

Below: *A detailed plan and description of the sick-bay and dispensary aboard HMS* San Domingo *(74). Ship's surgeons had to deal with a wide range of wounds, diseases, and sicknesses, which collectively killed far more sailors in this period than did the enemy.*

In the early years of the 19th century life was a risky business. Many children died at birth or shortly afterwards for lack of adequate medical care. For those who survived into adulthood, the limitations of medical knowledge at that time meant few illnesses could actually be cured, and when patients did recover it was often despite, rather than because of, the doctor's treatment. Doctors undoubtedly did their best, but disease was rife and death was accepted with some resignation. Against this background, the Royal Navy's

Estimated Fatal Casualties in the Royal Navy 1793-1815

Cause of death	Number	Percentage
Individual, non-combat (disease and personal accidents)	84,440	81.5
Collective, non-combat (foundering, shipwreck, fire, explosion)	12,680	12.2
Enemy action	6,540	6.3
TOTAL	103,660	100

(Source: *A Social History of the Navy*, M.A. Lewis, 1960)

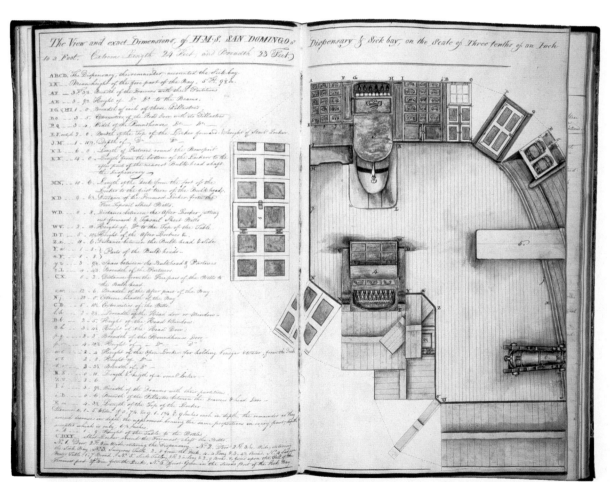

From these statistics it becomes clear that death in battle from enemy action was almost the least of a sailor's worries. The most likely cause of death during sea service was disease or accident. Certainly, as far as disease was concerned, matters differed little from the lot of the soldier in the army, for whom death by disease or illness was also far more common than death in battle.

For centuries the most prevalent cause of death at sea was scurvy, a disease caused by a lack of vitamin C in the diet. Fortunately it was discovered in the mid-17th century that citrus fruits provided an absolute cure and by the end of the century the issue of oranges and limes was general. Even so, supplies ran out on some longer voyages and the occasional outbreak of scurvy still occurred. A far worse killer during Aubrey's period was yellow fever, which was principally encountered in the Caribbean and Africa waters, and which on several recorded occasions killed every last man in a crew.

Typhus was general known as jail fever for the very good reason that it was prevalent in British prisons and was almost invariably introduced into naval ships by convicts who had been pressed. Its impact was reduced by the introduction of receiving ships in which ex-convicts were disinfected, scrubbed, and issued with clean clothing, but there were still outbreaks at sea. In *Desolation Island* Maturin has to deal with an outbreak aboard the *Leopard*

record of fatalities among its crews is hardly surprising, although the balance of the causes why the men died, as shown in the table, comes as something of a surprise to modern eyes.

Sometimes, however, rat colonies got out of hand. In such cases the ship had to be sailed to the nearest land, where every possible exit from below was sealed and then blocks of sulfur were ignited while the crew was evacuated for several days. Afterwards the ship was opened up and the dead rats disposed of, before sailing on.

Individual accidents were also a major problem. Ships had to operate by day and by night, in all weathers and conditions, and sails had to be shaken out, brought in, or reefed, which could only be done by sending men aloft. On the main deck, ropes had to be hauled and men on watch were directly exposed to the fury of the elements. Even below deck, the footing was slippery, headroom low, and the light was, at best, poor and at worst non-existent. As a result, accidents were a regular occurrence, ranging from being hit by broken cables or breaking spars, through gun barrels splitting in action or during practice fire, and

Left: *A ship's medicine chest shows only too clearly the paucity of drugs and equipment available to surgeons such as Stephen Maturin. It is easy to forget that before the days of antiseptic and antibiotics, medical care of the sick was still relatively primitive.*

Below: *Quite apart from disease and enemy action, the sailor was liable to physical injury from the dangers of his job, particularly when working aloft on tasks such as reefing sails, as shown here. Falls, whether onto the deck or into the sea, were frequently fatal, and muscle strains and hernias were common.*

bound for Australia. He fumigates the ship with brimstone section by section while many of the sick are put ashore in Brazil because all available medical supplies on board have been exhausted.

Doctors like Maturin certainly did their best but they were hampered by the limitations of contemporary medical knowledge, coupled with poor resources and an administrative system, stretching all the way up to the Admiralty, which was slow to acknowledge that a problem existed and slower still to react, especially if it cost money. One of the most immediate problems was the conditions under which the sailors lived aboard ship. The ventilation below decks was poor, and increasingly so as one descended deeper into the ship, while the men's clothing was almost perpetually damp and personal hygiene left much to be desired. To make matters worse, every ship was infested with rats. Normally a form of equilibrium was reached in which the nuisance they created did not exceed the outer limits of what was deemed acceptable.

Below: *Some ships disappeared without trace, while others were wrecked or foundered. Here, HMS Ramillies (74) is in danger, having lost her mainmast and mizzen, and with only the lower half of her foremast still standing.*

complete carriages breaking loose in a gale, to falling from the masts and yards aloft. The last hazard came about not only as a result of handling the sails in bad weather, but also from over-confidence and even dares among midshipmen. Nor were rank or privilege any protection: captains were as likely to die of yellow jack or be lost in a shipwreck as an

Royal Navy Ship Losses 1793-1815

Ship rating	Foundered	Ship-wrecked	Burnt/exploded	Totals
Line (64+)	3	17	8	28
Frigates	4	67	2	73
Sloops, brigs, etc.	68	170	5	243
TOTALS	75	254	15	344

(Source: adapted from *A Social History of the Navy*, M.A. Lewis, 1960)

Foundering

Foundering means that a ship sinks in the open seas, without hitting a rock or running aground on the shore or a shoal. Some of the losses listed in the table sank due to identifiable causes, such as being in poor repair or following action with the enemy, and survivors were able to relate what had happened. Others simply disappeared without trace or explanation, taking their entire crew with them, such as *Blenheim* (74) and *Java* (32) off Madagascar in 1807 and *York* (64) in the North Sea in 1803. Considering that wooden ships rarely sank in battle though pounded by cannon fire, the events which befell these ships must, indeed, have been cataclysmic.

Wrecks

Shipwrecks were by far the largest single cause of ship losses. Some of them undoubtedly were due to carelessness or bad navigation, but the great majority were essentially the outcome of the attrition caused by incessant operations conducted by many thousands of ships over a period of 20 years. The number of losses suffered by the three groups of ships in the table is also significant. In general terms, the ships-of-the line stood well out to sea, while frigates did much of the patrolling closer to the shore, and the smaller vessels were, by definition, mainly coastal craft. In addition, charts were frequently either incomplete, inaccurate, or non-existent, so operations close to the coastline carried a greater risk.

One other factor that could add significantly to the confusion and chaos when a ship was in serious trouble was the firmly-held belief among at least some sections of the lower deck that when wrecking became inevitable the "law of the sea" automatically absolved them from the navy's laws and

> **❝** Ship fires were made worse by the practice of leaving guns loaded, so that the charges would begin to "cook off" firing shots at potential rescuers heading for the ship. **❞**

able seaman, while Midshipman Lord Henry Lennox, the 14-year-old fourth son of one of England's leading aristocrats, the Duke of Richmond, slipped on a yard while furling sail aboard HMS *Blake* in 1812 and fell to his death.

Shipwreck and Loss

The loss of ships due to accidental causes is shown in the table. When you consider that losses due to enemy action in the same period numbered just ten major ships (one ship-of-the-line and nine frigates—smaller ships have not been counted), it is clear that, as with casualties among the men, action with the enemy was not the greatest threat.

Through Aubrey's Eyes

A fine description of the hazards of life at sea can be found in *Desolation Island*, Chapters 7 and 8. Aubrey in HMS *Leopard* is pursued through the huge, cold seas of the southern Atlantic by the Dutch 74-gun ship *Waakzaamheid*. A relentless gun battle develops between the fleeing *Leopard* and her pursuer, but when the situation looks most perilous for Aubrey, a single cannon shot carries away the *Waakzaamheid*'s foremast. The ship turns broadside to the waves and founders with loss of six hundred men—a dreadful vision that is burned indelibly into Jack Aubrey's memory.

Finding the ship now short of water, the *Leopard* heads further south to gather ice to melt for drinking. But the ship is driven onto an iceberg and severely damaged. The crew pump ceaselessly and attempt to mend the damage, but, when the situation appears hopeless, a portion of the crew determine to leave the "unlucky" ship. Mad to escape, they break into the spirit-room, consume the liquor and, led by Lieutenant Grant, leave the ship in small boats in a scene of terrible confusion.

on which he is taking passage to England is destroyed off the coast of Brazil, he and his men escaping on a small cutter and eventually being rescued by HMS *Java*. Once a fire took hold in a warship built of wood and in which many other combustible materials (such as straw and paper) were lying around, and which contained many narrow passages, low headroom, and a myriad small alcoves, it was difficult to fight the fire effectively.

Once firmly established, it was almost impossible to stop. The situation was made worse by the practice of leaving guns loaded, so that the charges would begin to "cook off" firing shot in an unpredictable manner at potential rescuers heading for the ship. This happened to *Boyne* (98) at Spithead on May 1st, 1796 and to *Queen Charlotte* (100) in Leghorn harbor on March 17th, 1800. Usually, it was just a

Above: Fire was an ever-present danger and, once started, it was hard to stop. Here, HMS Boyne (98) burns at Spithead in 1795.

regulations, and the authority of the captain and his officers ceased. In effect this amounted to a mutiny. Such insubordination did not always happen, but when it did, it nearly always started with an attack on the liquor room, following which the drunken men added to the confusion as they blundered about the deck, insulting the officers and warrant officers, looting the cabins in a search for yet more alcohol, and deriding those of their comrades still obeying orders. All this, of course, simply added to the confusion and seriously—sometimes fatally—interfered with the efforts being made to save the ship and its crew.

Fire and Explosion

Fire was an ever-present danger—it took just one careless act or oversight to start one. Jack Aubrey experiences a catastrophic fire in *The Fortune of War* when HMS *La Flèche*

matter of time before the flames reached the powder room and the whole ship blew up. On other occasions, ships simply blew apart without warning, obviously as a result of some mishap in the powder room, but without any survivors to offer some sort of an explanation. This happened, for reasons never established, to HMS *Amphion* lying at Plymouth harbor in September 1796.

Above: HMS Amphion (32) blows up, September 22nd, 1796. Although not proven, it was generally accepted that the explosion was caused by a gunner stealing gunpowder for sale ashore.

CHAPTER FIVE

The Eyes of the Fleet

By temperament Jack Aubrey is a man who relishes the challenges, and indeed the rewards, of independent command. In practical terms this means the command of a small vessel, and most especially a frigate. As a professional and exceptionally able naval man, Aubrey later rises to command squadrons of ships, but in such commissions he lacks the sheer joie de vivre *that he feels when free of the burdens of high command and able to concentrate solely on his orders and the responsibility he feels to his men and his ship.*

Right: *The main source of inspiration for Jack Aubrey was Thomas Cochrane, the finest frigate commander of his time.*

Opposite page: *The* Shannon *leads her prize, the captured Chesapeake, into Halifax, Nova Scotia, during June 1813 in this watercolor by J. C. Schetky.*

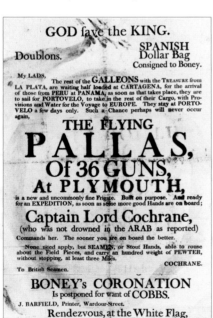

Above: *The number and value of his prizes made it feasible for Cochrane to advertise for crew, in this instance for the frigate Pallas.*

Modeled on Cochrane

As Patrick O'Brian readily admitted, a primary inspiration for his creation of Aubrey was Lord Cochrane, a celebrated (but at times infamous) British officer who excelled in the command of small ships. Otherwise immortalized in the novels of Captain Frederick Marryat, Thomas Cochrane was born in December 1775 at Annsfield in Lanarkshire, the eldest son of the 9th Earl of Dundonald, a man who had impoverished his family through scientific experiments. Cochrane joined the ship commanded by his uncle, Alexander Cochrane, in 1793 at the relatively late age of 17, and in 1800 he was appointed to the command of the brig *Speedy*. His brilliant capture of the considerably larger Spanish frigate *El Gamo* in 1801 brought him great fame, and later cruises in command of the frigates *Pallas* and *Imperieuse* won him a considerable fortune in prize money, as similar exploits do for Aubrey in HMS *Surprise*.

In 1806 Cochrane became the member of parliament for Honiton in the radical interest, and in 1807 was returned as MP for Westminster (a career move echoed by Aubrey in *The Thirteen-Gun Salute*), in the process gaining a reputation that earned him disapproval in official and government circles. In April 1809 Cochrane led a hazardous fireship attack on the French fleet in the Aix roads, but the results of this courageous effort were wasted by the commander-in-chief, Admiral Lord Gambier. Cochrane intemperately criticized Gambier, who was court-martialled but acquitted. This episode, combined with Cochrane's lack of popularity in government circles because of his vehement demands for parliamentary and naval reform, served to scupper any further sea-going command.

In February 1814 Cochrane was a member of a group that plotted to make money on the stock exchange by spreading false rumors about the abdication of Napoleon. In the subsequent trial Cochrane was sentenced to a period of imprisonment, and he was also expelled from parliament and deprived of the Order of the Bath with which he had been rewarded for his exploits in 1809. (At least Aubrey is innocent of the similar charges made against him in *The Reverse of the Medal*, even though he is found guilty.) This was the lowest ebb of Cochrane's fortunes, and it was at this stage that he accepted, during May 1817, Chile's invitation to command its fleet in the war of independence against Spain. Cochrane's capture of the Spanish flagship *Esmeralda* in the harbor of Callao was a major factor in the gaining of independence not just by Chile, but also by Peru. From 1823 to 1825 Cochrane commanded the navy of Brazil in that country's war of independence against Portugal, and was also largely responsible for the defeat of Portuguese forces. In *The Wine-Dark Sea* and *Blue at the Mizzen*, Aubrey also ventures to South America at the time of the struggle for independence by Spain's colonies.

Above: A satire on the court-martial of Admiral Gambier as a result of Cochrane's complaints—the nonconformist admiral is holding a service as Cochrane expostulates, "Why Admiral. Damn their eyes they'll escape if we don't make haste."

> 66 Cochrane had so incensed the Spaniards by carving up their coastal trade, that the government dispatched warships from several ports to intercept and either capture or destroy the British vessel. 99

Cochrane then returned to Europe, and was employed by the Greeks in their war of independence against the Ottoman empire. He resigned in 1828 on account of factional disputes and delays in the delivery of steam ships, which he proposed to use in war for the first time. Back in Great Britain, Cochrane struggled vigorously for reinstatement in the Royal Navy, just as Jack Aubrey does in the novels. Cochrane was reinstated in 1832, the year after he succeeded his father as earl. Cochrane then rose to flag rank, and from 1848 to 1851 Cochrane commanded the American and West Indies station, where he drew attention to the importance of Trinidad Pitch lake. It was only his advanced age of 79 that denied him command of a fleet during the Crimean War. Cochrane died in October 1860, and was buried in Westminster Abbey. Throughout his life he had also taken a keen interest in inventions, particularly those related to gas, tar, tubular boilers, and screw propulsion for ships. Truly it can be said without any measure of exaggeration that few men have ever led so adventurous, turbulent, and versatile a career.

The Capture of El Gamo

Cochrane's victory in the brig *Speedy* (14) over the Spanish xebec frigate *El Gamo* (32) was the model for Aubrey's capture of the *Cacafuego* (32), a xebec frigate (generally square-rigged on the foremast and lateen-rigged on the main and mizzenmasts) in the sloop *Sophie* (14) as recounted in *Master and Commander*.

In the course of one of the *Speedy's* Mediterranean cruises, Cochrane had so incensed the Spaniards by carving up their coastal trade, that the government dispatched warships from several ports to intercept and either capture or destroy the British vessel. Early in April one of the pursuers, the xebec *El Gamo* (32) decoyed the *Speedy* into hailing distance and then opened her gun ports, which generally numbered more than the guns actually mounted. Faced by a vessel apparently mounting 36 guns and carrying a very considerable crew, Cochrane, in a vessel armed only with 4-pounder guns, decided not to enter into action before trying a trick, escape being out of the question as the *El Gamo* was considerably faster than the *Speedy*. Cochrane decided to try to pass the *Speedy* off as a Danish brig of war in a legitimate *ruse de guerre*: flying Danish colors at her gaff-end, the *Speedy* was apparently commanded by a man dressed in a Danish officer's uniform and seemingly speaking Danish in the two ships' exchange of hails.

Not quite satisfied as to the national character of the *Speedy*, *El Gamo* sent over a boat carrying a Spanish officer.

range and tackle the Spanish ship, which was identified as *El Gamo* as the vessels approached one another. The *Speedy* was under *El Gamo's* lee, so Cochrane tacked and began his attack, the fire of the *Speedy* immediately being returned as the Spanish frigate maneuvered in an attempt to board. As soon as he heard the Spanish order to board, Cochrane ordered his vessel to sheer off. Once more the Spanish attempted to board, and once again Cochrane evaded their attempt. Knowing full well that the Spanish frigate carried a considerably larger crew and more numerous and powerful guns, Cochrane decided—after a 45-minute cannonade in which the *Speedy* had suffered at the Spanish ship's broadsides losing three men killed and five wounded—to put the boot on the other foot and board the Spanish vessel. The *Speedy* was run close alongside *El Gamo*, and the men of the British crew, led by Cochrane, stormed from every part of the brig's deck onto the Spanish vessel. There followed a furious 10-minute melee, which was most severe in the waist of the frigate, before Spanish struck their colors and *El Gamo* became the *Speedy's* prize.

Before the Spanish boat reached the *Speedy*, however, the Spanish officer was informed that the "Danish" vessel had recently left a port on the plague-ridden Barbary coast of North Africa, and that any physical contact between the crews of the two vessels would require the Spanish ship to be quarantined for a lengthy period. This deterred the Spanish from pressing their demand for an inspection, and the two vessels parted company.

On May 6th the *Speedy* was off Barcelona and spotted a sail standing toward her. Cochrane decided to close the

> **Truly it can be said without any measure of exaggeration that few men have ever led so adventurous, turbulent, and versatile a career.**

Below: *A drawing by Nicholas Pocock shows part of the action in which the smaller and less well manned Speedy took the theoretically superior El Gamo, a Spanish xebec frigate with a lateen-rigged mizzenmast.*

Above: *Another great frigate commander in the Cochrane mold was Captain Sir William Hoste. He led a squadron of British frigates in the Adriatic between 1808 and 1814. Hoste conducted a large number of amphibious assaults on French-held areas and attacked French ships whenever he found them.*

Through Aubrey's Eyes

Jack Aubrey's career, as recounted in the Aubrey canon, is linked inextricably with service in frigates in general and the small but beautifully handling *Surprise* in particular. In the various frigates he commands, or on occasion is aboard as a passenger, Aubrey is a participant in and/or witness to several frigate actions. Moreover, even when he rises to higher command, as senior captain in a two-decker or as a commodore in command of a squadron, Aubrey is able to exploit the particular nature of his missions to switch into a frigate. Such, for example, is the situation in *The Hundred Days* when Aubrey, commanding a squadron with his pennant on the 38-gun frigate *Pomone*, transfers his pennant to the *Surprise*. In his favorite ship Aubrey catches and sinks the Napoleonic frigate *Ardent* (*The Hundred Days* Chapter 5) and later forces a treasure-laden Algerian galley to take refuge in a land-locked bay. Aubrey lifts some of the *Surprise*'s guns to the heights above the bay and forces her to surrender (*The Hundred Days* Chapter 10).

During the fighting on board the Spanish frigate Cochrane yet again used a bluff. Finding his crew on the verge of defeat by the vastly more numerous Spanish, Cochrane hailed the *Speedy* and ordered her to dispatch another 50 men onto the deck of *El Gamo*. At the time the British vessel had only three men on board, but the Spanish apparently believed that British reinforcements would soon arrive to double the strength of the boarding party, and shortly after this their resistance began to diminish.

From her complement of 54 men and boys the *Speedy* lost only one man killed and three wounded during the boarding for a "butcher's bill" of four dead and eight wounded during the complete action. *El Gamo*, which mounted 22 long 12-pounders on her main deck together with eight long 8-pounders and two "heavy carronades" (probably 24-pounders) on the quarterdeck and forecastle, carried a crew of 319 including 45 Marines. Her losses amounted to 15 men killed (including the captain, Don Francisco de Torris) and 41 wounded.

With so many prisoners to guard and two vessels to man, Cochrane still had a difficult task ahead of him, but over the next few days he worked both his own vessel and the prize into the British base at Port Mahon on the island of Minorca. As soon as the dispatch with news of his victory reached England, Cochrane was "made post," or elevated to the rank of post captain.

Fighting Spirit

Cochrane is an excellent example of the type of man whose skill and courage abounded in the Royal Navy of the time. Such men quickly rose from command of an unrated vessel, in the rank of master and commander, to the command of a frigate in the rank of post captain. If left unfettered by the demands of higher commanders for scouting and repeating frigates to serve with the line-of-battle ships of the main fleets and squadrons, leaders such as Cochrane could continue their cruising operations and in the process considerably enrich themselves with prize money.

Command of a frigate was therefore seen as an important step in an officer's rise to more senior command. It was also an end in itself for in Aubrey's day the frigate was seen much as a destroyer was regarded for most of the 20th century: it was a ship that offered altogether better sailing and handling qualities than the larger and more cumbersome line-of-battle ships, and therefore appealed to the more dashing type of officer. Such men were Cochrane and Aubrey.

Despite its relatively small size, the frigate was large enough to carry a useful armament, but also fast and nimble enough to allow it to refuse combat with larger ships except under favorable conditions or, of course, if trapped. Most frigates were allocated a task largely independent of the

From a Sketch by Lieut.t the Hon. N.Waldegrave.   Engraved by W.J.Bennett.
SIR W. HOSTE'S ACTION OFF LISSA. March 13th 1811.

fleet, either in the provision of longer-range reconnaissance for the battle line or, as preferred by most frigate captains, wholly independent cruising in search of enemy ships, both naval and mercantile. Thus the frigate captain was freed from the apron strings of the fleet and squadron commander, whose heavy ships were normally allocated to the patrolling of the approaches to the enemy's naval bases in the hope of forcing and winning a major fleet or squadron battle should the enemy seek to force his way out onto the high seas.

The frigate not infrequently fought single-ship actions against enemy frigates, and these actions were the subject of huge press and public interest in much the same way that fighter pilots' exploits caught the imagination in World Wars I and II.

Above: Among Hoste's most celebrated actions in the Adriatic was a major frigate action against a French and Venetian force of 10 frigates off the island of Lissa in 1811. Hoste's British frigates captured two of the enemy and drove a third ashore. The French rear admiral commanding the French and Venetian ships was killed in the fighting.

Left: The essence of the frigate captain was to be found in his "nose" for finding the enemy and then his willingness to engage him with the maximum fighting spirit. This painting by Thomas Elliott of the action between the Venus and the Sémillante on May 27th, 1793, exemplifies the frigate-versus-frigate action. The more powerful Sémillante was suffering badly at the hands of Sir Edward Pellew's crew before a consort arrived and Pellew had to break off the action.

> ❝ **It was in the middle of the 18th century that the 32-gun frigate, armed with 12-pounder guns, first appeared in the form of the ships of the "Southampton" class. These became the standard British frigates for a period of more than a quarter of a century...** ❞

Frigate Design

Unlike the line-of-battle ship, the frigate was laid out with an unarmed lower deck. With all its guns well above the waterline, the frigate could be allowed to heel sharply without the loss of firepower typical of line-of-battle ships that had to close the ports of their lower gun decks in heavier weather for fear of being flooded. Thus, relatively speaking, the frigate could carry a larger quantity of sail in adverse conditions than a line-of-battle ship could. The frigate was also very much cheaper to build than a line-of-battle ship: toward the end of the 18th century the cost of building a 38-gun frigate was less than half the amount needed for a 74-gun two-decker.

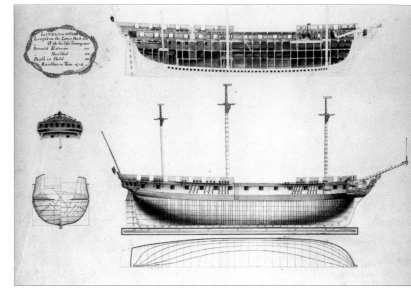

While it was expected that a frigate would fight another frigate, even one carrying somewhat heavier armament, as was often the case with American and French frigates, it was not expected to tackle a line-of-battle ship. The frigate's hull was weaker than that of a line-of-battle ship as it was designed for performance and the carriage of lighter guns. A typical 38-gun frigate could throw only half the broadside weight of a 64-gun two-decker, and only two-fifths of that offered by a 74-gun two-decker.

In terms of speed, both the frigate and smaller examples of line-of-battle ship had basically similar performance—both were recorded at 14 knots, for example—but the frigate generally was consistently faster as there was more opportunity for the underside of its hull to be cleaned of weed and other growths. The frigate could also maintain its speed in lighter conditions, and was definitely superior to windward as it could point up higher into the wind and additionally tack more swiftly.

With regard to guns, the design of line-of-battle ships had reached a formulaic stage after the universal adoption of the 32-pounder gun as its primary armament. But the same did not hold true of frigates, for which there was not any universal armament standard. At the start of the French Revolutionary and Napoleonic Wars, most British frigates were armed with 12-pounder guns, but early experience revealed that French frigates were generally more heavily armed. As a result, therefore, British frigates were designed to carry the 18-pounder gun, of which 32, 36, or 38 were mounted depending on the size of the individual ship. Then in 1812 British frigates encountered a new foe in the shape of the large frigates operated by the Americans. Though few in number, these were generally well-handled, mainly by volunteer crews, and almost universally outgunned their British opponents as their armament scheme was centered on the 24-pounder gun. This led to a series of humiliating British defeats in single-ship actions. The British responded from 1813 with a 24-pounder main armament in frigates that were either built as new to carry such guns, or cut down from smaller line-of-battle ships.

The Evolution of the Warship

It was in the middle of the 18th century that the 32-gun frigate, armed with 12-pounder guns, first appeared in the form of the ships of the "Southampton" class. These became the standard British frigates for more than a quarter of a century until their obsolescence was made evident by the appearance of larger 38-gun French frigates. Only a few more 32-gun British frigates were built after that time, the fir-built *Triton* of 1796 being the sole example of new construction until 1804, when the first of seven "Thames" class 32-gun frigates based on a design of the 1750s appeared. This did not mean that the 32-gun frigate was phased out of British service, however, for large numbers of older ships were still in commission. As late as 1810, for example, there were still 38 such ships, most of them dating from the time of the War of American Independence.

As built, these ships invariably carried 26 12-pounder guns on the upper deck, these guns generally being supplemented by four 6-pounder guns on the quarterdeck and another two 6-pounder guns on the forecastle. By the time of the Napoleonic Wars though, the surviving ships generally had carronades on their upper decks in at least partial replacement of 6-pounder guns. The size of the ships increased from a figure in the order of 680 tons for the early ships, via 720 tons for the ships of the time of the War of American Independence, to 848 tons for the *Triton*.

The threat posed by larger and more heavily armed French frigates led to the creation of larger British frigates, still armed with 32 guns but in this instance of the 18- rather than 12-pounder type. The first of the ships was the *Pallas* of 1790. From 1793 there followed the six "Cerberus" class ships that constituted the largest homogeneous group of such frigates; over the following years there appeared another ten such frigates. The 32-gun frigate with 18-pounder weapons was generally considered an intermediate type, and by 1810 there were only ten of them in commission with basically the same armament disposition as the 12-pounder frigates including the replacement and/or supplementing of the upper-works 6-pounder guns by "smasher" carronades.

> 66 ...the 49-strong "Leda" class was ordered up to 1815 and maintained in service long after this date. 99

36- and 38-Gun Frigates

Three examples of the 36-gun frigate were constructed in the 1750s, but only with 12-pounder guns. Then in 1778 there appeared a new type of 36-gun frigate in the form of the ships of the "Flora" class, which were the first British frigates with 18- rather than 12-pounder guns. By the end of the War of American Independence in 1783, the 36-gun frigate with 18-pounder guns had become relatively common, there being 17 of them (including captured ships) in commission. Thereafter construction of this type of warship became normal between 1794 and 1812, the total including 26 ships of the "Apollo" and "Euryalus" classes.

So far as the armament layout was concerned, the 36-gun frigate had the same main upper-deck armament as the 32-gun frigate in combination with eight rather than four quarterdeck guns; the upper-works guns were also 9- and 12-pounder weapons rather than the 6-pounder weapons standard on the smaller frigates. The nature of the naval fighting practiced by the British in the French Revolutionary and Napoleonic Wars meant that the ships were most generally armed with carronades rather than cannon, and in size terms the ships extended from a lower limit of some 950 tons up to 1,042 tons in the case of the three frigates of the "Penelope" class of 1797. Construction and captures brought into British service meant that the Royal Navy's total of these useful 36-gun frigates rose from 43 in 1805 to 63 in 1812.

The 38-gun frigate was not new to British service at the time of the start of the French Revolutionary and Napoleonic Wars in 1793, when the Royal Navy could number some 17 such ships (most of them captured from the French) in its overall strength. Thereafter British construction was increased, so that by 1801 only 12 of the 28 ships in commission were not of British construction. After this the 38-gun frigate, which differed from the 36-gun frigate mainly in the mounting of 28 rather than 26 18-pounder guns on the upper deck, became the norm: in June 1813 there were 80 38-gun frigates compared with totals of 70 and 35 for the 36- and 32-gun

Above: *Evident above the Trincomalee's beautiful stern gallery are two tops. In action these accommodated Marines who would fire down onto the enemy ship's deck.*

Quarterdeck

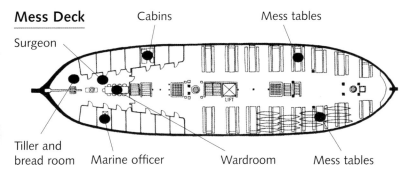

Ship's wheel — Capstan — The heads

Quarterdeck — Mainmast — Waist rail — Forecastle

Gun Deck

Capstan — 18-pounder gun — Galley stove

Captain's cabin — Starboard main hatchway — Manger

Mess Deck

Surgeon — Cabins — Mess tables

Tiller and bread room — Marine officer — Wardroom — Mess tables

Orlop and Hold

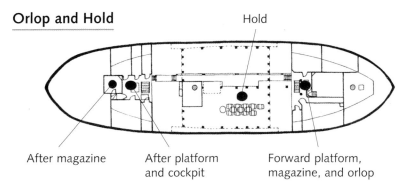

Hold

After magazine — After platform and cockpit — Forward platform, magazine, and orlop

The decks and main features of the frigate HMS Trincomalee

Above: *The wardroom was the communal space available to all but the captain of the ship's commissioned officers, although the captain was sometimes invited to dine with the officers.*

Above right: *The forward part of the Trincomalee's mess deck was where the men ate and slept. The deck's after part contained the officer's cabins, the wardroom, and the bread room.*

Above: *The gun deck carried the Trincomalee's two main broadside batteries, and in the center is the companion way linking the gun deck and the waist.*

frigate. However, an important caveat in the classification of most of these ships as British-built, is that the 38-gun frigate was more influenced by French naval architecture than any other type of British warship. Moreover, the most successful of the ships were either captured from the French or merely copied from the best of the captured ships.

The first 38-gun frigates of British design were the four ships of the "Minerva" class, which were launched in 1780-82. It was soon discovered that these 940-ton ships were too small for the effective carriage of their planned armament. There followed an interval before six more 38-gun frigates were ordered after the outbreak of the French Revolutionary and Napoleonic Wars. These were the "Artois" class of just under 1,000 tons, but experience revealed that the upper deck was too short for effective fighting of the two 14-gun batteries on the upper deck, and a decision was then taken to copy the *Hecate*, a French frigate captured in 1782 and known to be effective. The result was the 49-strong "Leda" class ordered up to 1815 and maintained in service long after this date. The British seemed determined to create an all-British 38-gun frigate, but the *Amazon* and *Naiad* of 1796 were not successful. Success came only with the "Lively" class, of which 16 examples were completed between 1801 and 1812.

Considerably smaller in number were the 40-gun frigates. There were just seven such ships in 1801 rising to 13 by 1813. Some of these were captured, others were prizes, and others still were razees (cut-down two-deckers), but in 1797 there appeared the *Endymion* derived from the French 44-gun *Pomone*, and the British-designed *Acasta* and *Cambria*. Finally, in 1813-14 and in direct response to the threat posed by large American frigates, British yards laid down five 40-gun frigates derived from the *Endymion* but of generally inferior construction in pitch pine.

Far right: A watercolor by Irwin Bevan details 1793 prizes of the Phaeton (top), the 38-gun frigate of Captain Sir Andrew Snape Douglas. They were the 28-gun frigate La Prompte and 22-gun corvette La Blanche (center left and right), the 22-gun Le General Doumourier with $2.4 million on board, the 16-gun privateer Domen and the merchantman St. Jago worth £300,000 (bottom left, center, and right).

The Spoils of War

Captured ships, especially those taken from the French, constituted a considerable proportion of British frigate strength right through this period: during 1801 one out of every three fifth-rate frigates was of non-British construction, and in the course of the French Revolutionary War the British sank or captured 206 frigates including 143 from the French. These were both national and privateer ships, the latter operating under letter of marque issued by the national authorities and so not pirates, even though they sailed for profit. However, in general the national ships were of greater size and superior capability. Of the captured ships, a significant proportion was felt unsuitable for anything but harbor service: as an example, during 1814 some 29 of 45 captured fifth-rate frigates fell into this category. Some captured ships bought into British service were notably successful, especially those of French origin. But while the British did bring into service captured Dutch and Spanish frigates, they did not think highly enough of them to base their own frigate designs on them.

The concept of cutting away some of the upper decks of a ship to reduce it to a smaller number of guns, and in the process translate it to a lower rate, was well established by the time that the French Revolutionary and Napoleonic Wars started. One of the first results of the outbreak of war was the reduction of three 64-gun two-deckers, the *Anson*, *Indefatigable*, and *Magnanime*, to 38- and 40-gun frigates of this razee type. The cutting-down process proved successful, and the *Indefatigable* in particular proved an effective ship that gained some notable successes.

The threat of the large American frigates in the War of 1812 prompted the British to undertake the same process in an effort to create frigates that were larger than those of the Americans, and armed with 24-pounder guns: a classic example of the process was the *Saturn*, a 74-gun two-decker that had been built in 1786, which was cut down to a 58-gun ship with 24-pounder guns on two decks but with no

Above: Though there was criticism of the Royal Navy's smaller frigates for their lack of gun power, the ships generally sailed well and were nimble in action. Thus on June 24th, 1795, off Toulon in the Mediterranean, the British 28-gun frigate Dido succeeded in battering and capturing an altogether larger ship, the French 40-gun frigate La Minerve. In the illustration, the Dido has lost her mizzenmast, while La Minerve has lost her foremast and main topmast.

quarterdeck or forecastle. Whatever the successes on individual razee frigates, however, it could not be ignored that the type as a whole could not be regarded as completely successful, for they carried their guns too close to the waterline by frigate standards.

Smaller Sixth-Rate Frigates

The above types were all fifth-rate frigates. One rung farther down the rating ladder there were the sixth-rate frigates. These were smaller than the fifth-rate ships, and were also distinguished at the technical level by the fact that they had no platform in the hold amidships, so their cables were stowed directly on the barrels in the hold. Moreover, like the smaller examples of the three- and two-deck line-of-battle ships, the smaller types of single-deck ship had largely fallen

Top left: *Though size and the number of guns was important in the naval warfare of the period, it was often the handling of the ship and the speed and accuracy of her gun crews that were the decisive factors. Thus it was in June 1813, when the 38-gun British frigate Shannon (side elevation left) challenged the larger but less well handled American frigate Chesapeake, and in a 15-minute battle outsailed and outfought her, firing 2.5 broadsides in 6 minutes and scoring 25 hits out of 30 shots fired.*

Left: *To create larger frigates the British cut down a few third-rate ships to powerful frigate standard. This is the Saturn after her 1813 reconstruction as a razee ship.*

from favor by the outbreak of the French Revolutionary and Napoleonic Wars. There were only 41 sixth-rate frigates in commission in 1793, and in the course of the wars that followed only a few more ships of this type were added.

The most common type of sixth-rate was the 28-gun ship, which was arguably the oldest type of frigate in service as it had first appeared in 1748. Armed only with 9-pounder guns, the 28-gun frigate was notably weak in armament terms even by the standards of the 32-gun frigate. It is hardly surprising, therefore, that no more 28-gun frigates were added to the Royal Navy's strength after 1793. Still weaker was the 24-gun frigate, which carried 9-pounder guns on its upper deck. There were a mere six 24-gun frigates in British service in 1793, rising to only seven in 1808, and all of these were old British or captured ships.

Oddly enough, it is a ship of this distinctly limited type that is most associated with Aubrey, for his beautiful and sweet-sailing *Surprise* was of this type. The model for the *Surprise* was the French *Unité*, a 24-gun corvette captured in April 1796 by the *Inconstant* and bought into British service as the *Surprise*. The *Surprise* was sold out of the

service in 1802, and this fact is used to good effect in the Aubrey canon to allow the purchase of the ship by Stephen Maturin, who later sells her to Aubrey.

The greatest feat of the real ship took place in October 1799 when, under the command of Captain Edward Hamilton, she cut out and recaptured, from under the noses of the Spanish garrison of Porto Cabello in what is now Venezuela, the frigate *Hermione*. The British suffered only 10 men wounded while the Spanish lost more than 200 killed or wounded. The crew of this ship had mutinied in October 1797 against the tyrannical rule of Captain Hugh Pigot: the mutineers killed Pigot and nine other officers before handing the ship and themselves over to the Spanish (see also Chapter 7). The *Hermione* re-entered British service as the *Retaliation* and was later renamed the *Retribution*. It was 1806 before the British effectively ceased to look for the mutineers after a process in which 24 of them had been caught and hanged. Aubrey encounters some of the mutineers on the American frigate *Norfolk* at a later date, these being captured and executed as recounted in *The Far Side of the World* and *The Reverse of the Medal*.

> ❝ The greatest feat ...took place in October 1799 when, under the command of Captain Edward Hamilton, she cut out and recaptured, from under the noses of the Spanish garrison of Porto Cabello...the frigate Hermione. ❞

Right: The efforts of the frigates in British naval service were supplemented by those of sloops of war. This aquatint by William Anderson shows the 12-gun Wolverine *in successful action against two French privateering luggers off Boulogne on January 3rd, 1799.*

To return to the sixth-rate frigate as a ship, it is worth noting that its only variant that underwent any development was the so-called 22-gun ship, of which two classes were ordered in 1805. Each amounting to six ships, the "Laurel" and "Banterer" classes were of 526 and 537 tons respectively, and both carried 22 9-pounder guns on their upper decks together with eight 24-pounder carronades on the quarterdeck and forecastle, and in the bows two 6-pounder chasers. Several captured ships

Frigates and Smaller Vessels—Typical Statistics and Crew Complements

Rate	Vessel type	Tonnage	Guns	Crew
5th	44-gun frigate	1380	20 x 18-pounder guns 22 x 12-pounder guns 2 x 6-pounder guns	250-280
5th	38-gun frigate	940-1,050	28 x 18-pounder guns 10 x 9- and 12-pounder guns	250
5th	36-gun frigate	950-1,050	26 x 12- or, later, 18-pounder guns 10 x 9- and 12-pounder guns	240
5th	12-pounder 32-gun frigate	680-720	26 x 12-pounder guns 6 x 6-pounder guns	220
5th	18-pounder 32-gun frigate	less than 800 to 900	26 x 18-pounder guns 6 x 6-pounder guns	220
6th	28-gun frigate	560-610	28 x 9-pounder guns	200
6th	22-gun frigate	430-470	22 x 9-pounder guns 8 x 24-pounder carronades 2 x 6-pounder guns	160
not rated	quarterdecked ship sloop	330-445	1) 14 to 18 6-pounder guns 12 or 14 swivel guns later replaced by 12-pounder carronades 2) 18 x 32-pounder carronades 8 x 12-pounder carronades 2 x 2-pounder guns	110-130
not rated	flushdecked ship sloop	up to 450	16 x 32- or 24-pounder carronades 2 x 6-pounder guns	120-130
not rated	brig sloop	250 or more	about 16 x 6-pounder guns or 24-pounder carronades	120-130
not rated	brig	150-190	14 x 18- or 24-pounder carronades 2 x 6-pounder guns	80-125

Note: There was never the same exactitude of data in Georgian times as there has been since the beginning of the 20th century, so the above figures should be treated as typical, rather than exact. It should also be noted that during the French Revolutionary and Napoleonic Wars ships were often revised with carronades in place of cannon in their main batteries.

were taken into the sixth-rate category, and in 1813 there were 52 such ships in commission.

Sloops and Smaller Ships

Smaller naval vessels also appear in the Aubrey canon. The largest of these non-rated vessels was designated as the sloop, a term that underwent considerable evolution from its original concept of a single-masted vessel. In naval service, however, the term sloop of war was applied to a non-rated vessel captained by an officer in the rank of commander. The sloop of war was armed with between 10 and 18 guns. The rank of the captain and the number of guns were about the only two things that all sloops of war had in common. Large sloops of war were akin to sixth-rate frigates in the layout of their decks (quarterdeck and forecastle with an armed upper deck between them, an unarmed lower deck, and two platforms in the hold), while flushdecked sloops had neither forecastle nor quarterdeck and only rudimentary platforms in the hold. Sloops of war could be ship-rigged with three masts or brig-rigged with two masts.

There was no consistency other than in their rigs between the ship- and brig-rigged sloops of war: the brigs were sometimes larger than the ships, and on occasion the same basic hull design was employed for ships and brigs.

The sloop of war was cheaper and quicker to build than the frigate, and could be manned and operated more simply. This type of light warship (increasingly armed with carronades) was therefore employed to carry out many frigate functions except for fleet reconnaissance which was likely to involve contact with hostile frigates that could destroy a sloop of war. Thus the primary use of the sloop of war was in the patrol and commerce protection tasks. There was a marked increase in the numbers of sloops of war operating in the last decade of the 18th century, the total increasing from 53 in 1793 to more than 200 in 1801.

The largest sloops of war were laid out as scaled-down sixth-rate frigates with armament on their quarterdecks and forecastles. There were 31 ships of this quarterdecked type in 1793 with 16 or 14 6-pounder guns on the upper deck. A further 23 of the type were built up to 1806 in the form of the "Cormorant" class vessels. From 1795 quarterdecked sloops of war were produced to a larger size (420

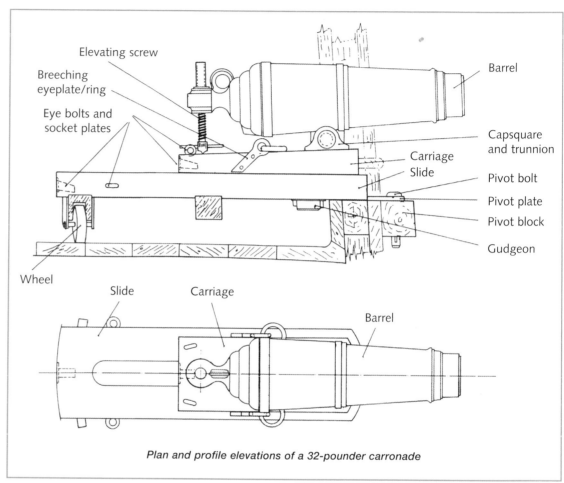

Plan and profile elevations of a 32-pounder carronade

rather than 330 tons) with 18 rather than 16 guns on the main deck. On their quarterdecks and forecastles, the early ship-rigged quarterdecked sloops of war carried some 12 or 14 swivel guns, which were generally of small caliber and designed mainly for use against personnel, rigging, and sails. But by 1795 there had emerged a tendency for these swivel guns to be replaced by carronades, normally of the 12-pounder type, and by the turn of the century new-build vessels were also being armed with carronades as their main weapons. The 10 vessels of the 1807 "Conway" class, for example, each carried 18 32-pounder carronades on the main deck, six 12-pounder carronades on the quarterdeck, and two 12-pounder carronades and two 6-pounder long guns on the forecastle. The quarterdecked sloop of war was never available in large numbers—its total in commission was 32 in 1801 and 57 in 1814.

Above: *The carronade was developed in the late 1770s as a short weapon of large caliber. Intended only for short-range work, the slide-mounted carronade required only a comparatively small powder charge to fire its projectile. It was widely mounted in all rated ships.*

Left: *During the action shown on the opposite page, Captain Lewis Mortlock defended his ship gallantly. Here, attended by his faithful dog, he accounts for a French boarder. The ship escaped but Mortlock was fatally wounded in the encounter.*

Below: In very light airs, the main part of an action could be undertaken by the vessels' oared boats, as happened in December 1808 off Martinique when the boats of the frigate Circe, sloop Stork, and schooner Express took the French corvette Cygne.

Thus most of the ship-rigged sloops of war were of the flushdecked type with either no quarterdeck or forecastle or only very small upper works carrying no guns. These vessels offered poorer accommodation for the officers, but were generally more weatherly than the quarterdecked sloops of war, often of a similar size, and not usually inferior in main armament with 18 or 16 carronades. First built

Brig Sloops and Bomb Vessels

The brig-rigged sloop of war had begun as a simple evolution from merchant ship design in the 1770s, but there were only 11 such vessels in service in 1793. By this time the brig sloop of war generally lacked a quarterdeck, but in overall size and armament at the upper end of its type it was comparable with the ship sloop of war. However, some of the more numerous brig sloop classes, such as the vessels of the 1807 "Banterer" class, were quite small at only 250 tons. Development of the brig sloop of war during the French Revolutionary and Napoleonic Wars began with the eight-strong "Diligence" class of 1795, followed by the same number of "Albatross" class vessels in the same year, and then came the most successful of all the classes, the "Cruiser" class that appeared in 1796.

This introduced lower-deck carronades in place of 6-pounder long guns, and although only one vessel was completed before 1800, orders were placed steadily between 1803 and 1814 for an eventual total of more than 100, making this the largest class of sailing vessels ever ordered. For so large a class built over a comparatively short time, timber was inevitably a problem, and while oak remained the preferred choice, many of the vessels were built in fir

> 66 **The cutter...was developed by smugglers in Kent and other parts of south-east England for speed and handiness, and then adopted by the Excise Service in an effort to catch [them].** 99

Right: Sloops and brigs played a major role in the campaign against French privateers in coastal waters. This engraving by William Elmes shows a British brig in pursuit of a privateer.

in 1796, the flushdecked sloop of war was in effect a product of the Royal Navy's increasing preoccupation with the use of the carronade in place of the longer-ranged cannon. The first flushdecked sloops of war were the four 1796 vessels of the "Snake" class, each carrying 16 32-pounder carronades and just two 6-pounder long guns as chases. In overall terms, however, it was the 24- rather than 32-pounder carronade that became the "standard" weapon of the flushdecked sloop of war up to about 1810, when the 32-pounder weapon was preferred once more. While there were 43 flushdecked sloops of war in 1801, by 1814 the total had fallen to just 20.

and teak. The numbers of brig sloops in British service were bolstered by the buying in of captured vessels—the total of 181 brig sloops of war in 1814 included 35 vessels that had been bought in after being captured.

Of all the types of naval vessel operated by the Royal Navy, the most specialized was the bomb vessel. This was intended not for the engagement of other vessels except, of course, to defend itself, but for the bombardment of shore targets. The primary armament was therefore one or two large-caliber mortars, which fired explosive shells in a high trajectory to plunge down onto their targets before detonating. Bomb vessels had to be very sturdily built to withstand the stresses imposed on their structures as the mortars were fired, and had special provision for the carriage of explosive shells. Although the first bomb vessels were ketch-rigged (i.e. with no foremast) to allow the mortars to fire forward, the poor sailing qualities of the vessels led to the adoption of a ship rig shortly before the start of the French Revolutionary and Napoleonic Wars. Most bomb vessels were built by private yards and then converted to their specialized role, and were generally of between 300 and 400 tons. There were two bomb vessels in British service in 1793, the total rising to 14 in 1799 and 19 in 1805, but falling to 13 in 1812.

Brigs and Schooners

By comparison with the brig sloop of war, the type known just as the brig was a smaller vessel that was again square-rigged on both of its masts, but captained in this instance by a lieutenant rather than a commander. With the exception of gun brigs upgraded from gunboat standard, most brigs carried an armament of 14 24-pounder carronades. In the "Confounder" class, though, the armament was 14 18-pounder carronades, and construction amounted to 39 vessels including 18 completed from 1811 to a standard revised by the addition of two 6-pounder long guns.

The British made only limited use of the schooner, which was a type of North American origin, but altogether more extensive use of the cutter. This type of vessel was devel-oped by smugglers in Kent and other parts of south-east England for speed and handiness, and then adopted by the Excise Service in an effort to catch the smugglers. Finally the Royal Navy adopted it as a utility type best suited to tasks such as dispatch delivery. By 1793 there were 18 naval cutters, but the number then rose and the single largest class comprised the 12 vessels of the 111-ton "Lady Howard" class crewed by 40 men and armed generally with 12 18-pounder carronades. The vessels were mostly schooner-rigged though officially classed as cutters. Other cutters were bought from merchant builders, and the Royal Navy had 42 cutters in 1813. Designed for speed, the cutter had a very large rig comprising both fore-and-aft and square sails on a single mast.

Above: A light vessel perfected in North America, the schooner was fore-and-aft rigged on two or more masts with one or two square sails on the foremast. Of shallow draft, fast, and capable of upwind performance better than that of a square-rigged ship, the schooner was ideal for operations in close waters. Based on John William's painting, this engraving shows the action in which the British schooner Monkey captured the Spanish slaving brig Midas on the Great Bahama Bank on June 27th, 1829.

Track of the action between the Java and the Constitution
(December 29th, 1812)

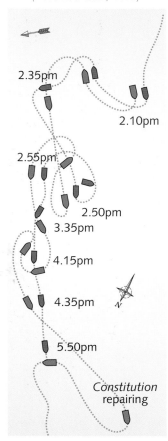

2.35pm

2.10pm

2.55pm

2.50pm

3.35pm

4.15pm

4.35pm

5.50pm

Constitution repairing

The action between HMS Java *(red) and the* Constitution *developed as each ship maneuvered to rake the other, the Java then trying to come alongside the American ship but losing her foremast. She was then steadily raked until she struck her colors.*

Above right: *A watercolor by Pocock reveals the stage in the action between the Java and the Constitution when the American ship—fouled by the Java's damaged bowsprit—has just struggled free to sail to a safe range from which she can cripple and overcome the already badly damaged British frigate.*

Eyewitness

"...the din of battle continued. Grape and canister shot were pouring through our port-holes like leaden rain, carrying death in their trail. The large shot came against the ship's side like iron hail, shaking her to the very keel, or passing through her timbers and scattering terrific splinters, which did a more appalling work than even their own death-giving blows.... Suddenly, the rattling of the iron hail ceased. We were ordered to cease firing. A profound silence ensued, broken only by the stifled groans of the brave sufferers below. It was soon ascertained that the enemy had shot ahead to repair damages, for she was not so disabled but she could sail without difficulty; while we were so cut up that we lay utterly helpless. Our head bracer was shot away; the fore and main top masts were gone; the mizzen mast hung over the stern having carried several men over in its fall; we were in a state of complete wreck."

An account of the defeat and capture in October 1812 of the British 38-gun frigate Macedonian *by the American 44-gun frigate* United States, *commanded by Captain Stephen Decatur. From* A Voice from the Main Deck *by Samuel Leech*

Such, then, were the types of smaller vessel possibly commanded by an officer before he rose to post rank and the command of a larger frigate. Early service in, and later command of, such small vessels gave officers an excellent schooling in the ways of the sea, and also helped to inculcate a spirit of daring. Gaining experience in this way, British frigate captains were not averse to tackling enemy frigates, even when they were notionally superior ships, and they had an excellent record of success up to 1812. Then, with the start of the War of 1812 against the Americans, Royal Navy frigate captains found themselves faced by frigates that were larger and also better armed. The American vessels carried long guns rather than carronades as the core of their main armaments and so could undertake a stand-off engagement that left the British frigates effectively impotent. The American ships were also well crewed and commanded by good captains.

The Classic Duels

Jack Aubrey is witness to two of the great single-ship actions that actually took place with the Americans. In *The Fortune of War* he is on board Captain Harry Lambert's 38-gun *Java*, as a passenger, in December 1812 when she is captured and burned by Commodore William Bainbridge's 44-gun *Constitution*. Later in the same book he sees, on the British ship, the classic action between the British 38-gun *Shannon* under Captain Philip Bowes Vere Broke (generally reckoned to be one of the most efficient ships in the Royal

Navy) and the American 44-gun *Chesapeake* under Captain James Lawrence, an officer who had made his name in the sloop of war *Hornet* when sinking the similar British *Peacock* off Brazil in an 11-minute engagement with a newly raised and untried crew.

Broke cruised off Boston and challenged Lawrence to bring his ship out for a frigate-versus-frigate duel, and Lawrence was unwise enough to respond. Broke outthought and outsailed his American opponent, and in only a few minutes the *Shannon* managed to rake the *Chesapeake* several times, killing or wounding about one-third of the American ship's crew. One of those who suffered a

mortal wound was Lawrence, among whose last words were the order "Don't give up the ship!," but then Broke brought the *Shannon* alongside the *Chesapeake*, and the British boarded the American frigate.

The Americans surrendered some 15 minutes after the start of the engagement, losing 146 men killed and wounded to the British casualty list of 83. The *Chesapeake* was brought into Halifax, Nova Scotia as a prize and after repair was taken into British service under the same name. She never saw any active service and was sold in 1819. Broke was knighted for his triumph in this action, and his success was a major fillip for British morale at a time in which it had

been severely dented by the news of several American successes at sea. In *The Surgeon's Mate* O'Brian evokes the atmosphere of huge excitement in Britain as the news of *Shannon*'s victory is received. Jack Aubrey lands in Portsmouth from the *Diligence*, and is besieged by well-wishers wanting to know more about the action.

Aubrey approves strongly of Broke's dedication to brisk, short-range gunnery, which reflects his own enthusiasm for this method of closing and crippling an enemy. He also shares Broke's interest in scientific matters, as did a number of other naval officers of the period: in the case of Broke this took the form of the invention of a new gun sight.

Above: *The capture of the US frigate* Chesapeake *by the* Shannon *in a boarding action of June 1813 was a great fillip to British morale dented by a string of American frigate successes. In the action the British suffered 33 dead and 50 wounded to the American ship's figure of 61 dead (including the captain James Lawrence) and 85 wounded. Here Captain Philip Broke is seen leading the boarding party.*

CHAPTER SIX

The Thunder of Battle

When questioned about their national character, the British may describe themselves as a pacific people who shun war and who only enter combat when it is absolutely unavoidable. But while they may not necessarily seek wars—and the wars with Napoleon were certainly not of Britain's choosing—Britons do make good sailors and soldiers, who, as the Aubrey novels demonstrate, fight with skill and determination.

Opposite page: Frantic activity on Victory's upper deck as Nelson falls at Trafalgar. Gun crews are hard at work (note the gun captain aligning the weapon, left) while sharpshooters pick off enemy crew.

Thus, during the Napoleonic wars a rather ill-assorted collection of officers whose selection in many cases depended upon social status and influence rather than intellectual capacity or professional skills, combined with a motley group of sailors, many of whom were dragged off the streets against their will, to produce a navy which swept its European enemies off the seas. These men proved their skill and abilities in two ways: by keeping going during the long and tedious months of patrols and blockade duties, and then throwing themselves, heart and soul, into the infrequent and relatively brief periods of violent action.

The Fighting Ship

The primary purpose of the sailing warship was to carry guns, and ships of the line were defined by the number of guns they carried. The various types of gun are described in Chapter 3, so it will suffice here to say that the naval gun of the Napoleonic period was a simple, unrifled tube, which was mounted on a heavy carriage with four, small-diameter wooden wheels on fixed axles. The gun could be elevated by adding or removing a quoin (wedge) which could alter elevation from about +10 degrees to –5 degrees, while the entire carriage could be aimed to a certain extent by differential use of the gun tackle, with fine adjustment by use of handspikes or crowbars.

Above The gun captain (standing left) stands well clear as he applies the match to the gun's touchhole.

Each gun had a crew led by the "gun captain" and if the ship was engaged on both sides, then each gun was served by a single crew, typical figures being seven men to a 32-pounder and six to an 18-pounder. When the enemy was engaged on one side only, however, the crews from the unengaged side would move across to join their comrades on the opposite side of the gun deck, thus improving manning and efficiency.

British crews were trained to fire on the downward roll of the ship, aiming at the enemy's hull or deck; thus, if the shot landed short it would ricochet off the water and still hit the target. This technique maximized both damage to the enemy's hull and casualties among his crew. The French, on the other hand, persisted in firing at their opponent's rigging, even though experience showed this to be less effective as a tactic of war. In a similar way, their army continued to advance in column right up to the end of the Napoleonic wars—even though their columns were regularly defeated by the British line.

The heavier "long guns" were probably capable of firing to a range of some 2,000 yards at maximum elevation, but their *effective* range in battle was about one-tenth of that, perhaps 200 yards at point-blank for a 24-pounder. As a result, the range at which actions took place was usually very short; 100 yards at most, reducing to 30-40 yards in some cases.

There is a popular notion that warships of the Napoleonic period fired a succession of "broadsides" in which all the guns on one side of the ship fired simultaneously, but, although this may sometimes have been the case for the opening salvo, the shock effect on the ship and crew would have been tremendous. It was much more likely for the guns to be fired under the orders of individual gun captains who fired as and when their guns came to bear on the enemy.

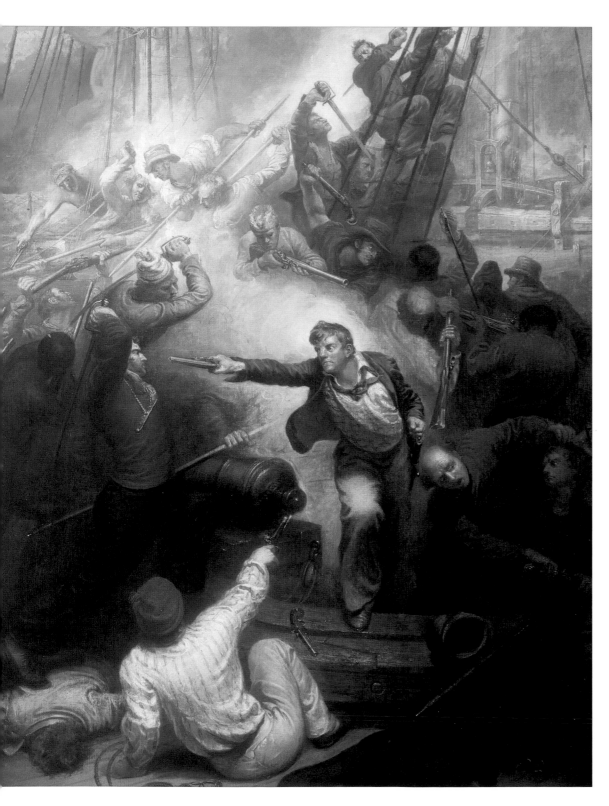

Virtually all a warship's guns and her thickest timbers were found along the sides of the vessel, whereas the bows and stern carried few weapons and were much more weakly protected. Thus, one effective tactic was to seek an opportunity to employ raking fire; i.e. attacking an opponent from directly ahead or astern, with gun captains firing in turn as their guns came to bear. Not only were there many fewer guns to retaliate, but there was a good chance that the shots would pass along the length of a deck, thus causing much more destruction—and many more casualties—than if fired across the deck, while the succession of firing considerably prolonged the agonies of the ship under attack.

A beaten enemy who had endured overwhelming death and destruction would sometimes signal surrender by hauling down ("striking") the national ensign, but frequently the issue had to be decided by the attacking ship running alongside its victim and holding the two together with grappling irons, whereupon an officer, usually the captain, would lead a boarding party, which usually consisted of men designated for such a task.

Conventions of Combat

There were no formalized rules-of-war in the modern sense, but there were a number of well-understood conventions, which were generally observed by both sides. For example, it was accepted that if a crew had done all that could reasonably be expected and that casualties and damage were such that defeat had become inevitable, or if the ship had been carried by a boarding party, then the captain could surrender with honor. The visible token of such a surrender was the hauling down of the national flag and the custom was already established for warships to wear several such ensigns when going into battle in order to avoid any misunderstanding should one be shot away.

It was also considered that there was little point in a demonstrably weaker ship fighting a much more powerful opponent, although a few daring and determined captains, such as Cochrane, did so and succeeded. Jack Aubrey's 14-gun *Sophie* manages such a feat, capturing the 32-gun Spanish xebec-frigate *Cacafuego* in an action described in

Left: *When the French privateer* Jeune Richard *attacked the packet* Windsor Castle *in 1807, the French outnumbered the* British three-to-one. Despite this the British resisted stoutly and the master, William Rogers, led a party which took the enemy ship.

Left: *Fire aboard a warship was always to be feared, but if it approached the gunpowder room the results were almost always catastrophic. Here the French L'Orient explodes during the Battle of the Nile in 1798, being totally destroyed with great loss of life.*

JOHN CRAWFORD,

Above: *At the Battle of Camperdown (October 11th, 1797) John Crawford nails HMS Venerable's flag to the head of the topgallant mast after it had been shot away, lest the enemy think his ship had surrendered.*

Master and Commander, Chapter 10. Normally, however, the honor of the smaller ship was satisfied by firing a token broadside and then immediately surrendering. In fleet actions, smaller ships, even frigates, were generally immune to attack by ships of the line, provided they kept out of the way, but if one did choose to fire first, as did the French frigate, *Sérieuse*, at the Battle of the Nile, then the ship of the line was immediately free to fire back and the effect was usually disastrous for the smaller ship.

One of the enduring naval myths of the late 19th and 20th century naval warfare was the so-called tradition of the captain "going down with his ship." Such self-sacrifice was totally unknown during the Napoleonic period. In fact, it was very rare for a wooden warship to sink in battle, such a catastrophic event being far more likely to be the result of a storm or a navigational error (see also Chapter 4). Even then, the captain did not voluntarily end his life. For example, when HMS *Pandora* hit the Great Barrier Reef off the coast of Australia on August 28th, 1791, it would never have occurred to Captain Edwards that his responsibility was anything other than to secure the rescue of his crew. There were, however, occasions during a battle when a spark ignited the magazine and as a result the wooden warship might be destroyed by explosion, as happened to the French *L'Orient* at the Battle of the Nile on August 17th, 1798.

In the case of the Royal Navy, a surrender was followed by a court-martial of the officer commanding at the first available opportunity. As prescribed by the Articles of War (see Chapter 4) loss of a ship was automatic cause for a court-martial. This event was usually conducted with scrupulous fairness and, if it achieved nothing else, it served to air all the facts and clear the air. Jack Aubrey is court-martialled in *Master and Commander* for the loss of the *Sophie* and is honorably acquitted, the court deciding that he had used "every possible exertion" to prevent the sloop from falling into enemy hands.

Convoy and Blockade

There were few activities that British officers and, more particularly, sailors seemed to enjoy more than landings, sometimes in the support of the army, but also in pursuit of purely naval objectives. They performed some prodigious feats during such operations, a prime example being the conversion of a Caribbean island into a temporary fortress under the designation HM Sloop of War *Diamond Rock*.

The British Isles depended to a large extent upon trade. Small trading ships moved ceaselessly around the coast or between the mainland and Ireland. Such trade need protection and this was provided by the "coastwise" convoy system, which was supervised by admirals and captains at the major ports and conducted by smaller warships. The Royal Navy also ran long-distance convoys to the Americas and to India and the Far East. In such cases the merchant ships virtually all belonged to the East India Company and all of them had a number of guns for their own protection.

The average British man-of-war and crew spent far more time on blockade duties than on any other activity throughout the war. The original strategy employed the open blockade in which frigates maintained observation of the French and Dutch ports while the main English fleets remained over the horizon, or even back in port, ready to put to sea at a moment's notice. This preserved the main fleet safely in harbor, but it was not especially difficult for

the French to escape the blockade and, in any event, it left most British sailors at anchor for protracted periods, leading to boredom and occasionally to mutiny. This system was superseded from 1795 onwards in the Mediterranean and from about 1801 in the Channel by the close blockade in which the British fleets stood off the main French ports, such as Brest and Toulon, sometimes simply anchoring off the harbor entrance in full sight of the enemy. This was far more effective, and, if more wearing for the men involved, it also ensured that the British crews were highly trained

Far right: Blockade duties were long and boring, but could be enlivened by cutting-out expeditions, such as this attack by sailors and Royal Marines on French fishing vessels in a Mediterranean port, as depicted in a diorama. Sailors found such exploits exciting and they generally joined in with gusto.

Right: From 1795 onward, the British navy imposed a close blockade on French and Spanish ports. This scene depicts the advance squadron, commanded by Admiral Lord Nelson, off Cadiz in Spain. The ships involved were at sea constantly for many months at a time, which was hard work for the men and their warships. In Aubrey's opinion, voiced in The Ionian Mission, there was "no duller life on earth" than a blockade.

and highly motivated. In both cases, the ships of the French and their allied navies were often confined to port for protracted periods, with correspondingly detrimental effects on the morale and training of their crews.

COMMUNICATIONS AT SEA

The complicated problem of communications at sea vexed the minds of naval officers during much of the 18th century, and was a live issue throughout the Napoleonic wars. Admirals could hold face-to-face meetings with their captains, either in port or at sea, and written orders could also be

distributed at sea by calling boats to the flagship to collect the document. To a limited extent messages could also be passed by voice, using a megaphone, but this required the two ships to be in very close proximity, which was not always possible. All such procedures were, however, slow and, in any event, were impossible to conduct in the face of enemy action. So what remained were flags.

For most of the 18th century, signaling flags were given specific meanings, pre-assigned to them during a time of peace. But serving officers lacked the means to compose new messages to meet the demands of particular situa-

Above: A cannon is hauled from HMS Centaur to the summit of His Majesty's Sloop Diamond Rock, an exploit in which a tiny Caribbean island was transformed into a fortress. Manned by less than a hundred sailors, it took an entire French squadron and hundreds of soldiers to subdue it.

Right: *Various flag systems were developed during the Napoleonic wars, each composed of a number of colored flags whose meanings, both individually and in combination, were explained in a signal book, such as this.*

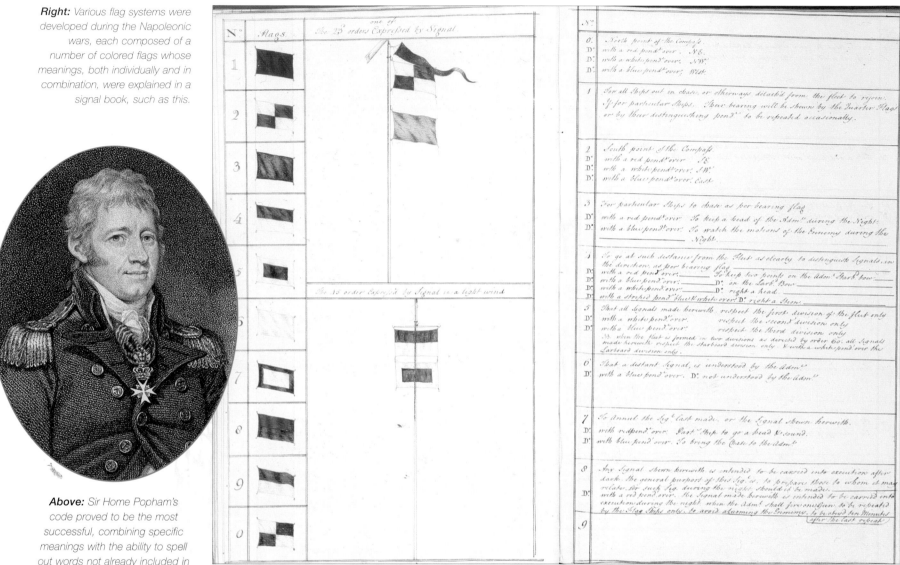

Above: *Sir Home Popham's code proved to be the most successful, combining specific meanings with the ability to spell out words not already included in the signal book's lengthy vocabulary. Devised in 1800, the code was progressively improved throughout the war.*

❝ **Sea battles of the period were slow and stately affairs.** ❞

tions. The result was an inflexible system, which effectively limited the admiral to those maneuvers which had previously been envisaged in peace, and enshrined in the *Fighting Instructions*. Admiral Howe devised a system which involved 14 flags of different design, which was incorporated into the Signal Book of 1790. These comprised ten flags representing the numbers 1-9 plus 0 (then known as the "cypher"). Each of the numerical flags had a specific meaning. Four more flags represented "substitute," "preparative," "finishing," and "affirmative," respectively. The substitute flag was used to repeat the top flag: thus, the number

44 was represented by 4 plus the substitute, while the number 404 was represented by 4 plus 0 plus substitute. This system enabled some 260 messages to be passed and was progressively refined, with the number of flags being increased and their design improved.

Then, another innovator, Admiral Sir Home Popham, realized that this was still too limited. So, he took matters a stage further and, using the same flags as the Howe code, devised a system which was first published in 1800 and was then widely adopted. Popham's ingenious system allocated combinations of flags to represent words and phrases, which enabled many thousands of words to be sent quickly and efficiently. Its most significant advance, however, was that words not already in the vocabularies could be spelt out letter by letter. This was achieved by using numbers 1 to 25 to represent each letter in the alphabet (at that time the letter "J" was not officially a part of the alphabet and was covered by flag 9 (letter "I"). In the most famous signal ever sent using this system—Nelson's "England expects…" at Trafalgar—the only word not covered in the vocabulary tables which had to be spelled out was "duty."

Apart from the admiral passing orders, these flag systems had many other uses, the most important being to pass intelligence. Thus, frigates could be deployed around a fleet at the extremity of signaling distance and give the admiral timely warning of the approach of the enemy. Such a screen could be deployed even further away by placing a ship half-way between it and the fleet to serve as a relay station. In such a situation the height of the mast on which the lookouts were stationed and the optical power of telescopes became important factors.

In a flagship the admiral had the service of a flag lieutenant, but in other ships the brighter midshipmen were told off for the duty. One of the many complications was that the position of the signaling ship's sails and the relative position of the intended recipient of the signal had to be taken into account in order to select which mast (and, sometimes, more than one mast) was most suitable for the signal to be hoisted. All personnel on duty kept a particular lookout for signals directed toward their ship, especially from the flagship, and woe betide the captain whose lookouts' attention had to be gained by the firing of a warning gun!

Signals could also be transmitted at night using a combination of guns, flares, and lights, the latter being displayed on wooden frames. Various combinations of lights and guns enabled some 70 messages to be passed, such as "turn to larboard/starboard," "investigate strange ships," and so on.

THE NATURE OF BATTLE

Sea battles of this period were slow and stately affairs. Everything depended upon the strength of the wind, but speed was almost invariably reduced by sailing under topsails. Speed was also affected by fouled bottoms, i.e. the growth of weed on the hull which impeded forward motion. This particularly applied to British ships which spent much longer at sea than their opponents did. Some ships sailed more slowly than others due to differences in design and the relative abilities and seamanship qualities of their crews. Thus, the maximum speed in battle of even the fastest ship was probably no more than about 5-6 knots, and the rate of advance of a formation was, of necessity, determined by the speed of the slowest ship. Alternatively such ships had to be left behind, thus weakening the line.

Above: Admiral Lord Nelson aboard his flagship, HMS Victory, just before the Battle of Trafalgar, as his famous signal—"England expects that every man will do his duty"—is prepared. His flag-lieutenant pores over the signal book (bottom right) while the crew assemble the flags in the correct order. So flexible and extensive was the Popham signaling system that the only word that needed to be spelled out in full was "duty."

Right: A page from the Admiralty's "Signal Book for Ships of War" published in 1799, with each flag indicating a specific point of the compass. Everything aboard ships of this period was influenced by the direction and strength of the wind and each ship's ability to take best advantage of it. During the advance into battle holding the weather gage generally conferred a great advantage.

Below: Many engagements culminated in a boarding action, such as that depicted here by George Cruikshank. These frequently became a matter of "every man for himself," with every type of weapon being used, although firearms were of limited value since there was no time for the lengthy reloading procedures. Swords, daggers, spears, axes, even tomahawks were all used to lethal effect.

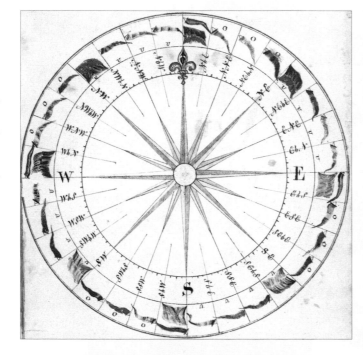

The Weather Gage

In discussing the naval tactics of the sailing era, the term "weather gage" (sometimes spelt "gauge") often arises. In such a nautical context gage means the position of one ship in relation to another and to the wind; thus "to have the weather gage" means that one ship is to windward (i.e. upwind) of another. Possessing the weather gage usually meant that an admiral or captain could choose whether or not to attack, and, in the latter case, when and where the attack should take place. This was usually a successful tactic, but, like all rules-of-thumb, there were always exceptions—at the Battle of Cape St. Vincent, for example, the Spanish fleet had the weather gage, but still failed to defeat the British.

The admiral's job was to position his fleet and then to commit his ships to battle to give them the maximum prospect of success. Once the fighting had started, he had very limited ability to influence matters any further. As the ships of the two fleets intermingled and the noise and smoke increased, it was difficult for the admiral to see what was going on, let alone communicate by flag to his subordinates. So, once the two fleets were engaged, it was up to the individual captains to fight their ships as best they might.

The captain had to achieve a balance between offense and defense, all of which revolved around a finite resource—his crew. The great majority of his men were allocated to the guns and it was essential to keep these weapons in action. If the ship had enemies on only one beam, the gun crews from the disengaged side could reinforce their shipmates across the deck. A proportion of the crew was involved with the sails in action, but if a major effort was required, designated men had to be removed from the gun crews. Similarly, if it was decided to board the enemy, then other designated men were called to join the boarding party.

Once the ship was engaged, the chaos aboard would steadily increase, with casualties from enemy cannon and sharpshooters increasing, dead bodies and wounded men cluttering the decks, spars and sails falling, probably some fires breaking out, men snatching breaks to carry wounded comrades below to the surgeon's station on the orlop deck, and, all the while, continuing to fight the ship. Most sailors were brave—they had to live with the sea every day of their lives—but perhaps British sailors tended to triumph in such battles not only because they were aggressive and had an expectation of success, but also because they went on being brave for a little bit longer than their enemies.

Single-Ship Actions

Of course not all engagements were full-scale fleet encounters. In fact, very few were. Throughout the wars from 1793-1815 numerous single-ship actions took place and, as the Aubrey novels make abundantly clear, the victors were showered with acclaim and honors. Such actions were often the

result of a chance encounter and generally took place between frigates or sloops, since larger ships (i.e. third-rates and above) rarely sailed alone. The engagements were seldom inconclusive and the losing ship normally ended up in a battered state being taken as a prize. The resulting promotions were of even greater importance to most officers.

There were numerous single-ship engagements between the British and French, and the War of 1812 was characterized by such actions, most of them between frigates, in many of which the United States' ships triumphed (see Chapter 5). Chance encounters frequently led to a chase in which both ships piled on every bit of sail that the wind—and prudence—permitted, with additional stays, such as preventers, being deployed to add strength to the masts. Sometimes, however, the limits were exceeded and a sail ripped or a spar—sometimes even a mast—broke. If the

damaged ship was the pursuer, then its victim escaped; if it was the pursued, then the crew's struggles to repair the damage were spurred on by the approach of the enemy.

It was not infrequent in such encounters for one or other of the parties to use subterfuge. False colors or misleading flag signals might be displayed in order to lull the opponent into a false sense of security, although honor required that the proper national flag should be flown immediately before the first shot was fired.

The reminder of the chapter is devoted to an examination of three actions that demonstrate how the Royal Navy conducted itself in battle in three very different types of engagement—a significant fleet action (Cape St. Vincent), a major amphibious operation (the Walcheren expedition), and a smaller-scale battle fought by small vessels acting in combination (Lake Erie).

Above: *HMS* Defence *(74) led the line on the Glorious First of June (1794), but despite being surrounded by enemy ships and losing first her main and mizzenmasts, and then her foremast, she was not captured. She was eventually towed away by HMS* Phaeton. *Despite the extensive damage, only 17 men on board were killed and 35 wounded. This painting of the action is by Nicholas Pocock.*

Battle of Cape St. Vincent
February 14th, 1797

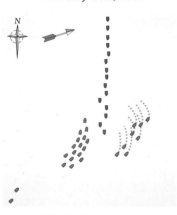

The fleets converge:
position at about 11.35a.m.

The British split the Spanish fleet:
position at about 12.30p.m.

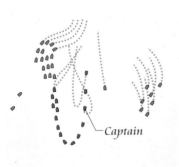

Captain

Commodore Nelson's attack:
position at about 1.05p.m.

➡ *British fleet*
➡ *Spanish fleet*

THE BATTLE OF CAPE ST. VINCENT

The Battle of Cape St. Vincent (February 14th, 1797) was an archetypical example of a fleet action in which superior naval intelligence and energetic use of frigates for scouting brought two fleets together, and the ships of the line then slogged it out until one of them was overcome. The battle had its origins in that bugbear of so many British governments down the centuries—the threat of invasion—a danger that particulary troubles people who live on an island. In early 1797 the Royal Navy knew that such an enterprise was being planned by the French and that an essential prerequisite for the enemy must be a concentration of the Franco-Spanish fleet at Brest. The English sought to prevent this by positioning a strong fleet under Admiral Sir John Jervis off the Atlantic coast of the Iberian peninsula. Its aim was to intercept and destroy the Spanish Mediterranean fleet as it sailed north toward its junction with the French.

Commodore Nelson was aboard the frigate *La Minerve* (38) in the Mediterranean and on January 29th, 1797, having escorted a convoy out of Elba, he sailed alone to look in on the French fleet at Toulon. All appeared normal, so he headed down the coast to Cartagena. There, to his alarm, he discovered the harbor to be empty—the Spanish fleet had sailed. Nelson immediately set out to inform Admiral Jervis, and calling at Gibraltar on February 11th, he was told that the British garrison had seen the Spanish fleet pass through six days earlier. Realizing that time was of the essence, Nelson pressed on to find Jervis, in the course of which he experienced one of the most extraordinary encounters in naval history.

Contrary winds had forced the Spanish fleet to head out into the Atlantic and it was several days before the wind veered sufficiently to enable the ships to head back toward their next port-of-call, the Spanish Atlantic port of Cadiz. As a result, during dense fog on the night of February 11-12th, Nelson and *La Minerve* found themselves passing through the main body of the enemy fleet. Nelson was one of those commanders upon whom fortune frequently shines and the Spaniards failed to see the lonely English ship slip through their columns, but Nelson and his crew certainly saw them. Nelson managed to be out of sight by daybreak and he duly found Jervis and his fleet off Cape St. Vincent on February 13th, where he passed on the news.

The Two Fleets at the Battle of Cape St. Vincent

Britain		Spain	
Ship	Guns	Ship	Guns
Britannia	100	*Santìsima Trinidad*	130
Victory	100	*Prìncipe de Asturias*	112
Barfleur	98	*Conde de Regla*	112
Blenheim	98	*San Josef*	112
Prince George	98	*Mexicano*	112
Namur	90	*Purìsima Concepción*	112
Captain	74	*Salvador del Mundo*	112
Colossus	74	*San Nicolas*	84
Culloden	74	*Oriente*	74
Egmont	74	*Atlante*	74
Excellent	74	*Soberano*	74
Goliath	74	*Infante de Pelayo*	74
Irresistible	74	*San Ildephonso*	74
Orion	74	*San Ysidro*	74
Diadem	64	*San Pablo*	74
La Minerve	38	*Neptuna*	74
Lively	32	*San Domingo*	74
Niger	32	*Terrible*	74
Southampton	32	*Glorioso*	74
Bonne Citoyenne	20	*Conquestada*	74
Raven	18	*Firme*	74
Fox	10	*San Genaro*	74
		San Francisco de Paula	74
		San Antonio	74
		San Fermìn	74
		Bahama	74
		San Juan Nepomuceno	74
22	**1422**	**27**	**2292**

The Opposing Fleets

Admiral Jervis's fleet comprised 15 ships of the line and seven smaller vessels, with three rear admirals and one commodore, Nelson, who, in view of the impending battle, had transferred his flag to HMS *Captain* (74). Jervis had his ships cleared for action and they remained at that state throughout the night. The following dawn (February 14th) found the English fleet sailing in two parallel columns and eager for battle. Shortly after first light their enthusiasm was rewarded when a frigate reported "enemy ships in sight" fine on the port bow. Lookouts quickly confirmed there were some nine ships which were judged to be warships,

Through Aubrey's Eyes

Regrettably from the reader's point of view, Jack Aubrey does not participate in a fleet action in the course of the canon, so we are unable to enjoy O'Brian's evocation of the thunder of a battle in which a multiplicity of ships are involved. Typically throughout the novels, Aubrey is seen fighting smaller actions, either ship-to-ship or as part of a small squadron of vessels.

However, it does become apparent in the course of the novels that Aubrey saw action in February 1797 at Cape St. Vincent in *Orion (Post Captain)* and *Colossus (The Thirteen-Gun Salute)*—an inconsistency that was evidently not noticed by O'Brian—and in October 1797 at Camperdown in the *Ardent (Desolation Island)*. And in August 1798 he was at the Battle of the Nile in *Leander (Master and Commander)*. In Chapter 2 of *Post Captain* Jack explains that he likes to celebrate the anniversary of the Battle of Cape St. Vincent with all the friends and shipmates that he can muster, and so he throws a ball at Melbury Lodge on February 14th at which both Sophia Williams, his future wife, and Diana Villiers, Stephen Maturin's future wife, are present.

The ships in the Spanish fleet commanded by Admiral Juan de Cordova were of good quality and well-armed, the total number of guns far exceeding that of the English fleet (see table); indeed, the flagship, *Santìsima Trinidad* (130) was the most powerful ship afloat. However, the ships in this formidable fleet were undermanned, and had spent many months confined in their harbor. As a result, the officers were not well-trained and were far less used to fleet work than their English opponents, while many of the crew were soldiers or landmen with little or no experience of life afloat. To add to their woes the ships were also short of supplies.

Below: *Victory passes under the stern of Salvador del Mundo at Cape St. Vincent and rakes her opponent, a devastating tactic with all her guns able to fire down the full length of the enemy ship.*

Right: *Admiral of the Fleet Earl St. Vincent while still Sir John Jervis, in his pre-1795 rear-admiral's uniform. Note the large lapels, buttons bearing the Admiralty anchor, and embroidered insignia.*

although it was later learnt that they were two ships of the line, three frigates, and four large merchantmen carrying a valuable cargo of mercury.

Shortly afterward the English lookouts sighted some 20 ships fine on the starboard bow and Jervis correctly judged this to be the main fleet, the first group of ships having been a detached division. His first priority was to prevent the two meeting and forming a single line. Largely by good fortune, the wind conditions and his position relative to the Spanish gave Jervis a distinct advantage, and he was able to hold his course and formation until just before 11a.m. when he signaled his fleet to form line of battle "as most convenient." Superbly trained as they were, his captains quickly slid their ships into position. At about 11.50a.m. a further signal announced that the admiral "...intends to pass through the enemy line."

Below: HMS Captain *capturing the Spanish* San Nicolas *at the Battle of Cape St. Vincent. Within moments the British ship was alongside the Spaniard and Commodore Nelson personally led the boarding party which quickly overcame the enemy crew. The watercolor is by Nicholas Pocock.*

The main Spanish fleet was heading east-south-east in three columns, each headed by its commanding admiral, but as soon as he saw the English fleet, the commander-in-chief, Cordova, signaled his fleet to tack to port and form line-of-battle thus retaining (as he hoped) the advantage of the weather gage. The result was confusion as the Spanish captains sought to slot into a line, while the admirals found their divisions dispersed at random along the line and outside their control. To add to their difficulties, three ships, one of them the flagship of Admiral Moreno, failed to turn in time with the others and fell behind. Seeing this, Jervis, leading the English line in *Culloden*, sailed between the

> 66 A victory is very essential to England at the moment. 99

two Spanish groups, his ships firing to starboard into the main Spanish fleet as they passed. He then ordered them to tack in turn, and they drew abreast of the detached group of three which, finding themselves heavily engaged by the English port batteries, temporarily abandoned their attempt to rejoin Cordova's fleet and fell away to port .

At this point (approximately midday) the Spanish fleet was in three groups, with Jervis intent on overhauling the main group and destroying it, but several events intervened. First, Admiral Moreno reversed course and closed on the English, his three ships attacking *Colossus*, fifth in the English line, which missed stays in the confusion and fell away to leeward, causing problems for the ships astern. Secondly, Cordova ordered his fleet to turn to starboard and cross the rear of the English fleet, but his signals were either not seen or could not be implemented and only a very few ships followed his lead. The third event, however, was even more significant.

Nelson's Master Stroke

By shortly before 1p.m. the leading four ships of the English fleet (*Culloden*, *Blenheim*, *Prince George*, and *Orion*) were engaging the rear of Cordova's main fleet, *Colossus* was recovering from her adventure and most of the remainder were following Jarvis's order to tack in turn and then catch up with the van. It became clear, however, that there was a possibility that the forward elements of the Spanish fleet might escape, which Nelson in *Captain*, third from rear of the English line, was quick to spot. Totally on his own authority, he ordered *Captain* to haul out of the line to port, reverse her course, and then turn to pass between *Diadem* and *Excellent* in order to attack *Santìsima Trinidad*. Seeing what Nelson was up to, *Excellent* (Collingwood) turned to support him, followed shortly afterward by *Diadem*. At approximately the same time as Nelson made his turn out of line, Jervis made a flag signal instructing his captains to "take suitable action" and the engagement became general and very fierce.

Nelson moved in to attack *Santìsima Trinidad*, which was supported by two other Spanish first-rates, *San Josef* (112) and *San Nicolas* (84), which led to some of the hottest fighting in a hard-fought day. *Captain* was isolated for a period and incurred very heavy damage before *Excellent* came up and fired a series of broadsides into *San Nicolas*, which then collided with the equally badly damaged *San Josef*. *Captain* was almost out of control but managed to fire a broadside into *San Nicolas*'s starboard side at very short range before the two ships came together, so that the three ships were locked together, with *San Nicolas* in the middle. Nelson immediately led a very enthusiastic boarding

Eyewitness

"...I pushed immediately onwards for the quarter-deck, where I found Commander Berry in possession of the poop, and the Spanish ensign hauling down. I passed with my people, and Lieutenant Pearson, on the larboard gangway, to the forecastle, where I met two or three Spanish officers, prisoners to my seamen: they delivered me their swords. A fire of pistols, or muskets, opening from the stern gallery of the *San Josef*, I directed the soldiers to fire into her stern; and calling to Captain Miller, ordered him to send more men into the *San Nicholas*; and directed my people to board the first-rate, which was done in an instant, Commander Berry assisting me into the main chains. At this moment a Spanish officer looked over the quarter-deck rail, and said they surrendered. From this most welcome intelligence, it was not long before I was on the quarter-deck, where the captain, with a bow, presented me his sword..."

Commodore Nelson's report on the Battle of Cape St. Vincent

party aboard *San Nicolas*, where quickly and very successfully they carried the day and then also took the *San Josef*.

This unprecedented action of taking two enemy ships by boarding one from the other was later described in English newspapers as "Nelson's patent bridge for boarding enemy vessels." Two other ships were captured, while *Santísima*

Trinidad was also taken but she subsequently escaped. The remainder of the Spanish fleet, badly battered, fled to Cadiz. The battle put paid to the Spanish naval threat and also confirmed the melee as a more successful tactic than the formal line of battle, at least when initiated by a more aggressive force exhibiting superior seamanship.

This battle showed the Royal Navy at its best, with frigates, such as Nelson's *La Minerve*, serving as the eyes and ears of the fleet and then delivering the news in timely fashion to the fleet commander. Then the commander-in-chief outmaneuvered his opponent and established a position of supremacy, after which individual captains took matters into their own hands. Nelson's performance was masterly and it does not detract from the credit accorded to Jervis's overall victory since battles seldom go exactly according to plan and subordinates sometimes have to use their initiative.

Above: *Nelson leads a boarding party of soldiers and sailors aboard the Spanish ship, San Josef. Fortunately, however, a Spanish officer signals from the quarterdeck that the crew has surrendered, which Nelson described as "most welcome intelligence."*

Far left: *A painting by Sir William Allan showing Captain alongside the San Nicolas and the boarding party pouring onto the Spanish ship. The San Josef is also part of the melee.*

THE WALCHEREN EXPEDITION
JULY-DECEMBER 1809

Throughout the Napoleonic wars the British took pride in their command of the seas surrounding the country which made it so difficult for the French to invade their islands. Unfortunately, the corollary was that in order to take the war to the enemy it was necessary for the Royal Navy to carry the army to some distant shore, sustain it there throughout a campaign, and, not infrequently, to withdraw it after the project had failed. Between 1793 and 1815 there were some 70 major amphibious operations and many more minor ones, and it should never be overlooked that ships of the Royal Navy sustained and supported Wellington's army in the Iberian Peninsula for no less than six years. But, despite the undoubted successes, such as the Peninsular War, there were also some dismal failures.

By 1809 the British government was very concerned about the French activities in the Low Countries, which included major defensive works and shipbuilding in several local yards (and the Dutch built very good ships!). As a result, it was decided to conduct a major raid, which would combine the necessary destruction of materiel with a way of diverting Napoleon's attention from his invasion of Austria. The plan involved an army element of some 45,000 men and 15,000 horses, together with field artillery, two complete siege trains, supporting troops, and considerable amounts of stores and supplies. The Royal Navy's involvement was also great, and included some 40 ships of the line, five two-deckers, 24 frigates, about 60 smaller warships, and over 100 smaller naval vessels. The Naval Transport Service provided 400 vessels, but even these were insufficient for the task and many warships also had to carry soldiers and horses. This huge force was greater than that devoted to Wellington's campaign in the Peninsula. Its assembly was widely reported in the press which led to accusations by government ministers and military commanders of conduct likely to prejudice national security.

> **The British aimed to penetrate as far as Antwerp, securing the islands and river banks as they went.**

Above: The *Naval Chronicle's* map of the mouths of the River Scheldt. Some parts, particularly Walcheren Island, were inhabited by malaria-bearing mosquitoes, as the British found to their cost.

Right: The British fleet (bottom) sets off up the Scheldt toward Antwerp (top). The approaches were protected by fortresses, a boom across the river just above the town of Lillo, and numerous French warships—a daunting and, as it eventually turned out, impossible prospect.

Eyewitness

"Lord Chatham with his sword undrawn, Kept waiting for Sir Richard Strachan; Sir Richard, eager to be at 'em, Kept waiting too—for whom? Lord Chatham!"

A popular song about the commanders at Walcheren

The Invasion Plan
The River Scheldt has two main entrances which are cluttered with sandbanks and low-lying islands, while navigation is further complicated by strong tides with a large drop between high and low water. The British aimed to penetrate as far as Antwerp, securing the islands and river banks as they went, thus enabling them either to capture or destroy enemy shipping, demolish dockyards and arsenals, and

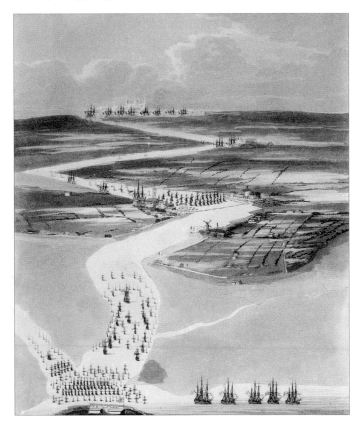

then to sink block ships to prevent the enemy from using the river.

After many delays, the force sailed on July 28th, 1809 and it achieved some initial success. Frigates and small boats marked the channel so that when the first transports arrived the following day they were able to pass through without mishap. The headquarters ship, *Venerable* (74), also arrived in the Westkapelle anchorage carrying the two British commanders, Rear Admiral Richard Strachan, renowned for his quick temper and dashing courage, and his army counterpart, Lieutenant General the Earl of Chatham, notorious for his idleness. Not surprisingly, there was considerable personal animosity between two such contrasting personalities.

On July 30th, Major General Hope's division anchored off Zierikzee (between North Beveland and Schouwen) but it was unable to land immediately due to the weather. Next day some 17,000 men under Chatham's second-in-command, Sir Eyre Coote, also arrived according to plan. The naval force included bomb (mortar) vessels and gunboats, which anchored off Veere on the northern coast of Walcheren on July 31st, and bombarded the town. Meanwhile, Coote's men captured Middelburg and then moved north to invest Veere from the landward side, where they were assisted by a naval "brigade" formed of men from HMS *Caesar* and the sloop *Harpy*. Recognizing the inevitable, Veere capitulated on August 1st.

Next, ten British frigates forced the entrance to the West Scheldt (August 11th) and two days later British warships, gunboats, and mortar vessels began to bombard Flushing. They were reinforced the next day by ships-of-the-line and on August 15th, after some 4,000 troops and civilians had been killed, the townspeople forced the French commandant to surrender. Over 5,000 troops were taken prisoner and the British moved on, with Hope's division being transferred by ship to the next island of Zuid Beveland where it

occupied Bathz. Meanwhile, lighter vessels moved onward nosing through the narrow creeks, working their way eastward toward Antwerp, pushing the main French fleet under Admiral Missiessy back until it took shelter behind the boom at Lillo.

The shallow water and twisting channels meant that there were frequent groundings, involving the crews in backbreaking labor, as they lightened ship and then kedged and worked over the shallows. The sailors also landed ships' guns and sailors to assist the army ashore, while other guns were put into empty transports, which, because of their shallower draft, could move further up river than warships.

The islands of Schouwen and Duiveland (then separated) fell to the British on August 17th and Chatham motivated himself sufficiently to move his headquarters forward but he began to dither and delay even more than usual, proving particularly susceptible to unfounded rumors. Meanwhile, sickness was steadily increasing and "Walcheren fever" (now known to be malaria) laid many thousands of men low, so that the medical staffs were quickly overcome by the sheer scale of the problem. Walcheren was already widely known

Above: *A British amphibious landing during the Walcheren expedition. Throughout these wars, major ships had too deep a draft to approach close to the shore, leaving no alternative but a long and arduous row.*

66 **...Rear Admiral Strachan, renowned for his quick temper and dashing courage, and his counterpart, Lieutenant General the Earl of Chatham, notorious for his idleness.** 99

Opposite page: A depiction of
the Battle of Lake Erie by an
American artist. Although all the
vessels engaged were small—
the largest was a corvette—
both commanders deployed and
fought their forces as if they were
admirals engaged in a major fleet
action. Commodore Perry's
resounding victory message
became part of American naval
history: "We have met the enemy
and they are ours."

Below: The Dutch town of
Flushing being besieged by the
British. The bombardment was
so intense that on August 15th,
after 31 hours, the inhabitants of
the town persuaded the French
garrison commander to
surrender. There were some
4,000 deaths in the town and
around 4,500 prisoners had to
be accommodated aboard the
ships of the fleet.

as the home of a virulent disease, particularly in the months June-September (just the time that had been chosen for the British invasion) and it had been widely reported only a few years earlier that a French force had lost no less than 80 per cent of its men. The British figures speak for themselves: 106 men died from enemy action, but Walcheren fever claimed 4,000 dead and a further 8,000 who were never again fit for service.

By mid-September the British situation was deteriorating, with land progress slow, some 10,000 sick and north-westerly gales making life difficult aboard the ships. At this, on September 14th, the Earl of Chatham simply returned to England, leaving a more junior officer in command of the army. A commission was sent from England to work out what to do and it recommended withdrawal.

Thus the British gradually withdrew. In continuing operations the French retook Zuid Beveland and by November British sailors were employed ashore destroying the defenses of Flushing, while a continuous succession of transports kept moving the sick back to England. The whole sorry affair drew to an ignominious close with the last ships departing on December 23rd. As an example of an amphibious operation, the whole expedition was a sorry story. However, the Navy performed its part of the job ably and emerged with considerable credit.

THE BATTLE OF LAKE ERIE

The Battle of Lake Erie (September 10th, 1813) is an interesting example of a naval action in that it was fought by small vessels—the largest was a 20-gun corvette—but both sides employed tactics as if they were grand fleets composed of line-of-battle ships. It also illustrates the problems arising from ships sailing at different speeds.

In the War of 1812, both the Americans and the British realized the strategic significance of Lake Erie, but both had only a handful of poorly armed ships there, and they were equally short of men and stores. The British squadron, under Commander Robert Barclay, was based at Amherstburg, at the western end of the northern shore of the lake. It comprised the corvette *Queen Charlotte* (20), schooner *Lady Prevost* (12), brig *General Hunter* (6), two armed schooners, and an armed sloop, while a further 20-gun corvette, HMS *Detroit*, was under construction. Barclay was short of everything, including men, weapons, and equipment, all of which had to be transported from Kingston, some 400 miles away. Despite his shortages, Barclay's small squadron gave him naval command of the lake.

This supremacy was, however, about to be disputed by Master Commandant Oliver Hazard Perry, United States Navy, who arrived at Presque Isle Bay on the southern shore of Lake Erie on March 27th, 1813, accompanied by one of his

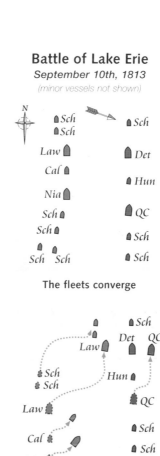

Battle of Lake Erie
September 10th, 1813
(minor vessels not shown)

The fleets converge

The contact

The final phase

Great Britain	United States
Det: *Detroit*	Cal: *Caledonia*
Hun: *Hunter*	Law: *Lawrence*
Sch: *Schooner*	Nia: *Niagara*
QC: *Queen*	Sch: *Schooner*
Charlotte	

younger brothers, Alexander (13), and a draft of 150 seamen. Perry found two 50-foot brigs and four schooner-rigged gunboats under construction. He immediately gave orders for the work to be speeded up. There were five similar vessels at Black Rock at the eastern end of Lake Erie.

Both sides pressed ahead with their construction programs, while Barclay's ships patrolled the lake and the Americans carried out raids on various British forts. One of their major achievements was the capture of Forts George and Erie, which dominated the River Niagara preventing the Americans from dragging the vessels from Black Rock up the rapids and into Lake Erie. With the way now clear, the vessels reached Lake Erie on June 12th. Having evaded the searching British squadron in dense fog, the American reinforcements reached Presque Isle on June 18th, where they anchored off the bar.

When the last of his vessels was completed on July 10th, Perry was faced with the problem of getting them over the sand bar. This meant offloading everything moveable, including the cannon, and then raising the hulls even further by use of "camels" specially for the purpose. The dismounted cannon were emplaced on the beach to prevent the British from interfering and the newly-completed brig, *Lawrence*, was the first to be moved. Matters proceeded much more slowly than had been expected and the Americans were in a particularly vulnerable position when the British appeared. Fortunately for Perry, Barclay misinterpreted the situation

and thought that the American ships were already clear of the bar. So, since they appeared to outnumber him, Barclay decided not to attack but to await the completion of HMS *Detroit*. Perry eventually got all his ships across the bar and also received a welcome draft of some 200 men, enabling him to tail his squadron (August 10th).

On the British side, shortages became so critical that the men were on half-rations, forcing Barclay to make a "do-or-die" attempt. He sailed in search of battle on September 9th. Just after dawn the following morning American lookouts sighted the approaching British, who were running down toward Put-In Bay with a following wind.

Battle Is Joined

Perry's squadron was armed with fewer long cannon than the British, putting them at a disadvantage at longer range, but they had carronades, which delivered a heavy round but only over the relatively short range of some 260 yards. So Perry's plan was to get as close to the enemy as possible. In order to encourage his men, his ship flew a special flag embroidered with the message "Don't give up the ship." Fortunately for Perry the wind shifted through 120 degrees and he committed his squadron to action. Perry was aboard *Lawrence* which soon outdistanced its fellows and came under fire from the British at about 11.45a.m. The wind then dropped, leaving the *Lawrence* in a very exposed position and under very heavy fire from some 20 long guns.

Below: At the height of the battle, Commodore Oliver Hazard Perry transfers his command from the badly damaged Lawrence to the Niagara. This battle was fiercely fought and casualties were disproportionately high, a total of 68 killed and 190 wounded on both sides, as many as in some major fleet engagements on the open sea.

Opposing Forces at the Battle of Lake Erie

		British	United States
Vessels	Corvette	1	
	Schooner	2	4
	Ship	1	
	Brig	1	2
	Sloop	1	3
Weapons	Long guns	35	15
	Carronades	28	39

> They had the fortitude to...stand serving their guns in battle for just one minute longer than their enemies—but that was the minute that really counted...

Perry's second-in-command was aboard *Niagara*, under orders to follow the second-in-line, *Caledonia*, which proved to be a slower sailor. This forced *Niagara* to hold back and, on seeing this, the British *Queen Charlotte*, which was waiting to engage *Niagara*, sailed out of line to join the *Detroit* hammering the *Lawrence*. At this point, *Lawrence* was taking a pounding from both *Detroit* and *Queen Charlotte*. To add to Perry's difficulties, the smaller British ships were now coming within range and joining in. For some 30 minutes Perry tried to maneuver his ship within range of her carronades, but by the time he achieved this, *Lawrence* was in a dreadful state, many men were wounded and the ship was badly damaged. Finally, at about 12.15 p.m. she closed sufficiently to bring her carronades into action, only to discover that the balls bounced off the sides of the stoutly built British corvette.

After about an hour the wind freshened slightly and the *Niagara*—which had now pulled ahead of *Caledonia*—came slowly into the fray. Perry—who was unscathed—now decided to transfer his flag to her, so he lowered the "Don't give up the ship" pendant, and, with five crew men, transferred from the *Lawrence* in a long boat. Seeing the pendant being lowered, the British thought that this signified

surrender and ceased firing. It was several minutes before they realized that the American national flag was still flying. The British reopened fire, but Perry managed to complete the transfer and, seeing him safely aboard *Niagara*, the remaining crew of the *Lawrence* hauled down the US flag and surrendered their badly battered ship. Meanwhile, Perry dispatched his second-in-command to bring up the schooners as soon as possible

Perry was now aboard a fresh ship, which up to then had only been lightly engaged. The British, who were dogged by ill luck throughout this episode, eventually lost the commanding officer and first lieutenant of every vessel involved, all having been either killed or so badly wounded that they had to be taken below. Perry had by now formed his vessels into a line and he steered *Niagara* to break through the British line, firing both broadsides and raking the nearest British vessels as he did so. This action, combined with the lack of senior officers to direct the ships, caused *Detroit* and *Queen Charlotte* to collide with one another. Minutes later, realizing that defeat was now inevitable, the British surrendered. Perry made his famous signal "We have met the enemy and they are ours: two ships, two brigs, one schooner, and one sloop." Considering the small number of men involved, the losses were heavy —British, 41 killed, 94 wounded; US, 27 killed, 96 wounded. These casualties indicated the ferocity of the fighting and its cost in human lives, but, as was customary with wooden warships, none of the vessels involved sank.

THE NAVY'S ACHIEVEMENTS 1793-1815

The War of the French Revolution and the Napoleonic War lasted from 1793 to 1815, with but two short breaks. During those 22 years the officers, men, and ships of the Royal Navy fought dozens of major battles and many thousands of minor engagements. They were not always successful, as the Battle of Lake Erie proves, and there were problems, including mutinies, to resolve. But, on balance, they won far more frequently than they lost and any unrest was usually settled. With only a few exceptions, it was always made clear by the lower deck that were the French to "come out" and fight, then there was no question but that matters would immediately return to normal.

Virtually all Royal Navy warships were very efficient fighting machines which, either singly or in combination in

a squadron or a fleet, outfought their enemies on most occasions. But, while the commanders may have received the glory and the riches, the whole system depended upon the sailors and Marines. They had the fortitude to withstand the boredom of the apparently interminable blockade duties, live in cramped accommodation that was perpetu-ally damp and infested with rats, stand serving their guns in battle for just one minute longer than their enemies—but that was the minute that really counted—and then leap aboard the enemy ship wielding cutlasses to set about the crew before they cheered their captain as he received his defeated opponent's sword.

Above: *Harold Wyllie's painting of the British and Franco-Spanish fleets at the Battle of Trafalgar, the greatest fleet engagement in 22 years of fiercely contested naval warfare.*

CHAPTER SEVEN

Scoundrels and Malefactors

The worst crimes committed on the seas were those involving robbery and murder when preying on merchant shipping. Both pirates and privateers put to sea with the specific intention of capturing merchant ships for direct financial gain.

However there was a huge difference between the pirate and the privateer. Piracy was a crime punishable by hanging; privateering was a lawful occupation.

Above: "Equity, or a Sailor's prayer before battle." The sailor prays that the fire of the enemy may be shared amongst the officers and crew in equal proportion to the prize money— the greatest part among the officers! In fact, officers walking the quarterdeck were at greater risk in battle than the men below deck at the guns.

Privateers

Privateers should not be confused with what were termed private ships. Both figure prominently in the Jack Aubrey novels. A private ship was a naval vessel that was not attached to a squadron or flag officer. It operated independently under "private" orders. Usually such ships were cruising frigates operating directly under Admiralty orders. They were not assigned in the fleet and stations lists to any fleet or squadron. The advantage of this to the captain, officers, and crew was that if they were fortunate enough to take a prize, they did not have to share the prize money

Prize Money

Once a prize had been condemned and lawfully sold, the prize money was allocated to the captors according to rank. The following table is based on a typical 38-gun frigate with a crew of about 300 including Marines. The flag officer would earn his eighth whether present or not. All ships within sight would also share in the prize money.

Prize Money Distribution until 1808

Rank	Proportion	Approximate amount per person per £1,000
Flag officer	$\frac{1}{8}$	£125
Captain	$\frac{2}{8}$ ($\frac{3}{8}$ if a private ship)	£250 (£375 if a private ship)
Commissioned officers	$\frac{1}{8}$	£25
Warrant officers	$\frac{1}{8}$	£7
Petty officers	$\frac{1}{8}$	£2-3
Remainder of crew including Marines	$\frac{2}{8}$	£1

After 1808, the distribution was changed. Captains earned $\frac{2}{8}$, of which the flag officer shared $\frac{1}{3}$. Commissioned and warrant officers' shares remained unchanged, but petty officers, crew, and marines shared $\frac{4}{8}$ of the proceeds.

with a flag officer, who would normally claim one-eighth. The station lists indicate that private ships were generally vessels cruising in the seas around Britain for commerce and fishery protection, sent on a secret or confidential mission, or were vessels undertaking exploration or hydrographic surveys. Cook, Bligh, and Flinders, for example, would have commanded private ships.

Privateers however were small armed vessels, often luggers, brigs, or sloops, although they were occasionally as large as small naval frigates. They were privately owned, usually by an individual or a small consortium. In many respects they were very much like naval vessels except that they were not owned by the state, nor—in the case of British privateers—were their officers and crews subject to naval discipline. They were usually fast, handy, lightly armed vessels. Their prey was merchant shipping so they needed sufficient armament to intimidate their victim but they had to be fast enough to run from more heavily armed ships that might be escorting a convoy. Privateers carried large crews so that they might have sufficient men to put a prize crew on the ships they captured, yet still be well enough manned to pursue other shipping. Privateers did not exist simply to annoy the enemy but rather to return a profit for their owners

This sounds very much like piracy, but there were important differences. Piracy was illegal. The privateer was licensed by the state to attack enemy shipping. This license was called a letter of marque. It specifically detailed the nationality of the vessels that the privateer could capture. Jack Aubrey sails as a privateer with just such letters of marque in *The Reverse of the Medal* and *The Letter of Marque*. Prizes, just like those taken by naval vessels, had to be legally disposed of through an Admiralty court. To deliberately stray from the letter of the license was to commit an act of piracy. A privateer could not attack and capture the ships of a friendly power, nor—unlike pirates—would the crew of a privateer either murder or rob their captives. Any privateer that did so would be considered a pirate and subject to the full force of the law. Piracy was a capital offense and there was only one penalty: hanging. Privateers were therefore very much like naval vessels except that they were subject to civil law rather than naval discipline. There was also an advantage to the state because it was spared the expense of the vessel's upkeep and its operational costs. These of course had to be covered by the ship's owner from the profits of a cruise.

Above: Merchant and naval shipping was at risk from predatory privateers that sailed with the specific intention of taking prizes. In this action, the packet Antelope is fighting with a French privateer, Le Atalante, in the Caribbean in 1794.

There were numerous British privateers, and it is surprising that so many were able to turn a profit as much of the merchant marine of Britain's enemies was swept from the seas during the Napoleonic Wars. British merchant shipping was plentiful and must have provided great potential for the French and, after 1812, American privateers. Many of the French privateers operated out of the Channel ports so that they might make a quick dash to sea, pick up prizes, and return. Some might cruise further afield and indeed several operated in the Indian Ocean out of the island of Mauritius. Mauritius was well placed as it flanked the routes taken by East India Company ships on their way to Madras as well as the return route from Indonesia. It was also within striking distance of ships using the Mozambique Channel when sailing north from the Cape to Bombay.

Privateers would operate very much like naval vessels cruising for enemy merchantmen. They would need to cruise off major landfalls along the usual shipping routes. The open

ward bound from India would pass through or usually to the west of the Azores. Shipping bound for the West Indies would either make a landfall off Barbados or Guadeloupe. Homeward-bound Spanish ships would usually make a landfall off Finisterre or Cape St. Vincent. Any privateer cruising to intercept British merchant ships homeward bound from Jamaica, might cruise between the west end of Cuba and the Cape of Florida and stand a good chance of sighting a prize. If, however, a convoy assembled first at Antigua, or Road Town, Tortola instead of sailing round Cuba, it would be more difficult to make an interception unless the privateer was well in with the point of departure. Once in the open sea and out of sight of land, even a large convoy would be difficult to find. These were the best cruising grounds for privateers but likewise they were where naval vessels would be stationed for the protection of commerce, often meeting a convoy and joining its escort to provide greater protection in the most dangerous waters.

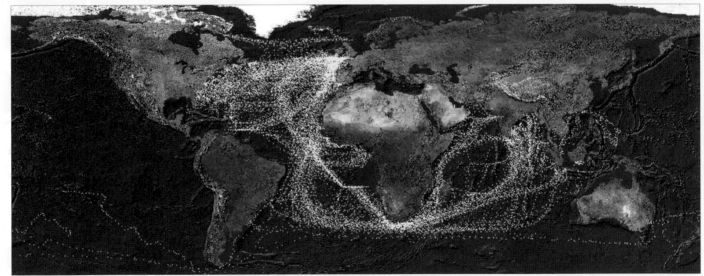

Right: Distribution of positional data for a selection of British vessels 1750-1785 showing the areas of the sea and routes favored by shipping. The data derive from daily logbook entries of Royal Navy warships and East Indiamen. The linear features clearly show typical trade routes. Clusters show concentrations of vessels off major landfalls such as the Channel approaches and the Cape of Good Hope.

ocean is so huge that the chance of meeting a prize in the open sea was extremely remote, even in the busiest shipping lanes. The best position to meet other ships was at the usual landfall any vessel would need to make after an ocean journey or a position where shipping routes would converge. The approaches to the English Channel were a potentially profitable cruising ground for the French. British merchantmen bound either to the West Indies or toward India passed near Madeira or the Canary Islands. Ships home-

Piracy

Piracy was all but eradicated by the beginning of the 19th century in the West Indies and North Atlantic. Other parts of the world, such as the Mediterranean and Indonesia, were much less safe. In the Mediterranean, shipping was subject to attack from the Barbary corsairs operating out of North Africa from ports such as Algiers and Tripoli. When ships were captured, their crews were usually sold into slavery. However, these corsairs were not like pirates in the

1804 one of the large American frigates, the *Philadelphia* under Captain William Bainbridge, was lured onto a sandbar off Tripoli where she stuck fast and was captured and her crew held for ransom. Shortly afterward, the *Philadelphia* was burnt by a boarding part led by Stephen Decatur. In August 1804, Preble in the *Constitution* took his squadron into Tripoli and bombarded the place. A treaty in which the Bashaw of Tripoli was "bought off" ended the conflict. The American attempt to eliminate the threat of the Barbary corsairs had proved too costly for a Congress reluctant to fund a war in the Mediterranean.

Other dangerous waters were those of the East Indies. Pirate vessels in these waters tended to be very small native craft that could usually be held off by any reasonably armed merchant ship. However, if a vessel was becalmed, it was possible for it to be overwhelmed in an attack by numerous heavily manned

Left: *British sailors boarding an Algerine pirate ship. Hand-to-hand fighting with cutlass and pistol was the most dangerous aspect of a sea battle. Against a determined enemy, casualties would be high. Pirates gave and expected no quarter, making the fighting hard and merciless.*

Below: *August 27th, 1816: a fleet under the command of Lord Exmouth in the Queen Charlotte bombards Algiers. With the war in Europe at an end, overwhelming force could be brought to bear against this stronghold of the Barbary corsairs.*

usual sense. Rather than being independent criminals, they were sponsored and protected by local rulers, such as the Dey of Algiers. The Dey was, in theory, subject to the Sultan of Turkey, as much of North Africa was part of the Ottoman Empire. Here, international law was complicated by diplomacy. The Ottoman Empire, though weak and disjointed, was nevertheless a power in the Mediterranean, having a small naval force, and therefore it figured in any alliance. It was not in Britain's diplomatic interest to take aggressive action to wipe out these pirates, as she did not need another enemy while at war with most of the rest of Europe. It was better to pay the tribute, a sort of protection money, levied by the Barbary corsairs. Action was taken against these pirates soon after the end of the war against Napoleon when the Royal Navy bombarded Algiers in 1816.

Only the Americans, unfettered by European diplomatic considerations, took any aggressive action against the corsairs before this time. Their Mediterranean squadron, under Edward Preble, retaliated against the corsairs. In

66 '...the exercise of the power of a master over his slave, must be supported by the laws of particular countries...such a claim is not known to the laws of England.' The Mansfield judgement released some 15,000 slaves in Britain. 99

vessels. East India Company ships were usually very well armed, and had the appearance of warships and so could often avoid attack. In areas where piracy was well organized, the navy took rigorous steps to stamp it out. In November 1809, two navy frigates with cruisers of the East India Company attacked Ras-al-Khyma in the Persian Gulf, destroying over 50 pirate vessels.

One did not always encounter pirates at sea, however, as the accompanying Eyewitness account illustrates.

Eyewitness

Log of John Douglas of the East India Company Ship *Dunira*, Captain Montgomerie Hamilton, at anchor Anjere Roads, Sumatra

30 April 1819, ...at 6p.m. Mr. Whiteman returned with the cutter and brought back the melancholy intelligence that Mr. Marsh (captain's clerk) had been murdered by the Malay pirates: they succeeded in bringing off the body; between 20 and 30 wounds were inflicted by spears and daggers in the corpse of this much lamented young man, although the injury was entirely unprovoked. 1 May 1819, ...at 9a.m., Captain Hamilton left the ship with three armed boats to Thwart the Way [Island] with intent to seize any remaining pirates, assisted with 2 boats by Captain Bunyan of the *Providence*. At 11a.m. sent a party of officers and men ashore with the corpse and interred it in the rear of the village. At 11p.m., Captain H. returned with the boats having destroyed two canoes and having seen 2 of the pirates, whom owing to the thickness of the jungle he could not overtake.

Slave Ships

During the Napoleonic Wars the hideous trade in black slaves from Africa to the New World was outlawed. Although slavery itself was not illegal and many of the British West Indian islands were economically dependent on it, trading in slaves by British subjects became unlawful in 1807. Slave ships were small vessels of between 80 and 200 tons burthen and carried between 200 and 600 slaves. Some vessels carried slaves as well as general cargo, while others were

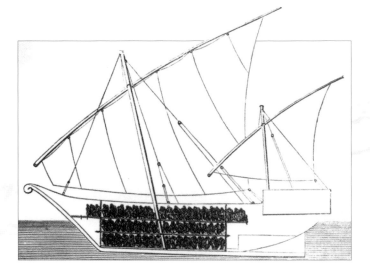

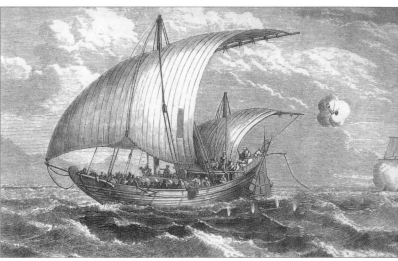

intended for slaving only. They were designed and rigged for speed, and were often fast schooner-rigged ships. Slaves needed to be transported to their destination as quickly as possible as the longer the voyage, the greater the mortality rate among the slaves was likely to be. The slaves were confined below decks in cramped and hellish conditions. Depending on the state of the wind and sea, the ship could cover anything from 50 to 250 miles a day on a voyage of about 5,000 miles. Therefore an average passage across the Atlantic would take about 20 to 30 days.

The route from West Africa, particularly from the Gulf of Guinea, was not direct. Any ship sailing to the West Indies, once clear of St. Thomas, the major island in the Gulf of Guinea, would sail south across the equator to take full advantage of the south-east trade winds, sail west below the equator before turning north to re-cross the line and then shaping a course for the West Indies. This avoided the worst of the doldrums and variable winds that would otherwise have hampered a swift passage. Other routes went to the southern United States or to South America. During the voyage, slaves would be exercised on deck in small groups providing the weather permitted it, as it was in the interests of captains to look after their cargo. This was not on the grounds of humanity but purely for reasons of profit. Bearing in mind the route and these other considerations, the best point to intercept a slaver was near her point of departure rather than in the open ocean or when she approached her destination.

The price of purchasing a slave on the African coast had risen from £3 in 1670 to £25 in 1800 (roughly the equivalent today of $2500-$3000). As long as demand for slaves was high, then profits were good. Humanitarian reaction to the slave trade developed fairly early in the 18th century and grew rapidly. Public interest was captured when evidence was published of the conditions on slave ships. In 1774, Wesley published his *Thoughts on the Slave Trade* and in 1783, the Quakers established a committee to petition Parliament for the abolition of slavery. In Britain there were strong legal arguments for abolition. Chief Justice Mansfield stated that "...the exercise of the power of a master over his slave, must be supported by the laws of particular countries...such a claim is not known to the laws of England." The Mansfield judgement released some 15,000 slaves in Britain.

In Parliament, William Wilberforce had been arguing that the British were a humane people and that this cruel trade was alien to their character. In the United States, all of the states north of Maryland abolished slavery between 1777 and 1804. However, anti-slavery sentiments had little effect in the main centers of slavery, those that were economically dependent on slave labor such as the plantations of the American deep South, the West Indies, and South America. Turning their attention to these areas British and American abolitionists began working in the late 18th century to prohibit the importation of African slaves into the British colonies and the United States. However, abolition was postponed due to the French Revolution and the wars that followed. Under the leadership of William Wilberforce and Thomas Clarkson, abolitionists succeeded in getting the

slave trade to the British colonies outlawed in 1807. Even though the British navy could not hope to police the seas effectively while still at war with France, the frigates *Solebay* and *Derwent* were despatched to the coast of Africa, and a token force was kept there until the end of the War. In the meantime, Denmark had already abolished the slave trade in 1803, the United States followed in 1808, Sweden 1813, Netherlands 1814, and France for the second time in 1818.

Yet abolition of the trade by Britain did not end slavery itself. The number of slaves taken from both West and East Africa continued to increase. In 1814, after the end of the Napoleonic War there was a new outcry. Petitions in Britain collected a total of 1.5 million signatures. As a result, during

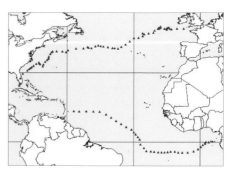

Above: *Track of HMS* Humber *in 1750 showing a typical southerly route from Africa to North America that slave ships also followed.*

the 19th century, Britain policed the seas with her navy in an attempt to stop the trade. Between 1825 and 1865, nearly 1,300 slave ships were captured and 130,000 slaves set free. Yet during the same period some 1.8 million slaves were transported. Slavery continued to exist even in British colonies like Jamaica. The trade had been outlawed but was not stopped, and slavery still existed in areas that were economically dependent on it. Parliament did not pass the Abolition of Slavery Bill until 1834.

Above: *The capture of the slaver* Boladora, *June 6th 1829. It was better to capture a slaver while she was empty of her cargo. Her fittings below deck would betray her occupation. The best course of action for the captor was to burn the vessel.*

> 66 *...extreme severity was usually a cloak for poor leadership and skill.* 99

Mutiny

The crew of any ship was a small floating community. It was a society with its own hierarchy, laws, customs, and professional language. Like society ashore, a ship suffered its fair share of petty crime, bad characters, and unsociable behavior as well as more serious crimes. The social welfare and the good behavior of the crew in the ships of the Royal Navy was the responsibility of the ship's officers. The captain himself was responsible for the conduct of the officers under his command. All of this was regulated by the Articles of War (see Chapter 4) and various sets of regulations and instructions that existed to underpin the lawful authority of the captain. It could be argued, therefore, that the navy's worst crimes, mutiny and desertion, were largely the fault of bad officers. This was certainly the opinion of John Jervis, Earl St. Vincent, with whom Jack Aubrey has an uncomfortable interview in *Post Captain*. St. Vincent was more severe with the officers of his fleet than the common seamen, but he would invoke without a moment's hesitation the severest penalties for mutineers.

The navy had been shaken by the great mutinies at Spithead and the Nore in 1797. The Spithead mutiny was over pay and conditions that had hardly altered since the 17th century. The mutiny had been largely settled, partly through the intervention of Lord Howe, when the Nore mutiny broke out. This mutiny was more militant in nature and more subversive to discipline. In the end the ringleader, Richard Parker and his followers were hanged. The mutinies shook the political establishment, already worried about the spread of revolutionary ideology from the Continent to Britain. The mutinies demonstrated how vulnerable the authority of officers could be, particularly the authority of unpopular officers, and how easily disaffected sailors could seize a ship. This is why in the months and years that followed, any mutiny in the navy's ships was dealt with quickly and severely.

Above: *Richard Parker was the leader or "delegate" of the Nore mutineers. This mutiny was more militant and dangerous than the one at Spithead. It had an immediate impact on the fleet of Admiral Duncan, tasked to deal with the Dutch fleet.*

Through Aubrey's Eyes

Jack Aubrey's thoughts on the subject of mutiny and sailors' reactions to a harsh and brutal captain are not as unequivocal as one might imagine. In *The Far Side of the World*, Aubrey discovers several *Hermione* mutineers serving with the Americans and takes them prisoner. In *The Reverse of the Medal*, he has the disagreeable duty of sitting on their court-martial, "this solemn farce," which is a mere formality as all the prisoners face the rope. In fact Aubrey feels quite uncomfortable throughout the whole of the proceedings. He reflects that had he been serving on Pigot's ship, then likely as not, he himself would have been swept up in the mutiny, not daring to support the much hated captain against a crew bent on murder and revenge. It was impossible to determine who had been innocently involved, and he wished that they had all been killed outright when taken.

In *The Mauritius Command*, O'Brian uses a conversation between Stephen Maturin and Cotton, the surgeon of the re-captured *Africane*, to inform us of the circumstances of Captain Corbett's death in the engagement between the *Africaine* and two French frigates. Corbett was such an oppressive and cruel officer that James' *Naval History* records that there was a rumor that Corbett's death wound had been inflicted by one of his own men. O'Brian not only uses the dialog to inform his readers of this, but also cleverly makes this fictional conversation the probable source of the rumor itself.

Cotton relates how after dressing a wound to Corbett's foot, the captain was taken back up on deck where he was again shot. Cotton does not know the exact circumstances of the shooting, but as Corbett's body disappeared over the side in the confusion of battle, he more than hints that one of Corbett's own crew may have done the deed.

However justified the Spithead mutineer's grievances were, particularly over pay and conditions, it should be noted that the mutiny was also about the removal of unpopular officers. Ideally a ship functioned like a patriarchal

society with the captain existing as a sort of father figure to
his officers and men. It was a community based on mutual
respect with discipline and order reinforced by the inter-
dependence of the entire crew in the safe running of the
ship. The greatest enemy to everyone on board was the sea
itself and survival depended on teamwork, discipline, and
skill. An individual sailor might desert his ship or commit
an act deemed mutinous, but when a large part of a crew
acted together to commit either mutiny or desertion, it was
the sign of a badly officered ship. Oppression and tyranny
in an officer might indicate an unbalanced mind, or simply
a cruel nature, but more often extreme severity was usually
a cloak for poor leadership and skill.

The "Black Ship"

The most famous mutiny in the history of the Royal Navy
was on the frigate *Hermione* in the West Indies in 1797.
Her captain, Hugh Pigot, was brutal to the point that he
would flog the last man down from the mast simply to
encourage the rest of the crew to be more brisk in their
duty. On one occasion, three seamen, anxious not to be
the last down from aloft under threat of punishment for
being last man down, lost their footing and fell to the deck.
Pigot ordered the dead bodies to be thrown overboard
without the least ceremony. This proved too much for the
disaffected crew who seized the ship, murdered all the

officers, and handed the frigate
over to the Spanish. The boats
of the frigate *Surprise*, Captain
Edward Hamilton, recaptured
the *Hermione* in 1799. The
mutineers were hunted down
for years after and many were
captured or discovered serving
in navy ships under false names.
In *The Far Side of the World*,
Jack Aubrey discovers several
Hermione mutineers from the
wrecked American frigate
Norfolk. In *The Reverse of the
Medai*, Aubrey sits at the court-
martial that condemns all the
men to death by execution.

Above: *On October 14th, 1799,
the boats of the frigate Surprise,
Captain Edward Hamilton,
boarded and recaptured the
Santa Cecilia, formerly the
Hermione, in Puerto Cabello
on the Spanish Main.*

Left: *The boarding and recapture
of the Hermione was one of many
such daring exploits in the
Napoleonic Wars. As her
name was charged with such
disgraceful memories of mutiny,
she was restored to the navy
as the Retribution.*

There were other captains who were, if not as brutal as Pigot, certainly as unappealing. In most situations men did not engage in mass mutiny without good reason. The captain and officers of a ship could drive a crew to mutiny by their behavior and there are a number of examples of officers whose behavior did little for the good of the service. When Robert Corbett first took command of the frigate *Africaine*, her crew, knowing his reputation, refused to serve unless another officer was appointed. They were persuaded to return to duty. However, their fears were vindicated as Corbett was later court-martialled for brutality. In *The Mauritius Command*, Barret Bonden returns to Aubrey's ship after having been flogged on Corbett's orders. Later when the

had not replaced him with the rather pathetic character of Lord Clonfert. Josiah Nesbit Willoughby was a daring but insufferably arrogant and reckless officer. It was he who actually commanded the *Néréide* and encouraged his senior officer Samuel Pym of the *Sirius* to engage the French at the disastrous battle of Grand Port in 1810. As a lieutenant in 1798, Willoughby had been placed under arrest for insolence to his captain, William Clark of the *Victorious*. When, after a short time, he was released from confinement, he refused to return to his duty until Captain Clark admitted that his arrest had been unjust. He was promptly court-martialed for contempt and disrespect and dismissed his ship. Again in 1801, he was court-martialed for insolence and contempt and this time dismissed from the service.

Insolence, and mutinous behavior was clearly not the exclusive preserve of the common seaman. Willoughby was reinstated in his former rank in 1803 after serving as a volunteer. In 1809, while commanding the sloop *Otter*, his admiral received a letter signed by the entire ship's company charging him with cruelty. He was reported to have said that he took as much pleasure in punishing a man as sitting down and eating his breakfast. A court-martial acquitted him, with the recommendation that he moderate his behavior. It is ironic that Robert Corbett sat in judgement at the enquiry.

Men like Pigot were unusual. However, there were rather too many officers like Corbett and Willoughby. Life at sea could be unbearable under stern officers, and it is this that accounts for the very high incidence of outright mutiny and the related crimes of mutinous expressions and mutinous assembly. Fortunately there were fair-minded officers in the navy as well. The *Otter* incident does demonstrate that the officers and crew of a ship had, at least in theory, recourse to senior officers,

Above: *The disastrous Battle of Grand Port, Mauritius, 1810 began as an attack on an anchored French squadron. All but one of the British frigates was run aground, burnt, or captured. The brutal J.N. Willoughby (top) commanded the Néréide during this battle.*

Africaine was in the Indian Ocean she met and engaged the French *Astrée* and *Iphigénie*. The *Africaine* was captured and it was rumored that Corbett had been shot by one of his own men. He in fact died shortly after his leg was amputated. The episode is dramatized by O'Brian in Chapters 8 and 9 of *The Mauritius Command*.

A brave and zealous but equally brutal officer would have appeared in *The Mauritius Command* if Patrick O'Brian

rather than to mutiny, if they were serving under a repressive captain. On an extended cruise in remote waters, a disaffected crew might feel the need to take matters into their own hands. The extract included in the Eyewitness box (right) tells of repeated attempts to seize a ship from its officers during the months of May to July 1799. The tension on board must have been unbearable for both the men and their officers.

Eyewitness

From the logbook of Lt. Augustus Brine commanding the brig *Hope* on the Cape Station

8 May 1799—off Madagascar, lat. 18:07 South
…at 9a.m. I was informed by one of the ship's company that a dangerous plan existed in the brig which was to confine the officers and take away the brig and run her back to St. Mary's [north-east Madagascar]….On this information being given every necessary precaution was taken by myself and the officers to prevent the intended attempt, and we waited all that day in expectation of their beginning for it was the decided determination of myself and the officers…to have put every man to the sword and to have worked the ship back ourselves to the Cape.

9 May lat. 18:31 South, long. 50:34 East
…at 9a.m., to show that I was acquainted [with the plot], by assembling the officers armed on the quarterdeck when I turned the hands up and after punishing Francis Foster…with 2 dozen lashes for being off deck in his watch, I seized and confined the remainder of the scoundrels [ten men in all]…without resistance from the ship's company.

2 July 1799 lat. 25:14 South, long. 40:23 East
From information that I received this morning from one of the prisoners, I find that the intended mutiny was of a more dangerous nature than I was aware of, that he feared they had not given up all thoughts of taking the brig. [A further eight men implicated]. These men were all at liberty and he advised me to watch them narrowly as well as the Quartermasters. If I had confined the whole of the ship's company, there would have been great difficulty in working the ship, the officers were therefore divided into two watches, armed with their servants who kept a constant and good lookout on those still out of confinement.

15 July 1799 lat. 29:57 South, long. 31:22 East
…a good deal of whispering among the people…at noon seized and confined James Gilbert and John Osborne two of the head men of the mutineers, having cause to suspect that they were trying to find an opportunity to let the others out of confinement, found it necessary to give orders to the respective officers having the watch over the prisoners and on deck to shoot any man who should come on deck when it was his watch below. Informed the ship's company…that any two of them who might be seen talking together before the main mast during the night would be shot.

22 July 1799 lat. 34:23 South, long. 25:15 East
…several officers were this day taken very ill, the symptoms violent reachings and pains in the bowels. The surgeon gave it as his opinion that an attempt had been made to poison us and what rather confirms the suspicion is that the two men Kinney and Thompson who refused to join the mutineers are also taken ill in the same way.

30 July 1799 At single anchor in Simons Bay, Cape of Good Hope
…came on board two parties of marines from HM ship *L'Oiseau* and *Camel*, confined the remainder of the ship's company at noon.

---

66 In most situations men did not engage in mass mutiny without good reason. The captain and officers of a ship could drive a crew to mutiny by their behavior and there are a number of examples of officers whose behavior did little for the good of the service. 99

Whereas some officers were clearly bad characters, or lacked authority or leadership qualities, the stress of command during a long war, and anxieties about one's career could also take their toll. One officer whose situation became too stressful for him to command effectively was James Athol Wood. In 1804 in the West Indies, he was relieved of the command of the *Acasta* by Sir John Duckworth who placed one of his own followers in command, forcing Wood to return to England as a passenger in his own ship. Wood naturally complained and called for a court-martial on Duckworth for oppression and illegal transport of goods. Duckworth declared that the goods (all forty tons of it) were presents. The charge, although proved in substance, was nevertheless considered malicious and Duckworth was acquitted. Wood suffered further distress by having his appointment to another frigate cancelled.

---

66 He was reported to have said that he took as much pleasure in punishing a man as sitting down and eating his breakfast. 99

Professional abuse by a senior officer and other disappointments caused such personal anguish that Wood's brother raised the matter of his professional mistreatment in Parliament. Utterly frustrated, Captain Wood vented his anger on the officers of his next ship, the frigate *Latona*. A complaint by the ship's master told of Wood singling officers out for verbal abuse, often shaking his fist in their faces. He made the master and a Marine officer perform their duty in such a way that they were deprived of sleep. He would issue orders that could not be performed and then threaten his victim with a court-martial for neglect of

against regulations and an officer could risk being dismissed the service. Captains could ignore a number of regulations if they chose to risk their careers. As noted above, Admiral Duckworth was accused and acquitted of transporting merchandise in the *Acasta*, which was strictly forbidden. He was certainly guilty even though he claimed the merchandise were all "presents." His superiors considered that no good would come from prosecuting an officer of his standing.

Officers were even known to falsify logbook entries, a very serious offense considering that logbooks were the chief source of evidence concerning the conduct of a ship in any court-martial. Officers might also commit offenses under civil as well as naval law. For example, Jack Aubrey is accused of fraud in *The Reverse of the Medal*. This incident is based loosely on the Stock Exchange fraud of 1814 in which Lord Cochrane, a model for many of the Aubrey stories, was accused of illegal trading in shares and dismissed the service. Cochrane became a mercenary admiral for the emerging states in South America, just as Aubrey does in *Blue at the Mizzen*.

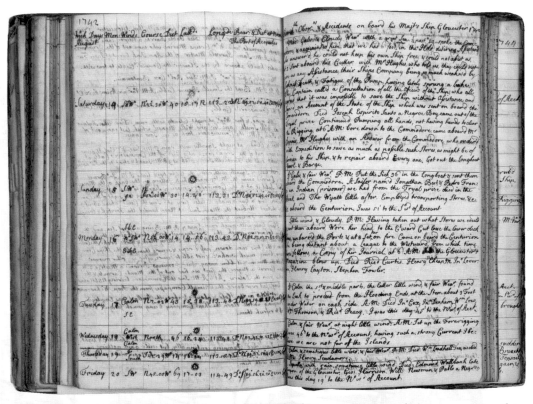

Above: *Logbooks recorded information on a ship's day-to-day proceedings. It would detail position, course, speed, weather, and any events worthy of notice. The log was important for navigational and legal purposes. It was a serious offense to falsify logbook entries.*

duty. Apparently the master's complaint came to nothing but Wood was held in low esteem by a number of senior officers. Even so, Wood served throughout the entire war but could not have commanded a happy ship.

There were a host of lesser offenses other than brutality for which ships' officers could be brought to account. A captain might keep a relative on the ship's books so that he earned "sea time," important for early promotion. The captain could pocket the relative's pay. Although keeping a false muster had been quite common in former times, it was

Desertion

A man might desert his ship for a number of reasons. Desertion during a sea battle was rare if not impossible, and was considered an act of cowardice for which the penalty was death. A sailor unhappy with his situation was more likely to desert when a ship was in port or, if there was an opportunity, to steal a boat or swim ashore. The man would have "R" or "Run" marked against his name in the muster book.

This was to distinguish him from those discharged, "D," or discharged dead, "DD." Shore leave was therefore only granted to those who were trusted to return to the ship. Statistics on naval manning and desertion indicate that during the 18th century desertion was rife.

It is likely that over 40,000 men deserted from their ships between 1793 and 1802, a total that accounts for nearly half of the men employed in any one year. Not only did this contribute to the already desperate problem of manning, but the scale of desertion suggests that many men deserted one ship merely to sign on board another rather than to escape entirely from naval service. By doing so they forfeited their pay and any prize money due from their previous ship, and possibly any rank or privileges they had acquired. Why would they do this? The answer is simple. Some wanted to escape a disagreeable situation, serving under officers who took no care of their welfare. Others might want to serve on another ship with former shipmates or with offi-

cers they knew and trusted. Ships were always short-handed so getting transferred was nearly impossible unless a senior officer requested a man, and even then a sailor's release had to be agreed.

Jack Aubrey often agonized about taking one of his former crew from another ship. Desertion was frequently the only way for a sailor to serve on the vessel of his choice. If a captain knew the man who wanted to join his ship, or if he was short-handed, the matter of the sailor's desertion from his last ship would be conveniently overlooked. Flogging a man whose skills and experience were much needed was against common sense and indeed many deserters were either not caught or had their crime overlooked. The severe penalty of flogging for desertion was therefore more of a deterrent than an absolute certainty. As a deterrent it clearly did not work, even when there was in prospect the most extreme punishment of flogging round the fleet (500 lashes or more) for the most persistent offenders.

> **❝ Shore leave was only granted to those who were trusted to return to the ship. ❞**

Above: *Most towns and cities had stocks and pillories where miscreants were sentenced to be publicly humiliated. In* The Reverse of the Medal, *Aubrey is sentenced to confinement in the pillory but is protected from harm by his friends and shipmates.*

Left: *Shore leave was a rare treat. A ship could spend months or even years on blockade duty. Once back in port, shore leave was restricted to those trusted to return. The attractions and amusements of the shore all too often lured the sailor from his duty. Too drunk to wander off entirely, he was often retrieved by his shipmates or officers.*

> 66 Hundreds of
> men...cooped up in a
> small wooden world
> afloat on a wide,
> empty ocean... 99

Of course this leniency did not hold true if a sailor deserted to avoid naval service, or if he joined an enemy vessel. He could then expect the most severe flogging or even hanging. British sailors found the American Navy very attractive and its ranks held many men who had served in British men-of-war. This caused all sorts of problems when Britain and the United States went to war in 1812. One of the main reasons for the war in the first place was the

ship were easily available and the Americans positively encouraged desertion, though not officially. The problem was further complicated by the very cosmopolitan nature of British crews. As well as British subjects, many Irishmen and Americans served in the Royal Navy. Many British officers had the attitude that no matter what a man's nationality, any period of service in a British warship gave them some sort of claim on his person. This is what made the

Above: The midshipman's berth was the home of future officers. Here they would study navigation, seamanship, and write their journals. At the same time it was a den for drinking, gambling, pranks, fights, and practical jokes. Any offense against the ship's laws would be punished.

routine stopping of American vessels by the Royal Navy to look for British deserters. The matter had almost led to conflict in 1807 when the *Leopard* fired on the American frigate *Chesapeake* and removed some of her men. It was an affront that injured the pride of the Americans, hence the extreme hostility encountered later by Aubrey while innocently in command of the much-hated HMS *Leopard.*

It was already difficult to determine whether a man was English or American, particularly as false papers of citizen-

problem of desertion to the Americans such a tricky issue. Once war broke out sailors would have faced the prospect of punishment for serving in an enemy vessel or the alternative of fighting against their countrymen.

Lesser Crimes and Misdemeanors

A ship was a floating community and, like any community on shore, was never entirely free of petty crime or unsociable behavior. Hundreds of men, many in their twenties,

Eyewitness

Log of Captain James Athol Wood,
HM sloop *Favourite*—12 October 1795

At 6 David Peters represented to Mr. Dawson the Gunner that Henry Washer the prisoner had requested him to go down into the hold and search under the ballast on the starboard side and he would find a tin case (like one the prisoner took out of his pocket and showed him). Agreeable to the prisoners direction, the said Mr. Peters found a tin case wherein was contained a watch that had been stolen some time before in the ship. From the gunner's making the above known to the captain he ordered him with Mssrs Johnson and Cumming, midshipmen to go down to the prisoner and have his hands secured until they could get a light but from their negligence and inattention to the Captain's orders, the prisoner had an opportunity of throwing the watch overboard.

it was important to keep the men at their work for good order to prevail. Logbooks would frequently record that the men had been "usefully employed" during the day. Bearing in mind the legal nature of the logbook, this record was important to show that the officers were doing their best to keep order. Unfortunately many of the tasks set would be of a very tedious nature, often routine labor to keep the ship trim, tidy, and well-maintained.

Theft

Theft was probably one of the more serious of the anti-social crimes on board a ship. It was subversive to good order and destroyed trust. As it was a crime against a ship-mate, it was not uncommon for the captain to let the crew

cooped up in a small wooden world afloat on a wide, empty ocean could not be expected to be model citizens. Confine-ment in such a cramped and overcrowded world inevitably led to boredom, drunkenness, gambling, and fighting which even the most disciplined regime could not hope to eradi-cate. In this context the general behavior of Jack Aubrey's crews seems far too good to fit the pattern of the time. An examination of the Royal Navy and the East India Company logbooks in the Napoleonic period clearly shows that there was always trouble of one sort or another. Insolence and drunkenness was very common, and it was not unusual for some member of the crew to be flogged nearly every week even in a well-run ship.

Offenses and punishments were recorded separately in the logs, as it was rare for a man to be punished on the same day as the crime as committed. The logbooks also indicate that shipboard offenses were most likely to take place when there was little to keep the men occupied. Petty offenses were more common in port or if the ship was at sea and the sailing was either easy or slow. As soon as the weather turned lively, the incidence of insolence, drunkenness, or misbehavior quickly declined. This is why

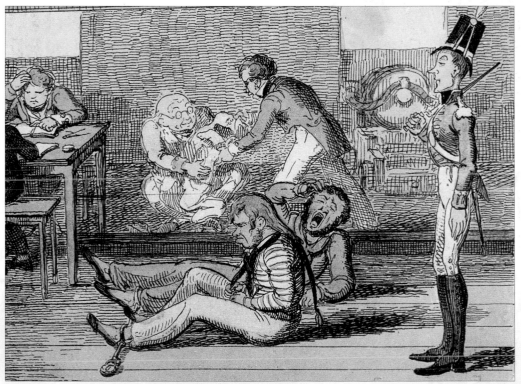

administer justice. This only formalized the existing justice of the lower deck. Some thieves were not simply criminals but spiteful people with no consideration for others' prop-erty, as the Eyewitness log entry (left) demonstrates.

As already noted, insolence and drunkenness were quite common. The latter often led to fighting or neglect of duty. Neglect of duty was particularly serious as the safety of the

Above: Being placed in irons was a convenient way of confining a prisoner prior to punishment.
Above top: The bosun's mate would perform public floggings on prisoners. At other times he would use a rope's end to "encourage" the sailors in their duty.

Below: *Mastheading was a minor punishment usually reserved for the midshipmen or "young gentlemen" when caught out in some prank or inattention to duty. It was most effective when the weather was rough.*

Right: *All officers and crew were expected to attend at punishment. The offense would be read out, the sentence declared, and the punishment administered to the roll of a Marine drum. The Marines were armed and assembled on the quarterdeck, a vantage point from which they could ensure that the sentence was carried out without interference from the prisoner's shipmates. This depiction of a flogging—entitled "The Point of Honour"—is by George Cruikshank.*

ship and its crew could depend on a good lookout or some equally important duty being carried out properly. Uncleanliness was another offense that was not tolerated. The crew were expected to keep themselves and their clothes as clean as circumstances allowed. This was to help prevent disease. In the mid-18th century, shipboard diseases such as typhus (sometimes called jail or ship fever), flux, dysentery, and scurvy had decimated the crews of ships on long voyages. Advances in diet and hygiene had lessened the problem considerably by the time of the Napoleonic Wars, and regular inspection was deemed essential in maintaining a healthy ship.

Punishments

Punishments for shipboard crimes could be varied depending on the nature of the offense, the character of the culprit, and any extenuating circumstances (see also Chapter 4). The captain was frequently both judge and jury and, after interviewing the offender in the cabin, listening to the circumstances and taking into account the character of the prisoner, would pronounce the nature of the punishment. An officer might be confined to quarters or stand a double watch. The common sailor might be dis-rated if he held a position of responsibility. He could be confined in irons, have his daily ration of rum suspended, or be ordered

Eyewitness

Log of Captain Charles Graham, William Pitt, East Indiaman—March 16th, 1816, Lat. 25:35 South, Long. 60:46 East

AM with the approbation of all the officers, punished Richard Symonds [ordinary seaman] for repeated thefts by marching him three times round the deck with the Rogues March playing and a halter round his neck, after which gave him four dozen lashes on the backside at a gun in the presence of all the crew. When punishment was over made him stand on the gundeck with the word Thief stuck on his back.

[Note: Symonds was presumably young as he was lashed, probably with a rope's end or cane, on the backside over the breech of a gun rather than flogged across the back.]

to clean the ship's heads. A captain would often try to make the punishment fit the crime. A man guilty of insolence might be gagged. A thief might have to run the gauntlet. Running the gauntlet involved the crew lining up in two columns each with a stick or rope's end. The offender would have to pass between the two lines and suffer a beating. The Admiralty abolished this punishment in 1806. A captain might still find a fitting punishment for theft. A young boy might be turned over the breech of a gun and publicly caned. As in the case of Richard Symonds on the *William Pitt* (see Eyewitness box above), some sort of public humiliation was expected to prevent re-offending.

Flogging was the usual punishment for any crimes deemed serious. The offender would be lashed to a grating or hatchway cover. It would be placed upright with the prisoner spread-eagled and tied to it. Something might then be placed in his mouth to prevent him biting his tongue. He would be lashed across the back and shoulders with a cat-of-nine-tails, an instrument made up of nine lengths of line, knotted along its length. A boatswain's mate would administer the flogging publicly in front of the officers and crew and would be replaced by another man once either six or a dozen lashes had been given. Officially there was a limit to the number of lashes a captain could award. The relevant Article in the *Regulations and Instructions Relating to His Majesty's Service at Sea* stated that:

"No commander shall inflict any punishment upon a seaman beyond twelve lashes upon his bare back with a cat-of-nine-tails according to the ancient practise of the sea. But if the fault shall deserve a greater punishment, he is either to apply to the commander in chief or inform the Secretary of the admiralty if the ship is at home in order to the offender being brought to a court martial…"

It is quite plain from the evidence of ship's logs and punishment books that this regulation was not adhered to. In many respects it was impractical. Putting aside for a moment the issue of the brutality of this sort of punishment, it is clear that the captain of a ship needed wide discretionary powers when awarding punishments. The extensive list of possible crimes and misdemeanors required a range of punishments of different severity. A prisoner might therefore be found guilty of several crimes at once. The act of making oneself drunk might inevitably lead to insolence and neglect of duty. A captain could therefore justify the award of three dozen lashes on the grounds that three crimes had been committed. It could further be argued that with persistent offenders, if a dozen lashes had not reformed them, then a more severe flogging was required. Life on board a British man-of-war could be harsh and brutal, particularly for those who transgressed the rules of naval discipline. However, it should also be considered that life ashore could be equally harsh and our attitude to the rigors of life at sea should be viewed in this context.

> **He would be lashed across the back and shoulders with a cat-of-nine-tails… A boatswain's mate would administer the flogging publicly in front of the officers and crew…**

Above: *The cat-o'-nine-tales would scar a man's back for life, an unmistakable mark of his profession.*

A Cast of Characters

Dramatis personae of the major characters and ships that feature in the Aubrey canon

Adams, David: clerk, secretary, and occasional purser to Jack Aubrey in a number of ships.

Ariel, HMS: a sloop—ex-French—commanded by Aubrey during the secret mission in the Baltic which involves landing Stephen Maturin on Grimsholm island; on the return voyage toward Spain she runs onto rocks on the coast of Brittany and is lost.

Aubrey, Charlotte and Fanny (Fan or Frances): twin sisters, the eldest children of Jack and Sophie Aubrey.

Aubrey, General: father of Jack Aubrey, a coarse throw-back to an earlier age and, as a result of his radical speechifying while a Member of Parliament, a severe impediment to his son's advancement.

Aubrey, George: son of Jack and Sophie Aubrey, and the younger brother of Charlotte and Fanny.

Aubrey, John (Jack): hero of the Aubrey canon, which covers his life, vicissitudes as well as triumphs, between his time as a master and commander (1800) to his eventual elevation to flag rank (1815).

Aubrey, Philip: Jack Aubrey's considerably younger half-brother, taken to sea by Heneage Dundas as a midshipman.

Aubrey, Sophie (Sophia): née Williams, much loved (but not infrequently betrayed) wife of Jack Aubrey.

Babbington, William: a well-connected naval follower of Jack Aubrey, who in the

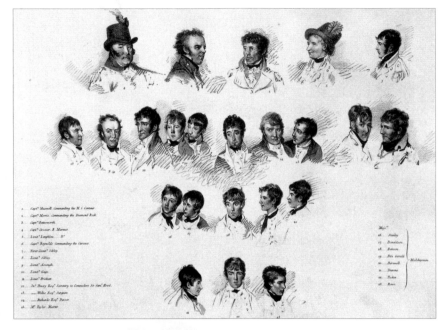

course of the Aubrey canon rises from midshipman to the verge of post captaincy.

Banks, Sir Joseph: a rich naturalist and politician (1743–1820) on one occasion given temporary rank as a post captain in the Royal Navy, and one of the real persons much admired by Jack Aubrey and Stephen Maturin. He was President of the Royal Society and accompanied Cook on his first voyage of discovery.

Barmouth, Admiral Lord: commander-in-chief in the Mediterranean in succession to Admiral Lord Keith, and in the estimation of Jack Aubrey a man better suited to command of a frigate than of a fleet.

Bertie, Admiral: commander-in-chief in South Africa (1775–1824), and the man under whose overall supervision Jack Aubrey is ordered to take Mauritius and Réunion but then denied the triumph of the resulting success.

Blaine, Sir Joseph: celebrated entomologist and intelligence chief, in the former capacity a colleague of Stephen Maturin and in the latter Maturin's primary contact with British intelligence.

Bligh, Admiral William: the celebrated navigator and seaman (1754–1817) best remembered for his loss of the *Bounty* to a mutiny in 1787, but also a good fighting officer who was finally appointed governor of the penal colony of New South Wales.

Boadicea, HMS: A 38-gun frigate which Commodore Aubrey commands during his campaign against the French off Mauritius in the Indian Ocean.

Bonden, Barret: Jack Aubrey's coxswain and right-hand man on the lower deck until his death in *The Hundred Days*.

Bowes: purser on the *Surprise* denied a

full naval career by his club foot but ever a volunteer for cutting-out parties, in the course of which he is fatally wounded.

Broad, Mrs.: owner of the Bunch of Grapes in London where Maturin keeps a set of rooms, and frequent provider at short notice of sustaining meals for Aubrey and Maturin.

Broke, Captain Sir Philip: the victor (1746–1841) of the celebrated frigate duel between the British *Shannon* and American *Chesapeake* in 1813.

Calamy, Peter: a son of a deceased former shipmate whom Jack Aubrey takes into the *Surprise* and *Worcester* as a midshipman.

Canning, Richard: a rich Bristol merchant who offers Jack Aubrey command of a privateer but is turned down and then becomes an admirer of Diana Villiers before being compelled by the scandal to move to India, where he forces a duel on Stephen Maturin and is killed.

Casademon, En Ramon d'Ullastret: Catalan godfather of Stephen Maturin, initially allied to the French until subverted by Maturin.

Christy-Pallière, Guillaume: French naval captain who captures Jack Aubrey in 1800 before becoming a friend and admirer, and later, as a royalist officer during Napoleon's "100 days" in 1815, an ally.

Clarence, Duke of: third son (1765–1837) of George III and an erstwhile shipmate of Jack Aubrey, and later a friend and supporter of both Aubrey and Stephen Maturin.

Clonfert, Lord: a well-connected but insincere shipmate of Jack Aubrey once dismissed from the navy but then reinstated, suspected of cowardice and finally allowing himself to bleed to death in hospital in Mauritius to avoid any form of commiseration from Aubrey.

Cochrane, Captain Thomas: the heir to the earldom of Dundonald, Cochrane (1775–1860) was a superb fighting seaman who is much admired by Jack Aubrey, but he is also severely hampered in the advancement of his naval career by his outright criticism of superiors and political opponents.

Colman, Padeen (Patrick): giant and somewhat slow Irishman taken up by Stephen Maturin, who cures his cleft palate and lack of English, and then makes him his servant.

Cook, Captain James: the explorer and navigator (1728–1779) much admired by Jack Aubrey for his seamanship and navigational skills.

Cuvier, Georges and Frédérick: members of a celebrated French family of scientists much admired by Stephen Maturin (Georges 1769–1832) (Frédérick 1773–1838).

Davies or Davis, Awkward: a very large and aggressive seaman who tries to follow Aubrey (often successfully) from ship to ship, and is thought by Aubrey to be a cannibal.

Day, George: gunner of the *Sophie* whose depressed cranial fracture is cured by the first of Stephen Maturin's several trepanning operations, and who thus gains the nickname "Lazarus."

Dillon, James: a wealthy Irish aristocrat and member of the United Irishman society fighting for Irish independence, and a dashing naval officer later killed while serving under Jack Aubrey's command.

Dray, Amos: a bosun's mate on the *Surprise* who, after losing a leg, becomes a servant of the Aubrey family.

Dubreuil: French intelligence agent operating in Boston at the time of the War of 1812; killed by Maturin.

Duhamel: French intelligence agent of dubious attachment to the French cause, who is instrumental in freeing Jack Aubrey and Stephen Maturin from captivity in exchange for Diana Villiers' huge diamond, which he later returns after reaching London. There he reveals the traitorous dealings of Wray and Ledward in exchange for a passage to Canada but he drowns while boarding the ship because of the weight of his money belt.

Dumesnil, Jean-Pierre (Pierrot): a nephew of Christy-Pallière and later opponent of Jack Aubrey in the Far East.

Dundas, Heneage (Hen): a close friend and naval colleague of Jack Aubrey right though the Aubrey canon. Fictional son of Henry Dundas (1742–1811), Lord Melville, First Lord of the Admiralty, and brother of Robert Dundas (1771–1851), also Lord Melville and First Lord of the Admiralty.

Dutourd, Jean: a French privateer captain and visionary with the idea of founding a utopian society in the South Seas before becoming the enemy of Jack Aubrey and Stephen Maturin in their South American dealings.

Fielding, Charles: a British naval officer and husband of Laura Fielding, held prisoner by the French but who manages to escape and make his way back to Gibraltar.

Fielding, Laura: virtuous Sicilian wife of Charles Fielding unsuccessfully pursued by Jack Aubrey and forced to spy by the French agent Lesueur.

Fox, Edward: a British diplomat send to the Far East in Jack Aubrey's ship to secure advantages in the area, but lost at sea while trying to make a hasty return to London to secure preference for himself for a treaty actually made possible by Stephen Maturin.

Garron, Lord: a midshipman in the *Lively* under Jack Aubrey; he later rises to higher rank and has his son accepted by Aubrey as a midshipman in the *Surprise*.

Gill: a pessimistic sailing master who serves under Jack Aubrey in the *Worcester* and then the *Surprise*.

Grant: an excellent but insubordinate junior officer under Jack Aubrey in the *Leopard*, and who disagrees with Aubrey's plans after a collision with an iceberg. He is permitted to take one of the ship's boats and other dissenters in a successful attempt to sail back to Cape Town.

Grimshaw, William (Bill): a sick man left ashore in the East Indies by another British ship and brought on board the *Nutmeg of Consolation* as Killick's assistant.

Hamond, William: captain of the *Lively*, whose command Jack Aubrey takes over so that Hamond can devote more time to his duties as a member of parliament.

Harding, William: first a master's mate in another ship, Harding later joins Jack Aubrey as an officer, remaining with him as a volunteer after the *Surprise* becomes a private ship.

Harte, M.: an admiral and the primary service opponent of Jack Aubrey in the first half of the Aubrey canon, before coming into an inheritance, changing his name to Dixon but remaining no more supportive of Aubrey than hitherto.

Harte, Fanny: daughter of Admiral Harte, who marries her off to the traitorous Andrew Wray rather than

William Babbington, Jack Aubrey's subordinate and friend.

Herapath, Michael: son of a loyalist American smitten by love for Louisa Wogan, impressed as a seaman after stowing away on the *Leopard* taking Wogan to Australia, and then rescued from an opium habit by Wogan before the pair settle in the USA.

Herschel, Caroline: unmarried elderly sister (1750–1848) of the celebrated astronomer Sir Frederick William Herschel (1738–1822), and a great aid to Jack Aubrey as he builds his observatory and telescope.

Hollom: a shipless midshipman taken on board the *Surprise* by Jack Aubrey but then detected in an adulterous affair with the wife of the gunner, who murders the pair.

Jacob, Amos: a Jewish doctor who accompanies Stephen Maturin on a secret mission in North Africa, providing information of various Jewish and Islamic sects in the region.

Jagiello, Gedymin: a Lithuanian cavalry officer in Swedish service, who is of great aid to Jack Aubrey and Stephen Maturin in their mission to the Baltic, but is then captured with the two British men and imprisoned in Paris before the trio escape to England, where Jagiello is suspected wrongly of having an affair with Diana Maturin.

Johnson, Henry (Harry): a wealthy American who becomes the lover of Diana Villiers in India before the pair travel back to London and thence the USA, where Johnson comes to believe that the British intelligence agent who has scuppered his plans for Louisa Wogan is Jack Aubrey rather than Stephen Maturin, whom he attempts to win to the American cause.

Keith, Admiral Lord: one of the Royal Navy's greatest commanders in the time of the French Revolutionary and Napoleonic Wars, Keith (1748–1823) and his wife Queenie (or Queeney) (1762–1857), who had been Jack Aubrey's unofficial mentor during his childhood, are great supporters of Aubrey.

Killick, Preserved: a querulous, mean-spirited, but loyal man who despite his many failings remains Jack Aubrey's steward throughout the Aubrey canon.

Kimber: a mining engineer whose fraudulent schemes for the extraction of silver from lead dross lead to severe problems for the Aubrey family at Ashgrove Cottage.

Ledward: a traitor who collaborates with Andrew Wray to aid the French, but the two homosexuals are betrayed by the defecting French agent Duhamel, flee to France, and are then sent to the Far East in the hopes of establishing a French presence in the islands off Malaya. They fall foul of Stephen Maturin and local interests and are assassinated.

Leopard, **HMS:** A 50-gun fourth-rate in which Aubrey is commanded to transport convicts, including Louisa Wogan, to Australia; she is pursued in the southern seas by the Dutch *Waakzaamheid* before striking an iceberg and struggling to Desolation Island where repairs are undertaken. She is later converted to a transport ship

Lindsey, Sir David: An ex-Royal Navy officer engaged as the commander of its naval forces by the rebellious southern faction who are attempting to free Chile from Spanish rule. Lindsey is contumacious and rash, and sees Jack Aubrey as a significant rival.

Lively **HMS:** a frigate that is Aubrey's first command in the rank of post captain and in which he helps to capture a valuable prize of Spanish treasure ships; the later distribution of the prize money, however, becomes something of a *cause célèbre*.

Martin, Nathaniel: a naval chaplain and naturalist who comes to play a prominent part in the Aubrey canon as a support for Stephen Maturin.

Maturin, Brigid (Brigit, Bridie, Brideen, or Breen): daughter of Stephen and Diana Maturin (née Villiers), a strange child generally left in the care of Clarissa Oakes and Padeen Colman.

Maturin, Stephen (Don Esteban Maturin y Domanova): Jack Aubrey's half-Catalan and half-Irish friend, a man who loves music and natural history and who sails with Aubrey as often as possible, especially when he can combine this with his other great task of working against Napoleon, the worst enemy of the freedom Maturin so dearly loves, as an agent of British intelligence.

Melville, Lord: Henry Dundas (1742–1811), First Lord of the Admiralty and an admirer of Jack Aubrey, whose career he seeks to advance despite the threats hanging over himself for supposed financial irregularities in fact resulting from his secret funding of the British intelligence service.

Melville, Lord: Robert Dundas (1771–1851), son of Henry Dundas from whom he inherits the title of Viscount Melville. Also First Lord of the Admiralty and an ally of Aubrey, he appears as a defense witness at Aubrey's trial for fraud.

Morris, the Hon. Mrs Selina: a friend of Diana Villiers involved in an illegal bookmaking business before running off to marry a man later discovered to be a bigamist.

Mowett, William (James): an important member of the followers who gather round Jack Aubrey and who move with him, whenever possible, from ship to ship as Aubrey's career develops; Mowett is an excellent seaman and also a good poet.

M'puta, Sally: a black women whom Aubrey as a midshipman conceals on the *Resolution*, leading to his disrating for six months, and the mother of Sam Panda.

Murad Reis: a celebrated captain commanding the treasure galleon of Sheikh Ibn Hazm, beheaded by his crew before they surrender to Jack Aubrey.

Nicholls (Nicolls): a lieutenant known to Stephen Maturin earlier in his life but appearing in the Aubrey canon as a man changed by an unhappy marriage into a drunk who is finally swept away after he and Maturin have landed on a small island.

Norton, Edward: a distant cousin of Jack Aubrey, who is offered a safe parliamentary seat by Norton. Aubrey inherits a considerable estate after Norton's death.

Nutmeg of Consolation, **HMS:** A 20-gun Dutch ship given to Aubrey by the Governor of Java, Stamford Raffles, and so renamed by him.

Oakes, Billy: a midshipman left in the East Indies to recuperate after an illness and then taken on board the *Nutmeg of Consolation* by Jack Aubrey as the starting point of the episode in which Clarissa Harvill is stowed away. She marries Oakes, who is later killed.

Oakes, Clarissa: a well-educated convict who as Clarissa Harvill is stowed away on Jack Aubrey's ship in New South Wales, is forced by Aubrey to marry her rescuer Billy Oakes, and later joins the Maturin household as a transformed person to help look after Brigid Maturin.

O'Higgins, Bernardo: South American revolutionary (1778–1842), the illegitimate son of Ambrosio O'Higgins, governor of Chile. Popularly known as the "Liberator of Chile," in conjunction with José de San Martin he led the northern faction seeking to secure the

independence of Chile from the Spanish; they engage Jack Aubrey as the commander of their naval forces.

Panda, Sam: Jack Aubrey's illegitimate son by Sally M'puta, Sam Panda travels to England from South Africa, meets Sophie Aubrey and Stephen Maturin, and later becomes a priest serving in South America, where he becomes confidential secretary to Bernardo O'Higgins, the independence-minded vicar-general of Spanish Peru.

Plaice, Joseph ("Old") and William: possibly meant be the same character, an elderly seaman who frequently serves under Jack Aubrey and is famously trepanned by Stephen Maturin after fracturing his skull.

Poychrest, **HMS:** ill-sailing experimental sloop that is Jack Aubrey's second ship in the rank of commander; she eventually runs aground on the coast of northern France and is sunk by gunfire.

Pullings, Thomas (Tom): one of Jack Aubrey's most loyal and capable followers, Pullings serves under Aubrey in both his naval and private capacities, and is eventually made post as captain of the 74-gun *Bellona*, in which Aubrey's hoists his commodore's pennant.

Raikes: a seaman who escapes from the accidental burning of *La Flèche* in Jack Aubrey's cutter but later dies of exposure and hunger, part of his corpse being eaten by some of the survivors.

Reade, William: a midshipman in the shipwrecked *Diane* who, injured in a Dyak raid on the island base of the stranded Britons, has an arm amputated by Stephen Maturin but makes a good recovery and remains one of Jack Aubrey's followers, often entrusted with command of the *Ringle*, Aubrey's fast-sailing private tender.

Richardson, Dick ("Spotted Dick"): a midshipman who possesses a great admiration for Jack Aubrey and is a sometime member of the older man's followers.

Rowan: a lieutenant who is exchanged into Jack Aubrey's *Worcester* and holds views opposite to those of William Mowett on poetry; he is another of Jack Aubrey's regular followers, and is present at Aubrey's pillorying on London in an effort to protect his senior.

St. Vincent, Admiral Lord: title of Sir John Jervis (1735–1823) after his great victory in the Battle of Cape St. Vincent, and one of the major figures in Royal Navy history in the period encompassing the French Revolutionary and Napoleonic Wars; he is opposed to the marriage of naval officers, and appears frequently in the Aubrey canon.

Saumarez, Admiral: James de Saumarez (1757–1836), a notably religious officer, he is Commander-in-Chief in the Baltic when Aubrey and Maturin carry out a secret mission in the *Ariel* to persuade Catalan troops on the island of Grimsholm to give up their allegiance to France.

Shape: the stockbroker of General Aubrey, who is used by Jack Aubrey for the share dealing that leads to his temporary disgrace and dismissal from the Royal Navy.

Skeeping, Mrs. Poll: a woman sailor, already known to Jack Aubrey as a previous shipmate, brought into the *Surprise* to look after the wounded and later encountered as a nurse at the Haslar Royal Naval Hospital.

Smith, Amanda: an unmarried lady living in Halifax, Nova Scotia who becomes Jack Aubrey's short-term mistress and whose love letters are later found by Mrs. Williams, Sophie Aubrey's mother, and shown to Sophie, causing a period of severe stress in the Aubrey marriage.

Somers, the Hon. Mr.: a well-connected and affluent lieutenant under Jack Aubrey's command in the *Worcester* but also an execrable seaman who makes as if to strike Aubrey, but is restrained before committing this capital offense and then transferred out of the ship.

***Sophie*, HMS:** A 14-gun brig-sloop that is Jack Aubrey's first ship as commander; he takes the Spanish privateer *Cacafuego* in her.

Stanhope: a British envoy who sails with Jack Aubrey in the hope of establishing amicable relations in the islands of South-East Asia, but who is prone to sea sickness; he is taken seriously ill and dies after being landed on Sumatra.

***Surprise* HMS:** A 28-gun small frigate in which he served as a midshipman, she is Aubrey's first permanent command as a post captain; she appears in the novel of the same name and either takes part in or is referred to in all the novels thereafter, initially as a King's ship, then—bought by Stephen Maturin—as a privateer operating under letter of marque, and finally as a ship hired by the navy.

Sweeting, Emily and Sarah (Sal): Melanesian girls rescued by the *Surprise* after being discovered as the sole survivors of a smallpox plague that has swept Sweeting's Island; the girls escape from an orphanage in New South Wales and rejoin the ship, becoming assistants in the sick bay before being delivered to Mrs. Broad of the Grapes Inn in London as god-daughters of Stephen Maturin.

Villiers, Diana: a widowed cousin of Sophie Williams (soon to be Mrs. Aubrey) and a notable beauty but of somewhat suspect moral character; she appears throughout the Aubrey canon in a number of capacities, and eventually marries Stephen Maturin and bears a daughter Brigid before being killed in a coaching accident.

Ward: Jack Aubrey's clerk in the *Surprise*.

West: a naval officer dismissed for duelling and who joins the *Surprise*, when operating as a private ship, as a mate; he is a good seaman for whom Jack Aubrey believes there may be a revived Royal Navy career, but he dies as a result of injuries received from the flying debris of an underwater volcanic eruption.

Whewell: a master's mate in the *Aurora*, and an expert in the transport aspects of the slave trade as a result of his previous employment on a slaver; he then becomes one of Jack Aubrey's followers, and later receives a lieutenant's commission.

Williams, Mrs.: the avaricious and stupidly ignorant but cunning mother of three daughters (Sophie, Cecilia or Cissy, and Frances or Frankie), and thus the mother-in-law of Jack Aubrey; at first comparatively affluent, she loses her money and becomes a dependent of Aubrey until killed in the coaching accident that also claims Diana Maturin's life.

Wogan, Louisa: an American agent separated from her husband and living in London until arrested and sentenced to deportation to New South Wales in Jack Aubrey's *Leopard*, which also carries Stephen Maturin to plant false information for Wogan to transmit in her letters home; Wogan is permitted to "escape" in an American whaler that arrives off Desolation Island.

Woods, Mrs. Christine: widow and naturalist, long known to Stephen Maturin and unsuccessfully wooed by him after the death of his wife Diana.

***Worcester*, HMS:** Ageing 74-gun ship-of-the-line of which Aubrey accepts temporary command for his mission to the Ionian isles as a way of escaping his worsening financial problems ashore; she is eventually sent to refit in Malta and Aubrey transfers to the *Surprise*.

Wray, Andrew: the senior of the two British traitors under the patronage of the Duke of Habachtsthal; Wray is a bisexual, and he and his homosexual partner Ledward are major opponents of Jack Aubrey and Stephen Maturin through much of the Aubrey canon until assassinated in the Far East, whereupon their bodies are dissected by Maturin so that they will disappear without trace.

Glossary

Note: For reasons of space the names of the various sails, masts, and yards are not included in this Glossary; instead illustrations of them can be found on pages 59-65.

aback: said of a sail that is being backed (i.e. trimmed so that the wind strikes its front side) to slow the ship or facilitate tacking; if variable wind or poor helmsmanship brings the ship to a stop, she is said to be **taken aback**, or, if tacking, **in irons**

abaft: aft of a given location on a ship

abaft the beam: indication of a position between a ship's **beam** (i) and her stern

abeam: opposite the center of a ship's side

abel-wackets: a seamen's game of forfeits; the loser received a blow with a knotted rope or kerchief

about: the position of a ship after she has tacked, or gone about

acockbill: having yards out of alignment; by extension, being out of place

Admiral of the Narrow Seas: a drunk man who vomits into the lap of one sitting opposite him

aft: behind, near the stern of a ship

Albany beef: British seamen's name for the North American sturgeon

all a-hoo: in disorder, perhaps from "all anyhow;" like **all a-tanto**, this favorite phrase of Aubrey's may be of O'Brian's own coinage

all a-tanto: all ship shape; perhaps from "all taut"

aloft: at the mast head or in the higher yards and rigging

amidships: the middle of the ship, either in regard to her length or breadth

amuse: to practice deception

anti-guggler: a hollow tube used surreptitiously to suck drink from a cask

ask bogy: see **ask my arse**

ask (or **ax**) **my arse** or **ask bogy:** said in answer to an impertinent question

astern: behind the ship

athwart: at right angles to a ship's course

athwartships: running across a ship from side to side

backing: a wind is said to be backing when it shifts in a counter-clockwise direction (to one looking into the wind)

backstays: ropes extending aft from mastheads to the ship's sides, supporting the masts against forward strain

banyan days: days when seamen were served no meat; the name derived from the East Indian "Banian" sect of Hindus, who neither kill nor eat animals

baptized: said of any hard liquor diluted with water

barge: (i) a 14-oared boat, principally used to convey senior officers; (ii) the dish for bread or biscuit on the mess table

bark(e)y: affectionate term used by seamen for their ship; from "bark," an early term for any small vessel, or **barque**

barque (US: bark): properly a three-masted vessel, square-rigged on the fore and mainmasts and fore-and-aft rigged on the mizzen; the term is often used loosely, especially in non-specialist literature

beakhead: see **heads**

beam: (i) measurement across the ship at her widest part; (ii) a timber that runs horizontally across the ship, supporting the deck

beam ends: a ship is on her beam ends when listing at an extreme angle so that her **beams** (ii) are near-vertical and she is in danger of capsizing (see **capsize**)

bear up: to change course so that the ship may run before the wind

before the mast: the state of being a common seaman, whose berth was in the **forecastle**; an officer or petty officer who was disrated was said to be "turned before the mast"

belay: (i) secure a rope by turning around a belaying pin; (ii) an order to cease or disregard

bend: to fasten to, or make fast

best bower: see **bower anchors**

betwixt (between) wind and water: at or near the waterline on a ship's hull

bible: (i) a bosun's axe; (ii) a large **holystone**

bight: (i) a loop or slack part in a rope; (ii) a large bay

"Billy Blue": Admiral Sir William Cornwallis (1744-1819), from his predilection for the **Blue Peter** flag; also nicknamed "Coachee" or "Mr Whip," from his rubicund and weathered complexion like that of a stagecoach driver

"Billy Ruffian": HMS *Bellerophon*

binnacle: the wooden housing for the ship's compass, usually situated beside or before the wheel

binnacle words: pretentious language; seamen would offer to chalk "affected" words on the binnacle

bitter end: the free end of a line

"Black Charley" or **"Mad Charley":** nickname for the bold but eccentric Captain (later Admiral) Sir Charles Napier (1786-1860)

"Black Dick": Admiral Richard Howe, Earl Howe (1726-99)

blanket hornpipe: sexual intercourse

blessing: a bonus; an extra portion

Blue Peter: a signal flag, blue with a white square in the center, hoisted on the foremast to signify immediate departure

bone: to acquire by stealth

boom: a **spar** extending the foot of a sail

bow or **bows:** the front end of a vessel

bower anchors: the two largest anchors carried permanently attached to their cables, the "best bower" to starboard and the "small bower" to port

bowline: a rope made fast to the sides of a sail to pull it forward so that it is steady when the ship is **close-hauled**

bowsprit: (i) a large **boom** running out from the **stem** to which the foremast **stays** are secured; (ii) the nose

box-haul: a method used in an emergency of making a ship turn on her heel by allowing her to make sternway

box the compass: (i)to demonstrate familiarity with all the **points** of the compass; (ii) to drift aimlessly, as when a ship loses steerage and faces successively in all directions

box the Jesuit: to masturbate

brace: a rope attached to the end of a **yard**, by means of which the yard may be **braced** in order to trim the sails

breaming: cleaning the ship's bottom by burning off marine growths while she is **careened**

brig: a two-masted vessel square-rigged on both masts

brigantine: a two-masted vessel, square-rigged on the foremast and fore-and-aft rigged on the mainmast

bring him to his bearings: make him see reason

bring to: to bring to a halt

bring your arse to anchor: sit down

broke: said of an officer condemned by court-martial to lose his commission

Brother Jonathan: an American

building the galley: a practical joke played on a new hand, in which seamen were made to lie on deck in the form of a ship; the victim was told he represented the figurehead and placed at the **heads**—and, on pretext of the figurehead being gilded, had his face smeared with excrement

bulkheads: the partitions in a ship

bum boat: small boat for carrying fresh food and other luxuries for sale to ships at anchor; the original "bum boats," in the 17th century, were also used to remove ordure and other garbage from ships in an anchorage

bunt: the center of a square sail

buntline: a rope used when **reefing**

burgoo: (i) oatmeal porridge; (ii) a "porridge" made of ships biscuit and molasses

burned or **burnt**: having a venereal disease

by and large: *see* **close-hauled**

(to go) by the board: to go over the side of the ship, as does a falling mast

cable: (i) the rope securing ship to anchor, and by extension any large rope; chain cable was sometimes used from c.1800; (ii) a nautical measurement of 100 fathoms (200yd)

Campbell's Academy: prison hulks; from their first superintendent

cant: to throw

capsize: (i) of a ship, to overturn; (ii) to fall down, as "he got drunk and capsized"

captain's servant: until 1796 (when it became Volunteer, First Class), the rating of a boy prior to becoming a midshipman

carcass: a hollow missile filled with combustible materials

careen: to tilt a ship on one side in order to work on, clean, or caulk the other; ideally done at a **careenage**, a steeply sloping, sandy beach

carry away: a mast, yard, or rope that breaks was said to "carry away"

catheads: (i) short, stout timbers projecting over the bows on either side of the **bowsprit** and housing the anchors; (ii) a woman's breasts

chains: the narrow projections on each side of the ship to which shrouds are secured and on which the leadsman stood when heaving the **lead**

chasse-marée: a French coasting vessel, usually employed in smuggling or privateering

Chatham Chest: a seamen's benevolent fund established since 1590 and merged with Greenwich Royal Hospital in 1814

cha(t)ts: lice

chowder or **chouder**: a stew with layers of fresh fish, salt pork, and sea-biscuit

clap on: to add something, as to hoist more sail

clews: the bottom corners of a square sail, or the aftermost corner of a fore-and-aft sail

clipper: from c.1812, a term for a fast sailing ship

close-hauled: sailing as near to the wind as possible with all sails drawing full; also called sailing **by and large** or **full and by**

Closh: a Dutchman; corruption of the common Dutch name "Claus"

club-haul: a method of tacking in an emergency which involved letting go the lee anchor and cutting its cable when the ship paid off

coach horses: the crew of a **barge**

coamings: raised sections around hatchways to prevent water getting in

cobbing: a punishment administered by seamen among themselves; the malefactor was beaten across the buttocks with a stick or rope's end

cockpit: the area beneath the lower gundeck which formed the surgeon's operating theater during action

condemnation: the judgement of a Prize Court that a captured vessel or her contents shall be confiscated

corvette: a type of small frigate

crank: said of a ship that is unstable when sailing

crocus: a surgeon (from "to croak" = "die")

crosstree: a horizontal timber that spreads the shrouds

"Dead Louse": HMS *Daedalus*

dead reckoning: determining the position of a ship without recourse to celestial observation; it is done by deduction from the ship's last conventionally determined location, making allowance for course, distance logged, drift, and **leeway**

decks: the various "floors" of a ship; those of a three-decker, from lowest to highest, were the orlop, lower deck, middle deck, main or spar deck, quarterdeck, and poop deck

docking: a punishment administered by seamen to a whore believed to have spread venereal infection; her clothes were cut off and she was thrust naked into the street

doldrums: a sea area near the Equator, out of the trade winds, where ships were likely to be becalmed; *see also* **horse latitudes**

earings: the upper corners of a square sail

(en) flûte: a ship was said to be *en flûte* when some of her guns were removed or relocated to make space for passengers or cargo

expended: slang term for killed in action

fathom: a measure of six feet used in describing depth, lengths of cable etc.

Fiddler's Green: the sailor's mythical heaven, where rum and tobacco are free and inexhaustible

fin: the arm

fir frigate: any one of the classes (some 50 ships in all, up to 1814) of frigates constructed of (largely Canadian) pine wood

flemish: to coil a line in a neat spiral on deck

flip: a mixture of small beer and brandy, flavored with sugar and lemon; *see* **"Sir Clowdisley"**

flotsam: floating wreckage or cargo from a sunken ship; *see also* **jetsam**

foot: the lower edge of a square sail

foot rope: a rope running below a **yard** and supporting the feet of seamen while **reefing**

fore and aft: running from **bow** to **stern**; the opposite of **athwartships**

forecastle (fo'c'sle): the area beneath the short, raised deck near the ship's **bow**; formerly a fighting platform, it became the location of the crew's quarters

"Foul Weather Jack": Admiral John Byron (1723-86), notorious for ill-luck with weather

full and by: *see* **close-hauled**

furling: bundling up a sail and securing it to a **yard**

futtock: a curved timber making up the rib of a wooden ship

futtock shrouds: small **shrouds** which secure the futtock plates of topmast rigging to a band around the a lower mast

gammoning: the skilled process of binding the rope that secures the bowsprit to the **stem**

gig: a four- or six-oared ship's boat

gingerbread work: carved and gilded embellishment to a ship's woodwork

give way: order for rowers to begin pulling on their oars

grog: rum and water; in 1740, Admiral Vernon, **"Old Grog,"** decreed that the pint of rum issued to a seaman each day should be diluted with two parts of water

ground squirrel: a pig

guffies: Marines

gunwale: the top edge of the side of a vessel; pronounced "gunnel"

halyards (halliards; haulyards): the ropes employed to hoist or lower **spars**, **yards**, or sails

haul the wind: to direct a ship to sail nearer to the direction from which the wind is blowing

hawse: (i) the area around the ship's **bow** containing the hawse-holes, through which the anchor cables pass; (ii) when anchored, the distance between the ship's bow and the anchor

head: the upper edge of a square sail

heads: seamen's lavatory, situated in the farthest forward part of the ship, the beakhead, forward of the **forecastle**; the term remains current

head rails: the teeth

heave to: to come into the wind with the minimum sail area exposed, and thus make no headway; a maneuver normally used to wait out rough weather

hen frigate: a warship in which the captain (as sometimes occurred) had his wife aboard and, it was cynically said, was ruled by her

herring pond: the North Atlantic ocean

hoist the blue flag: to leave the sea and take a public house; publicans traditionally wore blue aprons

holystone: a soft stone used by sailors for cleaning the wooden deck of a ship after it had been sluiced with water

horse latitudes: sea areas around c.30° North and South where ships were often becalmed and jettisoned livestock; it was supposed that the floating carcasses of horses might be encountered

hound: a projection or cheek below the masthead which supports the **trestletrees**

hull down: said of a vessel so far distant that—because of the curvature of the Earth—only her upperworks are visible; if her decks can be seen, she is **hull up**

in altitudes: drunk

in irons: *see* **aback**

Jack of (or **in) the dust:** the purser's mate responsible for the bread room, where flour was stowed.

Jack Nastyface: an ordinary seaman; a nickname current well before William Robinson (a deserter from the Navy in 1811) adopted it for an anti-naval publication in 1836

Jack Tar: *see* **tar**

jetsam: floating objects that have been deliberately thrown overboard, so as to lighten ship

jib: a large triangular sail set on a forward stay

Johnny Crapaud: a Frenchman

jolly: the **heads**; from c.1820, a Marine

jolly-boat: a six-oared ship's boat; the name's derivation is obscure, but it has nothing to do with Marines

jury leg: a wooden leg; *see* **jury rig**

jury rig: a temporary fix, as in a "jury mast" improvised from a stout **spar**, made out of necessity; perhaps from the French *journée*, "day" or "for a day"

keel: the bottom-most **fore-and-aft** timber of the ship, on which its entire framework depends

keelson: the line of timbers joining the **keel** to the upper framework

killick: originally a small anchor; post-1850, slang for a leading seaman's rating; noted here as a light on "Preserved Killick"

King Arthur: a seamen's game of forfeits; the loser had buckets of water thrown over him

(to) kiss the gunner's daughter: to be tied over a gun barrel and beaten on the buttocks, the usual punishment for boys aboard; hence the phrase "over a barrel" = "in an unpleasant position"

knot: a measure of ship's speed in

nautical miles per hour; so-called after the knots tied at regular intervals in the log-line

ladder: stairs aboard ship

Lady of the Gunroom: seaman assigned as a kind of batman (US: striker) to midshipmen

larboard: the **port** side (left, facing the **bow**) of a ship, possibly from Norse *hlada bord* or Old English *laddebord*, both meaning "loading side;" until 1844 this name was officially preferred to **port**

lateen: a triangular sail set on a very long **yard**

lead: a weight attached to a lead-line for determining the depth of water

leeches: the outer edges of a square sail

lee shore: a shore that lies on the **lee side** of the ship, which thus may be endangered by being blown toward it

lee side: the sheltered side of the ship; i.e. the opposite side to that on which the wind is blowing—*see also* **weather side**

leeway: the distance that wind or tide send a ship to leeward of her course

lie rough: to be obliged to sleep on deck

lifts: *see* **puddening**

live lumber: seaman's term for landmen aboard ship

loblolly boy: surgeon's assistant; from an old word for water gruel

lobscouse: a stew of salt meat, potatoes, broken biscuit, onions, and pepper; it came to be particularly associated with the port of Liverpool, whose inhabitants are still called "Scouse(r)s"

lobster: a soldier, from his red coat

log: an instrument used to measure the speed of a ship through the water

loggerhead: a tool—an iron ball on a long stave—for heating pitch; it made a handy weapon in a quarrel, hence "at loggerheads" (meaning violently opposed)

longboat: the ship's largest boat, usually fitted with a mast and sails

lubber: an unhandy or inexperienced seaman

luff: an order given to a helmsman to bring the ship's head up closer to the wind

marine officer: seaman's term for an empty bottle, implying the uselessness of Marines; by the 20th century, the usual term for an empty bottle was "dead marine"

marline spike: a pointed metal rod about 16in in length, used to separate strands of rope when splicing

messmate: comrade; one who eats at the same mess table

(the) more you cry the less you'll piss: traditional seaman's comfort on leaving his sweetheart

miss stays: to fail when going about from one tack to another

mizzen (mizen): the aftermost mast; the name probably derives from the French *misaine* or Italian *mezzana*—although both of these words mean "foremast"

nip-cheese: a purser, from his supposed pilfering of seamen's rations

offing: the distance from the shore maintained by a ship in order to minimize navigational hazards

"Old Grog": Admiral Edward Vernon (1684-1757), characterized by his boat cloak of grogram material, who also gave his nickname to **grog**

"Old Ironsides": USS *Constitution*, supposedly so named in 1812 when shot from HMS *Guerrière* failed to pierce her timbers; the nickname had earlier been given, for similar reasons, to more than one British warship

"Old Jarvie": Admiral John Jervis, Earl St. Vincent (1735-1823)

oldster: an experienced seaman of any age

orlop: the lowest deck of a ship

painter: rope securing a boat to a ship or quay

pay: to apply pitch or tar as a preservative to a seam ("the devil to pay" refers to a not easily accessible seam in the hull), mast, yard, or hull

(to) pay debts with the topsail: to go to sea leaving debts unpaid

people: a ship's company (excepting officers and petty officers)

pilot: a navigator expert in local conditions, often taken aboard to bring a ship into a port or anchorage

pinnace: an eight-oared (sometimes sixteen-oared) ship's boat, also fitted with a mast and sails

piping hot: newly served (and thus hot from the galley), as announced by the boatswain's pipe

pitching: the up and down motion of a ship in a **fore-and-aft** direction

point: the divisions of a compass; there are 32 points around the 360° circle, eight dividing each right angle between the the the cardinal points of North, South, East, and West

polacre: a Mediterranean type of **brig;** the three-masted version was often **lateen**-rigged on the fore and mizzen-masts

poop: the aftermost, highest part of a ship's hull

pooped: a ship is pooped when a high, following sea breaks over her **stern**

port: the left side of the ship, looking toward the **bow**; until 1844, officially called the **larboard**

pram (praam; prame): (i) a small rowing boat; (ii) a small flat-bottomed warship of 10-20 guns, used by the French for coastal defense

puddening: (i) matting used to prevent chafing; (ii) rope-work to prevent **yards** from falling if their supporting ropes (**lifts**) were severed in battle

pump ship: to vomit

quarterdeck: the portion of the upper deck **abaft** the mainmast

quarters: those parts of the **stern** within 45° of dead **astern**; an object not directly astern is described as being on the port or starboard quarter

quid: a mouthful of chewing tobacco

rake: to fire at a ship along her longitudinal axis to create maximum damage and injury

ratlines: small ropes across the **shrouds**, forming a kind of rope ladder for men going aloft

razee (rasee): said of a ship that has

been cut down by one deck

reef: a horizontal section of a square sail that can be rolled up to lessen the area of sail exposed to the wind

reefing: reducing the area of sail exposed to the wind by rolling up part of the sail

roadstead: an offshore anchorage

roll: the rocking motion of a ship from side to side

round robin: a petition drawn up by seamen; the signatures (or marks) were inscribed in a circle so that no "ringleader" could be discerned

running rigging: all ropes used in working the sails; *see also* **standing rigging**

salmagundi (salmon-gundy): cured fish (pickled herring or anchovies) minced with onions and dressed with lemon juice; minced veal or fowl might be used

salt eel: a rope's end used to administer punishment

salt junk: salt beef

schooner: a **fore-and-aft** rigged vessel, originally (c.1710) with two masts

sea lawyer: (i) a shark; (ii) an opinionated, argumentative seaman; this meaning was current from c.1820

sea william: a civilian

shallop: a small rowing (two-oared) or sailing boat

sheet anchor: the largest spare anchor carried aboard

shifting ballast: seaman's term for non-naval passengers aboard

shindy: a dance

ships' biscuit: hard, flat cakes of bread (*see also* **tommy**) with a life of as much as twelve months; it was not called "hard tack" until c.1840

ship shape: all in order

shrouds: ropes in the **standing rigging** that extend from the masts to the sides of the ship

sill: timber forming the top or bottom horizontal of a ship's square port

"Silly Billy": Prince William Henry, Duke of Clarence (1765-1837), later King William IV (reigned 1830-37), a career naval officer noted for rigid discipline rather than seamanship

"Sir Cloudesley": the drink **flip**; Admiral Sir Cloudesley Shovel (1659-1707) was said to have been inordinately fond of it

skylark: to indulge in moderate horseplay, as in "all hands to dance and skylark"

slings: ropes extending from a masthead to the center of a **yard**, used in conjunction with **lifts** and **halyards** to control the vertical movement of the yard

sloop: originally a single-masted **fore-and-aft** rigged vessel, but by Aubrey's time the definition had changed—there were two classes of sloops of war: the ship sloop (three masts) and the brig sloop (two masts), both of them square-rigged

slops: clothing for sale aboard ship—fit was approximate, hence the word "sloppy;" derived from the Old English *sloppe* or *slype* = baggy breeches

slush: fat skimmed from a pan in which meat was boiled, a cook's perquisite sometimes used to make candles

smart money: financial compensation for injuries incurred aboard

snow: a large, **brig**-rigged, two-masted merchant vessel found only in European waters

soldier's wind: a wind on the **beam** that makes sailing easy

son of a gun: seamen's term for a male child born aboard; by extension, a bastard

son of a sea-cook: term of abuse implying bastardy

spar: a general name for any wooden support—a mast, yard, boom etc.—for the rigging

Spithead nightingales: the bosun's mates, who conveyed orders by calls on their pipes; sometimes the pipes themselves were called by this name

spliced: married; from the joining or splicing of two ropes

standing rigging: rigging that supports the mast, as opposed to **running rigging**

starboard: the right side of the ship (looking toward the **bow**); the name may come from "steer-board," dating from the period when a steering oar was used rather than a rudder

start: to start a seaman was to urge him on with blows

stays: ropes in the **standing rigging** that run **fore and aft**, supporting the masts; they are named from their position, as **fore stays**, **back stays**, and so on. *See also* **miss stays**

staysail: a triangular sail set on a stay

stem: the "pointed end" of the ship; properly, the timber which unites the two sides of the ship at the fore end

stern: the rear ("blunt") end of the ship

swabs or **swabbers:** unhandy seamen, fit only to clean the ship

swipes: small (i.e. fairly weak) beer

tack: to go about, to change course from one board to another, by turning the ship's head through the wind

taken aback: *see* **aback**

tar (Jack Tar): an ordinary seaman; from his waterproof tarpaulin (tarred canvas) hat and trousers

tarry-breeks: as above; before Jack Aubrey's time, this term sometimes denoted an officer who had risen from the ranks

tartan (tartane): a small, single-masted Mediterranean trading vessel

toasts: in addition to the nightly drinking of the Sovereign's health after dinner, naval officers had traditional toasts for each day of the week. They were: Monday—"Our ships at sea;" Tuesday—"Our native land;" Wednesday—"Ourselves and no one like us;" Thursday—"A bloody war and/or a sickly season" (for faster promotion); Friday—"A willing foe and searoom;" Saturday—"Sweethearts and wives" (to which was usually appended "and may they never meet!"); Sunday—"Absent friends"

tommy: seaman's name for bread, as opposed to biscuit; often called "soft tommy" or "white tommy"

tops (fighting tops): platforms at the heads of the lower masts; marksmen were stationed here in time of battle

top lights: the eyes

touch bun for luck: as a final action before embarking, a seaman would touch his sweetheart intimately

trestletrees: parallel timbers that are fixed **fore and aft** on a masthead to

provide support for a topmast

tumblehome: the inward slope of the upper sides of a ship's hull

under way (under weigh): said of a ship that is moving through the water and answering to her helm (i.e. making way)

unship: to detach something, e.g. a mast or oar, from the place where it was fitted

veer: a wind is said to veer when it changes direction in a clockwise direction (looking into the wind)

warp: a rope attached to a small anchor; pulling on such ropes was a way of moving or **warping** a ship in a harbor, **roadstead** etc.

way: the progress of a vessel through the water

wear: to change a ship's course by turning her **stern** windward, as opposed to **tack**ing

weather gage (or gauge): to have the weather gage is to approach the enemy from the **weather side**, thus gaining advantage in maneuver

weather shore: a shore that lies to windward, so that the ship is safely blown away from it; *see also* **lee shore**

weather side: the side of the ship on to which the wind is blowing; *see also* **lee side**

weigh: to lift, such as heaving up or weighing the anchor of a ship

whaleboat: an open rowing boat of the type used in whaling, pointed at both ends for easy beaching and often steered with an oar rather than having a fitted rudder

xebec: a three-masted Mediterranean vessel, often **lateen**-rigged on the main and mizzenmasts, with a hull having a marked overhang at **bow** and **stern**

Yankee: an American

yard: a **spar** supporting a sail

yardarm: the outer portion of a **yard**

yellow admiral: an officer who reaches Admiral's rank by reason of seniority but is not appointed to a command and so retires

Index

PICTURE CREDITS

The publisher would like to thank David Taylor at the National Maritime Museum, Greenwich, Bryn Hughes at HMS *Trincomalee* Trust (www.hms-trincomalee.co.uk) and Matthew Sheldon at the Royal Naval Museum, Portsmouth for their help in providing many of the pictures that appear in this book. The picture sources are here credited by page number and position on the page (l:left, c:center, r:right, b:bottom, t:top).

Chrysalis Images: 10cl, 11cr, 15b, 16tl, 18tl, 20cl, 21bc, 25cr, 29tr, 30cl, 38, 39tr, 46cl, 50, 66tl, 68b, 71cr, 76, 84cl, 85cr, 85br, 138 both, 145tr.

HMS *Trincomalee* Trust: 102c, 104l, 104 diagrams, 105 all, 109 diagram.

Hodder & Stoughton: 6tl.

Frits Koek, Cliwoc Project, Royal Netherlands Meteorological Institute (KNMI): 136, 139tr.

National Maritime Museum: 1, 2-3, 4, 7, 10b, 11t, 14, 15tc, 15tr, 16b, 17 both, 19t, 20tr, 21t, 22, 23 both, 24 both, 25tl, 26, 27 both, 28c, 29cr, 30cr, 32, 33 both, 34, 35, 36, 37cl, 40, 41, 42, 43 both, 44, 45, 47 both, 48, 49, 51, 53, 54, 55, 57 both, 58 both, 59r, 61t, 62bl, 66b, 68cl, 69, 70 both, 72-3, 75 both, 77 both, 79 both, 81t, 82tl, 83, 84t, 85c, 86t, 88, 89 both, 91 both, 92, 93 both, 95 both, 96bl, 97, 98, 98-9, 99, 100, 101both, 102tr, 103, 106 both, 109bl, 110 both, 111, 112, 113, 114, 115, 116, 117 both, 118b, 119, 120tr, 121, 122t, 123, 125 both, 126, 127 both, 128 both, 129, 130, 131, 132, 133, 135, 137tl, 140, 142 both, 144 both, 145b, 146, 147 both, 150.

Royal Naval Museum, Portsmouth: 6bl, 8, 9 both, 13, 19b, 28bl, 31, 37tr, 39tl, 39b, 46t, 52, 56, 61b, 62t, 64, 72l, 78, 80, 81br, 82b, 86b, 87c, 90, 94, 96c, 108, 118cr, 120cl, 122bl, 134, 137br, 141 both, 148 both, 149.

BAKER & TAYLOR